A
MOUTHFUL
of
RIVETS

With Best wishes —

Nancy Wise

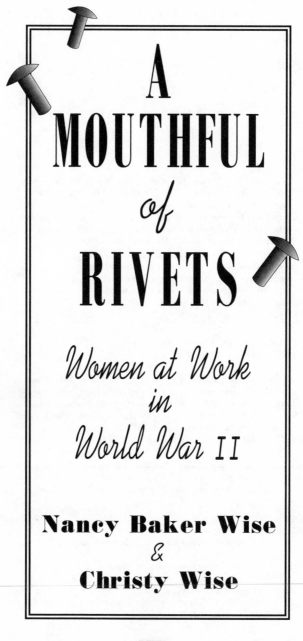

A MOUTHFUL of RIVETS

Women at Work in World War II

Nancy Baker Wise
&
Christy Wise

Jossey-Bass Publishers • San Francisco

Substantial discounts on bulk quantities of Jossey-Bass books are available to corporations, professional associations, and other organizations. For details and discount information, contact the special sales department at Jossey-Bass Inc., Publishers. (415)433-1740; Fax(415)433-0499.

For sales outside the United States, please contact your local Paramount Publishing International office.

Manufactured in the United States of America. Nearly all Jossey-Bass books and jackets are printed on recycled paper that contains at least 50 percent recycled waste, including 10 percent postconsumer waste. Many of our materials are also printed with vegetable-based ink; during the printing process these inks emit fewer volatile organic compounds (VOCs) than petroleum-based inks. VOCs contribute to the formation of smog.

Library of Congress Cataloging-in-Publication Data

Wise, Nancy Baker, date.
    A mouthful of rivets : women at work in World War II / Nancy Baker Wise, Christy Wise. — 1st ed.
       p. cm. — (The Jossey-Bass social and behavioral science series)
    Includes bibliographical references and index.
    ISBN 1-55542-703-0
    1. Women—Employment—United States—History—20th century.
2. World War, 1939–1945—Women—United States.   I. Wise, Christy, date.   II. Title.   III. Series.
HD6095.W62   1994
331.4'0973'09044—dc20   94-11929
                                                         CIP

FIRST EDITION
HB Printing   10 9 8 7 6 5 4 3 2 1   *Code 9493*

Contents

· ·

For Newt and Bob

. . . .

This book highlights a brief point in history when women rose to unexpected and surprising heights of achievement, then returned to more traditional roles, usually without protest.

Women stepped forward in unprecedented numbers and with unqualified enthusiasm when the extraordinary demands of the war became known. In many instances, they took over totally unfamiliar tasks and performed well, sometimes excelling beyond their predecessors. They found a special pride in accomplishing feats that surprised even them. Many said it was the best time of their lives.

A Mouthful of Rivets: Women at Work in World War II not only features women working in manufacturing fields; it also highlights stories of women in white-collar jobs and other professions where men's absences required women's participation and offered new opportunities. Rules or conventions restricting certain jobs to men fifty years ago are laughable today, now that women have moved into many of these positions in large numbers. For instance, Mary Jo Davis Owens broke ground in Missouri when she and a friend worked as movie usherettes. The theater was so ill-prepared for women ushers that the women had to wear the uniforms left by the men who were away at war, cinching their belts as tightly as they could to make the jackets flattering.

The book provides readers with touching and inspiring examples

of the courage, determination, and sense of humor these women dem-
onstrated as they performed their jobs, cared for their families, coped
with marginal housing and transportation, moved great distances,
and, rarely thinking they were doing anything special, survived physical and emotional challenges.

Virginia Tredinnick Denmark reported to work at the National
Weather Service in Missouri under the impression she would be typing
and filing, which she did for the first three or four weeks. Then she was
handed a brochure about radiosonde observation and told she would
be taking morning observations. This entailed sending up a six-foot-
wide balloon filled with helium from the local airfield. Her job training
consisted of reading "Circular P" and watching a demonstration. But
Denmark mastered her task quickly and soon found herself intrigued
with weather forecasting. In 1946, she married one of the men working
at the office and quit her job because of nepotism rules.

Kay Kane Whitney knew her husband would not approve of her
working as a welder while he was away at war, so she did not tell him
about it. But one day he came home on unexpected leave and was
sitting in her kitchen chatting with her mother when she walked in
wearing men's work pants, dirty shoes, and a lumberjack shirt over
wool underwear, with a laborer's bandanna covering her head. Her
husband was aghast. But she kept her job and felt liberated by it,
loving the camaraderie and the wildness of the Navy yard.

Author Nancy Baker Wise was hired to write advertising copy for
Swift and Company in Chicago during the war, a job that would not
have been available to women without the men's absence. She gained
confidence through her collaboration with the men in the department
and through giving presentations about agriculture and nutrition to
local high school classes. She also worked briefly for the Office of War
Information and the Phoenix Metal Cap Company—in the latter position, taking the place of a man who had gone overseas. Nancy's work
during the war gave her a special connection to the women we contacted. She conducted the majority of the first round of interviews and

was able to relate to their feelings and experiences, having worked during that period herself.

Author Christy Wise heard about women in the war more from her father than her mother. After serving for three years overseas, Newton Wise returned to Stanford University to complete his senior year, assuming the editorship of the *Stanford Daily*—the student paper where he'd worked before the war. As Christy remembers hearing the story from her childhood, the women editors stepped down from their leadership positions and graciously allowed her father and other men to take over. Christy was astonished by their acquiescence. Reality was slightly less dramatic than a child's impression. The women actually completed the remaining term and then the men took over. The process may have been gentler, but the result was the same: women stepped down and men took over.

It was this phenomenon that drew us to the book. While Nancy was impressed with the quick acceptance women gained in the workplace, Christy was amazed that women so willingly gave up those achievements. This is one time in our nation's history when the roles of women and men were strictly and unquestioningly defined.

In seeking their wartime jobs, the women's primary motivation was patriotism. They responded to the nation's call for help, desiring to help the country in any and every way they could. Their husbands, brothers, and fiancés were fighting overseas, their government was pleading for citizen contributions, and they wanted to be part of it, no matter how grueling the work or difficult their lives off the job.

Several women felt a pride separate from that of patriotism, a satisfaction that they were able to take on a new job or assignment and perform well. But a few resented the fact that they were asked to do their part for the war and then pushed aside, without proper appreciation or recognition, once the men returned. Most women were delighted to be asked to share their recollections. Many said this is a story that needs to be told and generously contributed their individual stories.

For some women, the war years were half a century ago and long forgotten. They had not given much thought to those years until reading a newspaper ad asking for women who had worked in nontraditional jobs during World War II.

Other women had entertained their children and grandchildren with tales about their war work, actively bringing the past into their present lives. In several cases, these offspring were the ones who responded to the ad, writing with great pride about their mothers and grandmothers and urging us to get in touch with them.

Curious about these offspring who wrote and wondering about others like them, we devoted a chapter to the oral histories of children and grandchildren of the women in our book, exploring the impact on them of their mothers' and grandmothers' wartime work. Several were inspired throughout their lives by the stories they heard about these contributions. They grew up with an attitude that women could and should tackle whatever they wanted. The women had a role model for their own lives, and the men felt supportive of the independence of their wives and daughters. A few who lived through it, however, did not have fond memories of their working mothers, resenting their time away from home or disliking the type of work they did.

Structure of the Book

Our book combines oral history with a thematic approach, grouping the women's histories into eleven categories. These start with the dislocation that occurred during the war. The first part of the book provides a glimpse of how women followed their husbands to different parts of the country, hoping to be with them a few more months before the men were sent overseas, or traveled for jobs or to be with their families while their husbands were away. The war triggered a transiency that continues today.

Once they were working, women encountered a huge variation in the training provided, ranging from an hour's worth to several weeks or months. Similarly, work conditions varied tremendously but overall were difficult, especially when combined with the stresses of finding housing, arranging child care, and using overtaxed transportation systems.

In recalling their experiences, women often mentioned harassment by male co-workers. The harassment varied from catcalls to threats of job loss by one boss unless the woman slept with him. But just as frequently, women praised the men they worked with for giving instruction and support. Women recalled the patience of male co-workers in helping them learn about the workplace and master the job skills. Male colleagues participated in one woman's baby shower—a first for that factory.

Several factory workers compared the coordination and concentration required by welding to more familiar handwork like crocheting and embroidery. Women brought fresh perspectives and a different spirit to the workplace, making suggestions that improved productivity and working conditions.

Many women talked about the self-confidence they gained from taking on new roles, learning new skills, and succeeding. This was often a lifelong boost, inspiring them to try other new things or to pursue related activities. One welder became a sculptor. A home economics major changed her career from working with food, such as being a kitchen tester, to becoming a personnel director.

Eventually, factories devoted to wartime production either closed or adapted to peacetime work, hiring men who previously had been employed there or new male workers and rather blatantly encouraging women to leave. A similar transformation occurred in professional jobs, where women were also viewed as placeholders.

When this time came, a great many women were ready. They were delighted to have their husbands return or to meet young men and marry. With the tragedy of the war behind them, they, like the rest of the nation, were ready for stability and rebuilding, and with that came a return to a life-style where men dominated the workplace and women stayed home to care for the house and children.

But this was not the scenario for all women. Divorced mothers needed to keep working and wanted the higher pay and greater challenge offered by the so-called men's jobs. Some single women were not ready to leave the workforce, not having married, and also were reluctant to leave work they found more interesting than what had been available to them before the war. They were offended by their employers' attitudes, resenting being cast aside. A few were able to stay, but usually not at the salaries being offered the men. A couple of women transferred to office work at the factories where they had been welders or riveters. Occasionally, women tried to remain in their field but without much success. One welder in San Francisco was laughed out of the commercial welding shops where she sought work as a welder.

Our Intended Audience

We wanted to capture these stories before they are lost, and we wanted to portray the human side of women's wartime experiences from the perspective of the women themselves. The stories in this book will bring the domestic scene during World War II back to the women and men who lived through those years. Those who have only read about the war or seen movies will enjoy reading the intimate side of it as told in these pages.

Although these women might not see themselves as pioneers, they deserve much credit for sparking the changes that occurred during the 1960s and 1970s when women joined the workforce in much greater numbers and in more fields. While barriers still remain to women in many positions and industries, the women in these pages, and women like them whom they represent, created a vital bridge to the present.

Acknowledgments

Our heartfelt thanks go to the women whose stories appear in these pages and to many women we spoke with who are not included here, all of whom spent many hours sharing their recollections with us. They generously repeated stories or expanded on incidents to help us fully understand their experiences.

We would also like to thank Marc Miller, who has been more than a legal advisor. His initial contact in the publishing world inspired us to keep pushing our project even in the face of several rejections.

Similarly, Bill Duddleson has been a long-standing supporter of the book, offering editing, advice, and information. Key counsel and editing help also came from Theda O. Henle and Jim Heig.

For newspaper mentions that garnered great response, we would like to thank Pat Holt of the *San Francisco Chronicle*, Jack Oglesby of *Senior Spectrum*, Don Thompson of the *Boston Herald*, Kathey Clary of the *Fresno Bee*, and Jane Heitman of the *St. Louis Post-Dispatch*.

Valuable research and reporting assistance was given by Mardy Baum and Anne Miller.

We deeply appreciate the patience and understanding of our family throughout our work, especially in 1993: Lee and Charlie Axelrod, and Jeff, Val, Jennifer, and Jesse Wise.

August 1994

Nancy Baker Wise
Novato, California

Christy Wise
Washington, D.C.

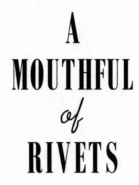

A
MOUTHFUL
of
RIVETS

. . . .

Introduction

When the Japanese attack on Pearl Harbor in December 1941 drew the United States into World War II, increased mobilization of the armed forces was immediate and intense. Within a year, hundreds of thousands of American men from eighteen to thirty-nine years old were fighting in the Army, Navy, Marine Corps, and Coast Guard, having left their businesses, offices, and factories. Ultimately, more than sixteen million Americans served in the armed forces in World War II.

Women, too, joined the armed services, becoming WACs, WAVES, and SPARS, taking desk jobs, driving jeeps, and becoming instructors to free the men for active duty.

A third force emerged to maintain the wartime economy and production so vital to victory—the women at home. Wives, mothers, sisters, and girlfriends left their families, schooling, or other jobs to learn the skills required to continue the work abandoned by the men, and to perform the new work of defense production. They were quick learners. By 1943, two million women were in war industries, and American production far outpaced that of Axis countries. At a Tehran gathering of Allied leaders in 1943, Russian premier Joseph Stalin gave this toast: "To American production, without which this war would have been lost."

For professional women, the war offered a chance to break into careers or management positions that otherwise would have been off limits, such as the civilian fliers and air traffic controllers. Some

1
..

women found themselves doing work they never would have imagined for themselves—and loved it. This happened to the New York office manager who gave up a good-paying job to contribute to the war effort but was employed as a secretary rather than at the plant. After her threat to join the WAVES, the management moved her to flight operations, where she became a clearance officer and flight tester.

Women's motives for working were primarily financial and patriotic. Having lost their sole wage earner to the battles overseas, many women had no choice but to go to work to supplement the small stipend they might be receiving. With the effects of the Depression still weighing heavily on many families, women and men alike were delighted with the prospect of work, often traveling thousands of miles to one of the two coasts, where much of the defense production was going on. Some women saw an opportunity to earn more money than was possible in the lower-paying, more traditional "women's" jobs of that period.

As critical as money was for most workers, the desire to help the United States win the war was equally important. Women responded to the nation's urgent call for help. In one poster, three women are featured in stateside jobs and at the bottom are identified as "Soldiers Without Guns." "Women in the War: We Can't Win Without Them" cried another poster. These were among thousands of flyers plastered in banks, department stores, post offices, on high school bulletin boards, and in magazines. Women on the home front wanted to bring their husbands, boyfriends, and brothers home as quickly as possible, and in a few instances, made financial sacrifices to do so. In other cases, the women sacrificed sleep, comfort, and time at home with their children.

Often, women discovered advantages to working outside the home that went beyond their paychecks. They enjoyed a camaraderie with each other and with their male co-workers that was a completely new experience after being isolated at home as housewives. Their confidence and self-esteem increased as they saw how well they could perform their work, conquering new, and sometimes frightening, tasks and circumstances.

They overcame discrimination, harassment, gritty working conditions, unfamiliar machines, acrophobia, transportation glitches, and homesickness. With gas rationing in place and all transportation systems overloaded, home-front workers had to find creative ways to get to work, either carpooling, walking long distances, or taking the few available buses.

Denying their preference for looking pretty and feminine, women factory workers grudgingly donned men's work clothes or uniforms, covered their hair with the hated "snoods" or bandannas, and tromped around in steel-toed leather boots. Women in office positions had it a bit easier. But with the shortage of nylons, they had to use leg makeup that streaked in the rain, and with cotton and wool reserved for the defense industry, their clothes were created with rayon and other less desirable fabrics.

In talking about these hardships, though, women laughed more than complained, pleased with their ability to adapt. Many wore their welding leathers with pride and found carpooling fun. Superimposed on the tragedy of the war was the energetic lightheartedness of what were, for the most part, young women. As with most people in their early twenties, they were thrilled to be out in the world—working, getting together with friends, dancing at the United Service Organizations (USOs), which were charitable social groups for servicemen. Almost apologetically, women said they had fun working during the war.

With the end of the war, the jobs that had been created specifically for the nation's defense disappeared. Plants closed or were converted to peacetime work. Employment preference was now given to returning veterans. Many women did not question the men's right to return to their jobs. They stepped aside willingly, delighted to return home to their families or to start creating families in the midst of the marriage boom that followed the armistice.

"I wanted to be home with those kids. They were too precious," said Lillie Cordes Landolt of Des Moines, Iowa. She and her husband both worked in an ordnance plant during the war while a retired school teacher cared for their five children.

But for other women, the veterans' return entailed wrenching change, forcing them angrily back to "women's work," with its accompanying reduction of responsibility and pay. They had proven they could do the work and were frustrated not to be allowed to continue.

"The guy came back to my specific job," said Vera-Mae Widmer Fredrickson, who was operating a punch press in Minneapolis, Minnesota. "It was union and the punch press was a man's job and had always been. They never had women on it. They put me to work putting labels on switches and I quit. I was furious. I went to the union about it, too. Didn't do a bit of good."

The women who share their stories in this book provide a glimpse of a special era when women came forward for their country and in doing so were accepted into the men's work world as riveters, welders, geologists, mail carriers, pilots, crane operators, and truck drivers. They learned faster and produced better than their male bosses anticipated. Their performance was extraordinary. But for nearly two decades after that, most women accepted the supporting role of homemaker and mother, not venturing into the workplace.

Today, with 57.3 percent of American women working outside their homes, compared to about 37 percent in 1950, women are taken for granted in some of the professions that were considered daring during the war. And in others, women still are in a minority.

Most women who participated in the workforce during the war consider it one of the highlights of their lives and retain the same pride and sense of accomplishment they felt half a century ago.

"When I show my grandchildren, I have a wonderful feeling of pride," said Jennette Hyman Nuttall, a crane operator during the war. "I say, 'See that crane way, way up there? Grandma used to run a crane like that during the war.'"

1

. . . .

The Shifting Scene

World War II changed the face and soul of the world forever. The boundaries of countries, the shapes of cities, and the minds and views of people were permanently altered. From the vast global changes to the new, individual awarenesses, people's outlooks would never be the same.

Families left familiar home settings to find jobs in strange and different places. Some forty million Americans left home, either to enter the armed forces or to find work in another part of the country. People relocating for work often had trouble finding places to live or schools for their children. Families following servicemen also were forced to be creative in their housing arrangements as the towns hosting military camps were pushed to the limit.

Moving this unprecedented number of Americans from place to place taxed transportation networks. Ninety-seven percent of the traffic was by train. Jammed, the trains gave priority to troop movement, and civilians often found themselves on remote sidings. Gas and rubber were rationed, limiting automobile travel, and getting from one coast to another by car required considerable planning: saving ration stamps, finding travelers headed in the same direction, combining travel modes. One war wife on her way from one coast to the other carpooled, took a train, got a last-minute plane reservation, and finished on a bus.

Workers found themselves next to people with different dialects and brand-new notions. New understandings evolved. Color lines blurred. A lasting change was the breakdown of regional barriers and a greater understanding of the variety of individuals who make up the American scene.

Mildred Admire Bedell was living in her Missouri home with her three children when her best friend, who was living in California, needed help with a new baby and asked if Bedell could come out. She packed her clothes and loaded her youngsters on the train.

"It took three or four days. The train was full of people, a lot of squalling kids, young men who would help me with my children. At that time, I was a young woman myself. I sat down and played poker with them. It was kind of fun. They put us to one side in Provo, Utah, on a siding, so the troop trains could get through. I don't know how many hours they left us there. We finally arrived in Richmond, California, our destination.

"I hadn't been with my friend very long when she and her husband suggested I take a job at the shipyards. So I went to the welding plant and the next thing I knew, I was welding. The class was eight or ten days. You had to pass the test. I became a journeyman welder—I did very well. I loved it. It was like crocheting or something. You lay the weld horizontally, but when you had to build on it and go up into a corner, you had to be very precise. If you're a good welder, it looks real pretty, because it's so precise.

"We were building troop carriers at Kaiser Shipyard. The men whistled at us—there were no married men. They were all single. Everybody looking for—a lot of flirting. Some of them were very protective. Later, after my husband came home, we attended church with a couple of them, and they assured him that I was a lady.

"Almost all the women were married. We had a leadman—we

were in crews. No leadwomen. The women were friendly. I had a lot of friends. Also, at the time, there were two black men, young men. The leadman came around and asked if we would accept them. And we did, and they were on our crew. Eight to ten were on a crew.

"I had to climb up and down and bring my wire, the wire that I was attached to the machine with, and it was an inch thick and heavy. I had to climb right up the ladder with that thing on my shoulder. It was about as high as a two-story house. One time I stepped on a board that was loose and almost fell. I caught myself. It was a really deep hole. It might have been a three-story house. I still feel frightened when I think about it.

"I worked there for two years, maybe even longer. After a while I became allergic to the smoke, and I had acute rhinitis, so they recommended that I get a job somewhere where I could breathe better. I went up to quit. I didn't have to work anyway, and, my gosh, you should have heard the sermon they gave me about helping our boys.

"They got me a job as a secretary. I worked in an office underneath the ship, where they were getting ready to launch, and my boss said, 'Take a letter, Mildred.' I said, 'Are you kidding?' I didn't know anything about that. Later, I did go to night classes and learned how to type. Well, I was able to type orders, and I notified everybody when a ship was going to be launched. There were maybe twelve launchings. It was really something. We got to see it all, if we wanted to. The flags waved, and someone hit the keel of the ship with champagne. Everybody cheered and they played the 'Star Spangled Banner.'

"Those years changed our lives and nobody ever recognized the fact that we gave something to World War II. I was a girl from a rural area. I'd never worked out. I was a mother with three children, and I had graduated from high school and had no idea of how to work. I had no career. All of a sudden, I was making money. I was head of a household, and it made a different person of me. I have never been without a job since that day."

When the war began, Geraldine Amidon Berkey was working as assistant to the traffic manager at the Diamond Magnesium Plant in Fairport Harbor, Ohio. She quit the position to be with her husband, who was going to Officer Candidate School in New London, Connecticut.

"I took a job with the Electric Boat Company, but my husband was a little bit hesitant about it because we had no idea what the job entailed. Submarines were being built there, and they needed a woman to replace a man doing the technical electrical inspection of all electric motors of the submarines.

"I learned how to read blueprints and I was trained to inspect the motor when it came in the yard and then follow it and inspect it after it was installed aboard the ship. I was checking the motors from the blueprints. I really had a wonderful job, when you stop and think how young I was and the responsibility I had. The training was only about six weeks.

"I was the only female in the North Yard and I guess they'd been told not to whistle and everything, and they didn't. They were respectful and I was treated very, very nicely. I had no problems at all. The men treated us like sisters. Many of the men at Groton were lobstermen. They would go out lobster fishing and bring in lobsters. It was a wonderful experience.

"Once I went down into a submarine and the power went off and you're walking just on beams, and I had to stay there for about two and a half hours and not move because of all the electrical equipment. A man had been electrocuted above decks, and that had caused the power outage. It was quite an experience—I think the most challenging experience I had during the war.

"I worked there for about six months because my husband was

transferred to San Francisco. They wanted me to stay at New London, but my husband didn't think it was safe for me to be alone there. So I went back to Ohio and worked at Ohio Rubber as a bucker. A bucker is the person who backs up the rivet for the person who rivets it. He rivets it, and you hold it so it doesn't bounce. Except since I only weighed ninety-six pounds, I wasn't heavy enough so they made me a riveter. I was adamant about getting a man's job. Every time I applied somewhere, I wanted to take a man's job.

"I was there probably a year. From there we went to California, where I worked at the lighter-than-air base. I had a top secret clearance and worked in the personnel department, corresponding with Washington, D.C. With my top secret clearance, I could always go aboard my husband's ship, no matter where they were. I traveled all over; I went to New York City to meet his ship.

"These jobs during the war certainly broadened my view, my outlook on life. They made me a better person. I was a narrow-minded girl who lived in a cloistered community and now after the war, and all my experience and everything, I could see the other side. My father was overprotective of us. He was a doctor and he saw the bad parts of life, and he protected us from it.

"Working during the war didn't change my mind about working. I was always going to be a career person. It never entered my mind that I'd do anything else. My father's sister was a doctor, his other sister was a lawyer. I come from a family where the women always had a profession."

Overnight, people became mobile. If they lived in a place where jobs were still scarce from the Depression, they could relocate to regions where airplanes and ships were being constructed, or, in Dee Davenport Callahan's case, where sugar was being refined. She and her

husband left Arkansas when their friends told them about the C&H
refinery in Crockett, California. But before they could take advantage
of the new employment opportunities, they had to cross the country.

"From Arkansas to Vallejo, California, we never stopped, except to
eat. There were six of us in the car, and we slept sitting up. Needles,
in the desert, was awful. No air-conditioning in the car. We had
friends who worked at the shipyard in Vallejo. We spent the first night
with them, then went to the Star Hotel in Crockett, an old hotel with
apartments. Later, the government built wartime housing, nice places,
about a block from the plant.

"I got a job at the sugar refinery in Crockett, which was considered a defense job during the war because of the need to produce
food. I was working with powdered sugar, packing 10-pound bags of
sugar into burlap bags, then 100-pound bags, and then later we used
paper.

"Then there was a job listed on the bulletin board that paid more,
working the centrifugals. I applied for it, got it, and worked with
twelve great big tanks in a big room upstairs. The tanks came down to
a funnel-type thing. I had to go around and hit them with a big
wooden hammer to make them each go down right. The sugar was
already made, and hitting these centrifugals would send it on down to
the floor below to be packed in one-pound boxes. It was very important that it got down to the scale so it wouldn't be kicked out. They
taught you how to judge it by the sound, and by doing your job well.
It's a little hard to explain. It wasn't much of a job.

"We took the train home once each year while we were in California. On one trip, we changed in Kansas City, and the train I was trying
to get on was so jammed, it looked like I wouldn't be able to get on.
I'd have to stay over in the station another twenty-four hours, with a
new baby, if I didn't make it.

"The soldiers made the people stand aside so I could get on. They
handed the baby up in the air over people's heads, person to person,

so the baby could get on, and then stood back for me. Once we were on the train, it was like one big happy family since now everyone knew I was the lady with the baby that the soldiers had helped get on the train."

Jane Ward Mayta was working at the ammunition depot in Mare Island, California, when Pearl Harbor was bombed. The depot became a scary place to work at times, with blackouts and a general fear of being blown up by the Japanese. Following her husband across the San Francisco Bay to live in San Francisco, Mayta briefly worked as a secretary for Southern Pacific Railroad before she got pregnant. Two months after her daughter was born, Mayta accompanied her husband—who was now a Marine—to San Diego, where she got a job at the Consolidated Aircraft Company.

"The people I worked with at Consolidated were a tremendous mixture from all kinds of places that I've never been, having always been in California. Fourth generation. There were people from the Midwest, from the East, the Deep South. The women came because their husbands were there. They were easy to work with. We were all in the same boat—wanting to work for the war effort.

"I started out trimming pieces of metal that were going into the plane. From there, I went to a riveting gun. I was putting bomb racks into what I believe were B-24s. And that is where I worked until almost the end of the war.

"We didn't encounter any trouble with the men, but they were lazy. They were protected. As long as they were in those airplane plants, they wouldn't be drafted. They didn't work too hard. As a matter of fact, I remember a couple of them that sat in the back of the plane making plastic jewelry. Oddly enough, the women didn't get resentful about that. It was normal at that time.

"The only thing I really got uptight about was that I thought I should be allowed to take my husband as a dependent because he was only making seventy bucks a month.

"I learned a lot in those years. For one thing, I got out of Vallejo and was able to get along on my own without the family background and all that I was used to. I learned to look for a job. I learned to do things I had never considered doing. I learned to be able to get along with and mingle with people from totally different backgrounds. We were all in little pockets before then. We were all the right age for it, in our early twenties. You're flexible. And you learned how to get along on very little."

President Franklin Roosevelt issued Executive Order 8802— forbidding racial discrimination in defense industries—in 1941. Before Pearl Harbor, one aircraft company was discovered to be employing only a dozen African Americans out of 33,000 employees. Annie Green Small's family left Louisiana for Marinship in California, becoming part of the 10 percent of African Americans working there.

"My cousin came out here to work in the shipyards from Shreveport, Louisiana. He sent for his wife, and she came out. Then her sister and husband, they came out here. Then they wrote us and sent us a ticket to come. My husband came out first, and he said if he liked it, he'd send for me, and if he didn't, he'd come back. So, in a week, he sent me a ticket, and then I came out.

"When I came here, it took me from Wednesday night to Sunday night on the train. I had $8 in my pocket when I got here.

"When I came to Marin City, I didn't like it. But I stayed on and went to work in the shipyards. I didn't like the climate. Back there it was hot, hot, and when I got here, it was winter. It was raining all the time. They called it fog, but I call it rain.

"I came out here and I went in the shipyards and I burned. I went to burning school, and I didn't like that. So then I went to welding. That's where I stayed.

"Every once in a while we'd have a meeting. They'd get the welders together and want to know about the bandannas. We had to wear bandannas and hard hats and keep them on all the time, but most all the women in the shipyards would tie their hair up and then leave a piece of hair out in the front—bangs—so you could look ladylike. So you could know the men from the women. They called a meeting and told us to put it in. 'You're a woman, you'll always be a woman, and if you don't put that hair in you'll have the damnedest permanent you've ever had because that weld is hot,' they said.

"I was making wonderful money from what I made back in Louisiana. We worked three shifts at the shipyards. I would go to work in the morning and my husband would go to work in the evening. We'd walk to the shipyard from Marin City. No buses, no one had cars. We'd walk up this hill. One man had a car here. The Greyhound bus was our transportation—not to work, but around the area. Every bus was loaded. Standees. The driver always said, 'No standees,' but there always were. They finally got a little yellow bus that would go up the hill here. Until then, we walked.

"On one visit to Louisiana, I had my son who was six and a baby, and my son got lost. Actually, I got lost. I had gone to the back of the train, the train was uncoupled, and he came to Los Angeles and I went to San Diego. They found him and he was waiting until I got in. He was really calm. They were holding him and said, 'You describe your mother when she gets here.' He said, 'She's got a little baby in her arms with a pink cap on.' It seemed like forever and a day before we got together.

"Those were the days when I could go out of the house and leave the door wide open. Nobody would go in. We could leave the money on top of the icebox and the man would come in, leave the ice in the box, take the money, and go. We stayed on because it was a nice place to raise children."

During the war, defense workers and servicemen from all over the country came through Middle River, Maryland, hometown of Ruth Vogler Fritz. Her family, and most residents, made rooms available "to let." There were no hotels in town. But before all that, Fritz experienced a Rip Van Winkle episode.

"I was sick with scarlet fever during my senior year in high school and was in isolation in the hospital. I went into the hospital in January 1942, and when I came out six weeks later, it was like a whole new world. All the military was there. It was like I'd died and come back to life. Everything was so different.

"The vice principal said I'd have to come back next year, since I'd missed so much school. I decided I wasn't going to do that, and I went to work as a riveter at Glenn L. Martin aircraft factory. We were doing men's work; it wasn't hard, but you had to keep on the ball.

"I worked on PBMs—Navy planes. They were like cargo planes. They carried a lot of equipment. I guess they lost quite a few of them because it was just at the time they were experimenting with a heavier plane to carry cargo. They used to kid us about the planes, and say, no wonder those planes don't fly, you girls have been out too late the night before. The PBM, I guess it was top-heavy. They had quite a few going down instead of up.

"We were trained for about two weeks and then they put us on the assembly line. I worked mostly on the door section. It was a big piece—one that opened up underneath. Sometimes we would get caught up and they would put us on smaller sections.

"The men made some remarks, but we didn't think too much about it. They'd whistle or something. We'd go by and they'd say things, but we never bothered about it. And we never had any problems as far as respecting women's ability to do the job.

"I enjoyed it. It was tiresome sometimes, but at night we'd go to the USO and dance. The servicemen all used to come there. That's how I met my husband. He was stationed with the Navy at Martin. Wrong-way Corrigan came in one day and shook everybody's hand. Burt Lancaster was there one time.

"My father had a bar and a restaurant and we lived upstairs. I was the youngest of ten children. My mother had a rooming house in a house we built next door. She must have had at least ten people. It was all bedrooms. There was a woman across the street that used to feed them. Workers from Pennsylvania and even New York would go home for the weekends.

"That was quite the thing in town. Everybody was taking in roomers, fixing up their big homes and taking them in. That was one form of income for people. Quite a few of them did give meals, but my mother didn't. I know we used to joke about the hillbillies from West Virginia, that they didn't know how to use the toilet, that they thought it was for washing their feet. It was a joke. My sister-in-law's sister married one. There were three brothers. One died, and she turned around and married his brother.

"I probably wouldn't have left Maryland if it wasn't for the war. It seems like Pennsylvania, Virginia is about as far as you'd go. You didn't travel like they do now. We lived in Massachusetts for thirty-two years because my husband worked there. He's originally from Massachusetts. We're now retired up here in New Hampshire."

The 1930s were not easy on Jennie Fain Folan. As a farmer in Arkansas, she lost a close friend during the Depression, and all her cattle and horses died due to drought and disease. Some bulletins came out from the West Coast in 1942 advertising jobs and she grabbed the opportunity, despite the challenge of traveling across the country.

"I loaded up the four kids that was left and I was twenty-seven and they were ten, eight, four, and two, and the only way we could get here was on the troop train, and we had to stand up part of the time. There was no food on the train, and I took a big basket of food, and then sometimes some of the soldiers would get off and get some milk and stuff like that. We finally got out here to Tacoma, Washington, after three days and three nights. It was a tough trip, but I was used to such a hard life that a lot of things didn't hit me like it hit a lot of people.

"I had just left a sad scene. The government had come in and shot our cattle because they were starving, our horses had died of sleeping sickness, we'd planted crops that were burned by June. There was no welfare then. It was a sad morning the day they rode in and herded up our cattle to be killed. Getting out was a new chance for me.

"My relatives and friends all thought I was going to get caught up with a lot of foreigners. They're all Scotch, Irish, English and were old settlers. Arkansas is one of the earliest settled places, going back to the 1600s. I have ancestors who fought with George Washington. And they wondered about my going away.

"When we got to Tacoma, I went to the housing authority and they gave us a place to live. It was built for the Navy. We had a three-bedroom house. We had day school there for the kids, and for the little ones, they went to nursery school. I went to school at Todd Shipyard for about six or eight weeks to learn welding, and then I started working in the shops. I had to join the union.

"I went from the shops out on the ways. We started on the keel and went clear to the top, climbing high. I was a strong kid, slim as a rail, but strong.

"There weren't any buses available because so many people were coming and going. We had to ride to work in trucks, open trucks with benches on the side, and we'd all pay so much a week. We were the first bunch of women to come in, and there weren't many there, only the older men, and they said, 'They won't last,' but we all hung in there, and we all got to be good friends. It was kind of like a family.

"We built ships for England, and then we built icebreakers, and then at the last part we were working on airplane carriers.

"Sometimes we were under a lot of pressure. They'd bring in those big walls—they called them bulkheads—and they were way up there. One time we got on the outside, and I was with two shipfitters, and they hit the bulkhead so hard, bringing the steel in and everything, that our scaffold went down, and we fell about thirty feet. I didn't get hurt so bad, just a black bottom. Two men got ribs broken and everything else. I had just started to weld and all at once I was on the dock. That was quite exciting and kind of shakes you up for a while.

"There were a lot of girls that got killed. Every day you'd see somebody in a stretcher, and maybe not all of them got killed, but a lot of them were hurt. Everything was going so fast. I think it was that way all over. I know people were killed here in the lumber camps. Everybody was working like mad. We were almost wiped out when they blew up Pearl Harbor, so we had to get some ships going.

"When they took the ships off the drydock, we got to see them launched, and that was a big thrill to see one go down. We kept on working.

"And the day the war was over, we were all laid off. No matter if we did have a union because it didn't stand for us because we were women. It was hard on women. There were a lot of them like me because a lot of them were young women that had men in the service, and some of them didn't come back and they didn't know what they were going to do. We had a lot of mothers working there.

"I stayed in Tacoma about six months, and I found out it was going to be pretty hard there with me alone with the kids. So I went to the

Yakima Valley, and during that time in the shipyards I saved up enough money that I could buy a house and a lot in Yakima. Then I got a job in a hotel and I worked for 29 cents an hour and kept the kids going."

In early 1941, Helen Kooima Dowling and her husband and two eldest children moved from Sioux Falls, South Dakota, to Chehalis, Washington, to care for her husband's brother. When the war started, they moved to Tacoma; they began working at Boeing in February 1942. Several relatives joined them from South Dakota.

"It was a complete change for me because there were so many different kinds of people working at Boeing from all over the nation and from all walks of life. I began work as a shop clerk in the machine shop. We were doing cost accounting, and I would go around and keep track of the time on the machines.

"So I met a lot of different people working there, and I think my ears were red and my face was red that first week that I worked. I heard and saw things that I just never had seen and heard. People from the South were coming, a lot of African American people, and I had not had any close contact with them to speak of, because in the Midwest there were not many people living there at that time.

"They came, and my experiences and my contact with them was good, but it was entirely different. Their language and their way of talking and the people with whom I worked, it was just a complete change. I benefited by that because it did broaden my horizon on the world. That was a good education for me to know of the different kinds of people who lived in the world and what were some of their problems.

"We, of course, shared rides at that time because of the shortage of gas and the rationing. The car I rode in, there were five of us women who rode back and forth together, and one of the women was a dear person, but she talked. She was talking when she got in the car and she never quit until she got in the plant. She became so tiresome. But she also worked in maintenance at Boeing, so she had some interesting things to tell. I haven't forgotten her because of her talking. The rest of us, we would go to sleep, and she would still be talking. She'd be talking when we'd go to sleep and she'd be talking when we'd wake up.

"I remember the balloons that were camouflage for the Boeing plant. They were colored like the Army uniforms now, and they were hanging just outside above the plant, all around. We were afraid of the Japanese attacking the West Coast, and all of us, while we still lived down at Chehalis, took CPR to be ready for the attackers in case they did try. We got black shades for our windows and we covered them, and at night we would keep these shades on so there would be no light showing through. That didn't last very long.

"The big difference to me was my contacts with the different kinds of people that I met. I got out of my Midwestern area and way of thinking and began to think about the world. I have memories of it and it did make a change in my life. Many, many changes were made in people's lives at that time, and it was a great upheaval. It was just a change in our complete society—the migration of people to different places, to war industries and Army posts, and it was a complete change.

"I remember the day that the war ended. Everybody was out in the streets and singing and shouting. Oh, it was a wonderful time. It was just a feeling of relief. It went on a couple of days, as I recall."

The Pacific Northwest was also the site of a broadening experience for Betty Kirstine Gannon, who was working at the telephone company

when the war started and living at home. She and two of her sisters
responded to a citywide call for help with the war effort. "Everybody
got together in downtown Seattle at rallies with Bing Crosby singing
and urging people to get to work. There was lots of patriotic fervor,
and we went to work because of the feeling of patriotism," Gannon
recalled. While preparing planes for bringing back wounded service
personnel at the Sandpoint Naval Air Station in Seattle, Gannon
made an important discovery.

"One thing I found out—we spent three or four years in the South and
before that I hadn't known any black people. When we were down
South, the blacks worked for us. We had a woman who came in, in the
morning, and cooked for us and did the wash. And she was very nice.
She came and went and that was it.

"Well, when I came to work at Sandpoint, I worked with—
probably every other person at the base was black. It was the first
time I really got to know blacks, and I can remember thinking that
they're just like us. The girls had boyfriends and husbands overseas.
We'd share letters. It was an eye-opener for me. We hadn't been
taught not to like black people. It just never occurred to us; they
weren't part of our lives.

"They were wonderful to work with—just like the white girls. No
different. We'd eat lunch together, share letters, and one time one girl
hadn't gotten a letter from her husband for a long time, and she was
worried sick. We all felt so bad and tried to cheer her up and keep her
going. But the color didn't have anything to do with it. The color was
gone.

"Our work at Sandpoint had to do with the PBYs, the Navy sea-
planes, that were being used to bring back the wounded. And when
there wasn't anything for us to do, they had us count nuts and bolts.
No one cared how many there were, they just wanted to keep us busy.
Made you feel as if you were doing something for your country. We did
a lot to make us 'feel good' about doing something for the country—

like saving tin cans. They said they were going to make bullets, but they didn't make bullets!

"My mother was a block warden, which meant she had to see that no lights showed in the houses. One time, they had a long bombing drill and they had to have survivors. Well, I was one of the survivors. Volunteers, like housewives and neighbors, were loading people, and Mother's basement was one of the places to bring victims. We lived on top of a hill, and I got wounded at the bottom, and they had to bring me up the hill. I remember one of the men was quite old and not too steady on his feet and he was helping load people, and he dropped me three times. When I got to the top of the hill, I *was* wounded. The only thing Mother could say was, 'Now what did you do?'

"For a while, I worked in the toolroom. I knew absolutely nothing about tools. To this day, I don't know how they got anything done with the women during the war. They put me in this toolroom all by myself. Somebody would come over and ask for a tool and what could I do? I asked what it looked like. One time this guy came over and he said he wanted some kind of a part and he said he wanted the female, and I said, 'Oh sure. Right. Is there something wrong with the male?' 'No, I want the female.' And I said, 'I've got things to do. I don't have time to mess around with this stuff.' So the people who needed the tools were the ones who actually taught me what they were. You didn't get any lessons. Nobody sat you down and said, 'This is a wrench.'

"Remember the stuff we put on our legs? It was the worst thing they ever invented. Leg makeup. I can remember every morning, putting it on. If it rained, you'd have stripes down your legs. And you had to stand in line for everything—cigarettes, nylons. You'd get off work and you'd be downtown for some reason. If you saw a line, you'd automatically get in it. You had no idea what the line was for, but you'd get in it. You knew it was something you couldn't get.

"However, I have to say something. That was one of the best times of my life, even though there was a war on and I had a dad that was overseas and I had a boyfriend that was overseas. Still, it was a really,

really nice time. For one thing, everybody was so kind to everybody. We all had somebody over there. So everybody understood."

Lyllus Runyan Butler and her husband moved to California from Iowa with their two children just before the war started, seeking a change of location and better weather. She was well placed to take a job at the machine shop at Mare Island Naval Shipyard in Vallejo, California, and her husband worked at Kaiser Shipyard in Richmond. The government sent Butler to machinist school for about six months.

"The job was interesting as could be. We made different parts for the subs or the ships that came in. We'd get a piece of steel or aluminum or whatever had been broken, and we'd make those parts on the lathe. Now I couldn't even make it to file it down. They'd give orders to you from the ship, and then they'd bring the order in to us.

"Then I worked on the bench a lot, which was filing. I remember one experience. They brought me a big piece of metal and the man who gave it to me said, 'This has to be made by hand because it has to be down to the very nth degree.' So I stood there and filed—and this is not an untruth—for three days to make it, and I could have taken it over to the milling machine and done it in two minutes. He said I had to file. So I filed it down and took it over to him. I was so proud because I got it right down to the right degree and everything, and took it over to my little supervisor and handed it to him, and he threw it into the garbage. The metal that I worked on all that time.

"I said, 'What in the world did you do that for?' And he said, 'To keep you quiet. We didn't have any machine work to be done and we didn't want you to take a day off because it's too busy.' Now, that's just part of our government. My husband said the theory was to have everyone on hand just in case a ship came in and needed to have a part made right away. The boss wanted to keep people from running around and visiting.

"When we first moved out there, we had this little house and we got an old washing machine. We'd get it started and the thing would stop right in the middle, and I'd have to empty the water, carry the water through the house, and then turn that thing upside down and there'd be a gear out of place or something. I don't know where I got my machinist's ability, but I was grateful for it then. Then I'd have to put that back together again and start it all over, heating the water on a little three-burner stove.

"Our house was a real hospitality house for friends and relatives whose husbands and sons were in the service and we were very happy to help any of them; even though it took both paychecks to give them a sample of home-cooked food and lodging. We had a two-bedroom house in El Sobrante.

"One lady, or one cousin, stayed, oh, periodically, she'd come and stay two and three weeks. We had one couple that we'd always been friends with, and she came and stayed. But I had some awful good friends and helpers. They were great. One cousin came and he had two children. We didn't know where we'd put all those people because we already had two women staying with us. So they bought a little trailer and lived in it out in our driveway.

"On the day that they said the war was ended, my husband came home. This time we had no washer in this nice home, either. I'm washing, and I had a lot of clothes on the line, and he came home and said, 'Get the clothes off the line. We're heading for Iowa.'

"With him, you did it sudden. I'm not a sudden-moving person either, but we folded up the clothes and folded up the kids and away we went. Then we had a terrible tragedy on the way home back to Iowa here. This is in August. I can remember this day—August 15.

"We stopped in Cheyenne to shower and everything and got to bed and nobody could sleep. Butler—I always called him Butler—got antsy and said, 'Let's just get up and go again.' So we drove from

Cheyenne, and neither one of us had had sleep. We got to Omaha and then we were both just exhausted. We got gas in a little station in Oakland, Iowa, then we went on from there. And Butler said, 'I can't drive anymore, and we've got to keep going.' I didn't think we had to, but he was so homesick, it was sad. I don't think anybody that gets that homesick can overcome it in any way.

"So we drove on, and I said I would drive. All at once, I had gone to sleep completely when driving, and a car—thank God to whoever it was—a car had seen that something was wrong and stopped and blinked his lights so it woke me up. They knew I was asleep, evidently, because I was probably weaving all over.

"Then when we got home to Bondurant, Iowa, my mother started out to the car and she was crying. My sister had been killed the day before at Oakland, Iowa, in a bus accident. The bus she was riding in had the accident and it had just happened and it happened close to where I had fallen asleep in the car. I just loved that sister. We were very close."

Katie Lee Clark Knight and her husband were living in El Paso, Texas, at the outbreak of the war and heard about jobs on the West Coast from a cousin who was working there.

"Of course, being young, we wanted to go where the big money was. At that time, that was good money. I remember I made, I think it was $50 a week.

"When I first arrived in Richmond, California, and applied for the job, they said, 'Oh, we can't hire you. You have to go back to school.' I was seventeen. And I said, 'Oh, no, I've graduated and I'm married.' They went ahead and let me go to work. I was in Yard One as a shipfitter. I was the one that marked all the portholes to those ships.

"You have a tape measure and you measure as far from the bottom of the ship up to where the porthole was to go, and then you would measure the size of the porthole, and then you'd have a center point, a center punch, and you would make the little punches exactly where that porthole was to go, and then later on the burners come along and cut the hole out.

"I stood on the deck. I could reach it. It was just about even with my eyes. I'm five feet three, so they weren't that high. At the time, I was the only one that marked off those. Then it got so cold there at Richmond, and the wind would come across the bay and nearly freeze me to death. I remember that. So I asked them to transfer me inside the building.

"There, I marked off the bulkheads. You'd get a template—it was like a lady's pattern for a dress. And you'd lay this on a huge sheet of steel and then take the little center punch and your hammer and punch little imprints of that center punch. You would mark places for them to work. The burners would come along and cut this pattern out of this big piece of steel.

"I wore jeans. Well, in the wintertime, I wore long underwear and my jeans and a shirt and a heavy sweatshirt over that, a jacket over that, and I had a bandanna on my head, with a hard hat, and then I wore the long, rolled socks and a pair of boots.

"The men were great. If I hadn't been married, I could have married a dozen of them. I remember this one short man—he didn't know I was married—came up to me one day and said, 'You know, if you'll marry me, I will buy you anything in the world that you want.'

"I remember my boss came in one day and said, 'I had a dream about you last night.' I said, 'Oh, yeah?' He said, 'And you know what you said? You said, "Just what I thought. You're just like all men."'

"People came from all parts of the United States to work there. People knew it was a good place to get a job. My husband and I saved a lot of money. We went back to El Paso after that, before we started traveling, and bought a home. I remember before we left Richmond, there was a beautiful, beautiful white wolf coat in one of the stores and I walked by and admired that coat. It cost $500. My husband told me, 'Okay. If you'll stay one more year, I'll let you buy that coat.' And I said, 'No, I'm homesick. I want to go home.'"

2

Quick Studies

Women's training varied tremendously as they assumed men's positions in factories and offices and behind the controls of airplanes. Preparation ranged from a full-fledged eighteen-month training course for civilian fliers to three weeks' instruction in shipyard welding to just learning on the job.

It was not unheard of for a woman to be trained on one machine and put on something completely different, as Edith Wolfe Tepper discovered. She was taught to read blueprints and asked to operate a lathe at Pratt & Whitney in Massachusetts.

Many wartime workers were given instruction in local high schools and vocational centers that were converted to training centers for the war, and just as many workers were trained at special centers at the work site or were given no preparation and learned on the job.

Some women had skills close to what was required for the war industry and needed only a small amount of additional instruction. For instance, art majors were trained to be drafters fairly easily. Others needed more extensive instruction in what they were undertaking, and in some cases, they got it.

Many professional women had all the education they needed before the war and could begin right away at jobs now available to them in the absence of men, gaining experience at a rapid pace.

Some college-educated women chose to postpone working in their fields, opting to help the country and earn some good money in shipbuilding or aircraft manufacturing.

In volunteering for defense work or taking advantage of special career opportunities, the women made the most of their training and skills, plunging right into their work.

Margaret Fraser Beezley was an office worker for the Anderson-Clayton Cotton Company in Memphis, Tennessee, when she heard they were taking women as civilians in the Air Force for plane inspection.

"There was a school down in Whitehaven, so I went down there one day, and they accepted me—to my surprise. It was an eighteen-month course and we had graduation and everything. They took care of our expenses. There were two women and thirty men. The men were from all over—California, everywhere. I wish I could find the other girl. Gertrude Rubinski.

"They taught us everything about the plane, inside and out, what to look for. They would fly that plane in completely from England. It was such a waste of money. They would take the British insignia off; anything that they put on in England they would take off and Americanize it. It would go through the line during all of this and when it came out, our job was to make sure everything was on that plane. We were classified as inspectors.

"That plane didn't move until we went over it completely. A lot of times the test pilots were there and we'd have to go in the air, and that was just great. One time I went up with them and they couldn't get the wheels down and we had to fly around for about forty-five minutes and it scared us all to death. Finally, they got the wheels down and we were able to land. These were B-24s.

"This was all in Louisville, Kentucky, on Standford Field, now a commercial field. We did that day in and day out for three years. The plant went day and night. I have asthma so they let me work days. It took an average of about three hours to inspect a plane.

"The men were great to us. Most were married, and if they weren't married, they found girls to marry. I was divorced at the time. We lived in a mansion that some lady owned and turned into a rooming house. It was real nice. We had to eat out. Gert and I lived there, just the two of us. She was married, from Minneapolis.

"I remember one funny incident. On the B-24s, on the pilot's side and the copilot's side, there's a tube and it has a little funnel on it. When I first got there they knew I was green and they had me go on these planes and blow on that. They said it was an interphone—that they could hear what I was saying in the back. But it really was what the pilots peed through. That was our initiation. Gert would blow on one side and I'd blow on the other. That's the only funny incident I can remember. It was strictly work.

"I loved the job, but it wasn't the easiest job in the world. It was the most rewarding work in my life. The glamour of it, and then I was helping my country, too. I wanted to do something for my country."

With two daughters to clothe and feed and a sister willing to care for her girls while she worked, Mildred Daniels Maguire of Corte Madera, California, took advantage of wartime employment opportunities. She signed up to work at one of Standard Oil's franchise gas stations and later worked in a local shipyard.

"For the service station job, I had to go to San Francisco for their school. The training program was in a conference room in back of a filling station. The class was all women. The first thing was pumping gas and not to waste it. We had to learn about checking oil, water, check the battery. We offered full service, including tires. You learned to greet people with certain words. You didn't call anybody 'Ma'am' or

'Sir.' You just said 'Good morning.' The school was for six weeks, and we were paid during the training period.

"The training was very well done. You learned procedure and all that. We were expected to always look nice and always treat everybody the same. By the same token, they told us there would be company spotters that would go through as customers. We had to wear those white uniforms and the little hat. We laundered and starched them.

"I worked at the filling station in San Anselmo. I could hear those church bells at 5:00 P.M. It was hard work. I was the only woman at the station. It was a breakthrough for women. The other two guys I worked with were great. They were 4-F. The one young man was married.

"I got to go up in the mountains of Ross to give rich clients a ride home and then drive back so their car could be serviced. That was one of the fun things. You'd check people's oil. Standard really impressed on you to get that hood up and try to sell them fan belts and everything. You noticed if a fan belt was worn, called it to their attention. That, people resented. I don't recall if I ever sold a fan belt. I thought, 'That's a man's thing.' It was expected, however.

"I didn't do a lot of servicing of cars because I was very fast at filling gas, and the lanes at the pumps were busy. I did a lot of windshield washing. You didn't put the gas in until you got their gas stamps. I was there at Christmas time, and you wouldn't believe the presents people brought. I felt they were trying to bribe me."

In 1942, Margaret Wolfe Berry left her home in southeastern Washington and joined her sister and twin brother in Seattle to work at Boeing's Plant 2, continuing there until the end of the war.

"I started as a bucker. We didn't have any special training, just on-the-job training. I worked in the tail section. There were several young men still in the plant when I started, but they were quickly drafted or volunteered. So pretty soon it was mostly women. The men treated us very well, rather like they might treat their sisters. There was only one person I remember giving me any smart talk.

"After being a bucker for a while, I went on to become a riveter, also with no special training. Eventually, I became the first woman to get the grade A level, the top grade. Of course, as you advance in levels, you get more money.

"When you rivet, you carry the rivets in your apron pocket. They're all different sizes and you have to figure out which one works where. They had a sort of oil treatment to keep them from corroding, so I didn't put them in my mouth.

"My brother lived in a boardinghouse, and my sister and I lived in a private home and then went to have our meals in the boardinghouse. Apartments were hard to get with all the people in town for work, but people were wonderful opening their homes to us. When my brother went into the service, he volunteered.

"Of course, it goes against the rules and regulations, but a lot of people did it. They wrote their name and address in the planes someplace. Well, the A mechanic that I worked with, he and I put in the flooring on one plane, and after the inspector did his work and before we put the flooring in, we wrote our names down. I received a letter from a master sergeant from Korea on one of the B-17s that I had put my name on. I corresponded with him for about a year after that.

"The only way they found it was, this person said they had been out dropping leaflets and they were hit by a bunch of flak and their hydraulic system was knocked out. So they had to do a belly landing, and consequently they had to do some repair work and that's how he found my name."

Virginia Tredinnick Denmark was working as a secretary for the Family Service Society in St. Louis when she received a call from the

Washington University employment office asking if she would be interested in an unusual job at the airport.

"I had always been attracted by anything in connection with flying, so I said yes, and they sent me for an interview with the weather service. They were looking for a young woman who had math through calculus and at least a year of college physics, which I had and which was a little unusual in those days. They said they'd like me to come to work. This was April 1942.

"So I did, and I was under the assumption it was a secretarial job, because that's what I'd been doing. Apparently, the man in charge, an elderly man, maybe in his early sixties, hadn't had a secretary for a while and he had a lot of backup filing to do, so for the first three or four weeks this is what I did.

"I kind of wondered about the place because it seemed like some of the people were always there when I got there in the morning, and some didn't leave when I did. I didn't realize people were on a twenty-four-hour rotation shift.

"I was kind of quiet and didn't ask any questions, so finally one of the men took me over to a great big machine that was sitting in the corner and he said, 'Now you're going to learn to do this.' And I said, 'Oh.' He said, 'It's a radiosonde observation and we'll give you this "Circular P" and you can read all about it.'

"They told me that there was a girl who worked—it was at that point that they said they made two observations a day and there was another girl who did the night one. I would do the day one at nine in the morning. That was my job training. I watched and got the 'Circular P.'

"Taking the radiosonde observation entailed sending up this huge balloon about six to eight feet in diameter. You went down on the field, out to a little garage-type metal building where there were helium tanks, and you filled this big balloon with helium. Attached to it was a long, heavy cord and a little red silk parachute, and below that was a small box. In that box was a little radio transmitter, and this was set off and you released the balloon.

"On windy, rainy days, sometimes you had to have two people; one would handle the balloon and the other would handle the box. When the balloon burst, you could tell on your graph that it burst. There was a tag on the box telling where to send it back to—to the weather office. Sometimes we'd have one of the little transmitters returned—this was Lambert Field in St. Louis—maybe from somewhere in Illinois or Missouri.

"The big machine in the office was a radio receiver, receiving the information from the transmitter. Attached to it was a paper and a pen that wrote on it, like a seismograph. You had tables to consult and eventually you worked up the sheet giving the information and then you put it on a graph and got readings of temperature and pressure and humidity. Weather service people were all at airport weather stations.

"When I first saw all this, I was floored, but it was very interesting, I thought. For the most part, everyone was very helpful. We worked 24 hours a day, 365 days a year, usually on eight-hour shifts.

"It was such interesting work, and you had contact with the airlines. The pilots would come in and if the weather was chancy and the ceiling was low, they would often ask us to do an extra ceiling check to see if they were within limits and all, and there was one time when they had done that, and the ceiling was too low to come in, and this pilot came in anyway. It was scary because if he had had a crash and it really was the weather that was involved, you'd have felt responsible.

"So I went over there and waited until he came in. One of the men said, 'This is a gal from the weather service.' He said, 'Oh, how was it out there?' I said, 'You know how it was. You know very well it was broken overcast and you came in. That's why I'm here. It's people like you that do things like that.' And I marched out and one of the men came in and said, 'Virginia, you don't talk to pilots that way.' And I said, 'I'm sorry, I do when they scare me that way.'

"It was exciting. When the weather was changing rapidly, and bad weather was coming in, you'd really be busy.

"Bill Denmark became the First Assistant to the OIC in 1944, and I left the weather service in June 1946 to 'marry my boss.'

With three sons in the service and a husband working for the defense industry at General Electric, Matilda Hoffman Becky Havers understood the importance of the nation's push to build more ships and planes as quickly as possible, but she thought she'd given enough. So, it took some persuading to get her personally involved.

"I was painting my house on the outside one day in 1942. I lived in Woodland, New Jersey, at the time. I was on a twenty-eight-foot ladder doing the second story, and a neighbor of mine who lived in the next block came down the street to talk to me. He saw me on the ladder and said, 'Hey, Becky, come down off that ladder.' So I came down and he said, 'Since you can do all these kinds of things, how about your coming to school? I'm starting a defense program and getting women to work in defense jobs, taking over the men's jobs so they can get into the service.' He was a machinist—a toolmaker and a machinist.

"I came down and said I would think about it. 'No, I'm not going to give you time to think,' he said. We were very good neighbors. He and another man had opened a special machine shop in a local high school to take in women defense workers and teach them how to run the machinery. 'You be there in the morning. Be there by 9:00,' he said. I said okay.

"I came and he took me all around the shop. I liked what I saw and signed up and started machine shop from 9:00 A.M. to 2:00 P.M., then went home for dinner and then back to school from 6:00 to 10:00 P.M.

"I never had a high school education, so I was real happy about attending school. I learned how to operate all the machines and saws, how to read blueprints and micrometers, and all the measures that went with machine work.

"The school lasted a bit longer than two months, but they needed the help so bad at the shipyard at the time that they let us out sooner. I got out in a month's time. I was the first woman machinist hired in the New York Shipyard, the south yard. They called it the New York Shipyard, but it was in New Jersey. Right away they put me on a machine.

"In the beginning, the men were terrible. They resented the women. I told them not to tell me how much they resented me, because I didn't like them either. I wasn't afraid of any of them. I said, 'You ought to be glad that someone's here to take over this work.' The boss that interviewed me and his helper were very nice to me. They told me what to do and not to bother the men. I said, 'You needn't worry. I won't bother them. They're going to talk to me first.' Afterward, they apologized.

"I was there only two weeks when they made me a woman counselor. They didn't call a woman a shop steward. Since the men didn't like having women in the shipyard, the girls had to come to me with problems and if I couldn't handle them, I had to take them to the north yard to have them cleared up.

"My second son was a tool and die maker and when he found out I was working at the shipyard, he told me to use his tools so I wouldn't have to buy any. When the men saw me coming in with my own tools, that made all the difference in the world.

"I moved around a lot as I could run all the machinery. I worked on the turret tops, set them all up myself. I had a tacker assigned to me. I did all the body bolts for the armorplate. I had to read all the blueprints and cut my own stock and everything, which I did. Most of the work I did was piecework.

"I worked at the shipyard almost four years and enjoyed every minute of it. I had a friend that had a motorcycle shop, and he sold me an old Indian cycle for $25, and I drove it to the shipyard with my sister on the back every day. I had the cycle for two years and one day I came out of work and someone had stolen it. After that, I took the bus."

Shortly after Mary Smith Ryder graduated from high school, her mother came home one day from her job working for the State of California and said the local junior college was giving tests for employment at McClellan Air Force Base. With a 98 percent score, Ryder was number two on the list of applicants.

"The test was for shipping ticket clerk, to track parts they were shipping. I went to school for about three or four weeks first. We were working on a type of booking machine. I worked at that for about a year, but then I had this big blowup with my boss because she never did anything. She sat around and filed her nails all day and expected us to do everything. You know how you get to feeling about things like that and all the other girls were always complaining about it but naturally, when I went forward with it, no one else joined me.

"So they sent me up to central personnel and gave me some aptitude tests. They gave me some complicated part to take apart and put back together. Well, shoot, I did that in nothing flat. So they transferred me right over to the maintenance department and put me to work installing radio equipment.

"The planes would come in for a complete overhaul. These were planes that had been in battle. First you have to remove all the radio equipment and the wiring if it had been damaged at all. The radios went to one shop to be repaired, and if we needed new wiring, we did that ourselves. At that time, they had antennas strung like clothesline on the outside of the plane. They had fancy wraps at the end of them that you had to do. No training for this job. They just handed you a screwdriver and said, 'Take this out.'

"There were various insects and things that came in from the islands, once in a while. You had to be on the lookout for things like that.

"All the guys I worked with were wonderful. There were a number of women working there, mostly young. Most of the men were older. They were deferred, or 4-F, or something. But we all got along very well. They weren't patronizing. I think that was because we all seemed to be pretty good at what we were doing.

"On the fighter planes there was a little hole we had to crawl inside to get the stuff out. I don't think it was even 2×2 feet. I was kind of a chubby girl, and they'd come by and say, 'Who's in there?' I'd say I was, and they'd say, 'How did *you* get in there?' They couldn't believe that I got in there.

"After the equipment was repaired, they'd send it back to the shop and we'd reinstall it. To handle the antenna, you had to climb way up on the plane, on the tail. I'm short, so some of the things were a little difficult, but not too bad. For some reason, I just took to this like a duck to water. I loved it. I liked working with my hands. I hated book work. When we were up in the shop working on wiring and things, there was always a lot of yakking back and forth. It was a pleasant work atmosphere. It was a very enjoyable period of my life, despite the fact that there was such a terrible war going on."

Armed with a college degree in theater arts and some acting experience on New York radio, Sylvia Rebarber Leff joined her draftee husband in Fayetteville, North Carolina. The available jobs were unappealing and paid poorly, so she tried the local radio station. She was in luck. With men leaving to join the service, management decided to take a big chance and hire a female announcer/disc jockey.

"To their amazement, none of the listeners objected to hearing a woman's voice on the air. It turned out to be a fascinating job, but my background had not completely prepared me. For one thing, announcers at small stations also were engineers in those days. This station had two network affiliations—the Mutual Broadcasting System and the Tobacco Network—and it carried programs from both. The announcer had to patch in all the shows that came in on his shift.

"Today, it takes six months to a year of formal training to get a basic engineering license. But when I reported for work at 11:00 on a Monday morning, the engineer showed me around for an hour and then said, 'I'm going to lunch—it's all yours!' And I had never touched a piece of engineering equipment in my life! Somehow I managed not to blow the place up, and by the end of the week I was quite adept at cueing up records while reading commercials or the news, bringing in the network shows as I read the station IDs, and even interrupting records to announce the location of a fire in town. The fire department automatically told the station when its engines were called out.

"Plus, the local organist and I did a weekly 'Words and Music' show. I read, not sang, popular song lyrics while he played. It was a 'remote' broadcast from the chapel of a funeral home, and for all the time we did it, I sent Bob ahead to make sure there wasn't a body in sight before I entered the room. The show developed quite a following and requests came pouring in.

"After I'd been at the station about three months, the bookkeeper came to me one day and said, 'My mother told me to tell you you're getting better and better every day because you sound less and less like a Yankee every day.' That night I told my husband that he had to start working on a transfer. I didn't want to come out of the war sounding like Scarlett O'Hara! But the people in that town were very kind to me. It was fascinating, and I made more money than if I had done anything else.

"A year and a half later my husband was transferred to San Francisco and I had to make my own arrangements to join him. There were no Pullman berths available, and I didn't want to sit up for five nights in a coach. I got permission from the station manager to ask, on the air, if there was anybody who might be driving to the West Coast.

"A woman from Wilmington, North Carolina, responded. She was going as far as Phoenix, Arizona. We arranged to meet at the Wilmington railroad station in a week's time. She met me in a Chevy coupe along with her two-year-old daughter, who she had never bothered to tell me about.

"It took ten long days to get to Phoenix. Gas rationing meant we traveled slowly, and there were floods so we had to take longer alternate routes. We took lots of rest stops for the child. Her Southern mother would discipline her by saying, 'See that big, black buck in that car over there? He's going to come along and take you away if you're not a good girl!' It was not an easy ten days.

"When we got to Phoenix, I asked to be dropped off at the USO and never looked back. The GIs were helpful when I asked how to get to San Francisco. They said there was a plane from Phoenix to Los Angeles and that once I got to LA it might be easier. This was in 1944 and I had never been on a plane. I hesitated and they said, 'Come on. We'll call the airport. There's a plane leaving at 10:00 tonight. We'll find out if there's space.' Well they did, and there was. It was a little American Airlines plane and they insisted on driving me to the airport, so I couldn't back out. But what choice did I have? I had to get to San Francisco.

"I tried to call my mother since I couldn't reach my husband. She wasn't home. I was furious. There was no reason she should have been home, but I wanted to tell somebody I was getting on that plane since I was convinced it would crash and no one in the world would ever know what had happened to me.

"I got on the plane and sat next to a middle-aged woman who was a buyer for the May Company. She saw my look of terror as the plane took off. She took my hand and said, 'Now, everything's going to be all right' and talked me through the turbulence. The run from Phoenix to LA was always a rough one and those were not pressurized planes. I'll never forget that angel of mercy.

"When I finally got to LA, I was told there was no plane to San Francisco that night and the morning flight was sold out. Somehow I managed to get to Union Station. It was past midnight. All the ticket windows were closed. I sat down on my big suitcase and tried to think positive thoughts when an elderly black porter came along and asked, 'Would you like me to put your bag in a safe place so you can try to get some sleep?' I said that would be just lovely. He said he'd bring the bag back in the morning.

"I managed to stretch out on a hard bench, woke up at 6:00 A.M., and could not remember what that sweet old man looked like. I had nothing in hand, no check or anything, and I thought, 'Dear God, what am I going to do?' Ten minutes later, he found me and gave me my bag. I'll never forget him, either.

"All in all, it was quite a trip. I started out on a train to Wilmington. Then I went by car to Phoenix. I took a plane to LA, a train to Oakland, and the ferry from Oakland to San Francisco. My husband met me at the Ferry Building and said, 'Now we have to take the bus to Petaluma.' We were staying in the old Petaluma Hotel, the closest available housing to Hamilton Field. I used every means of transportation then known to man."

Elizabeth Harrell Winter was married only a year before her husband volunteered for the armed services, leaving her to run his dry cleaning business in Alpine, Texas.

"I didn't know anything about the cleaning business, but the machinery is sort of automatic, if you know which button to push. I had been in the shop off and on, with Bill. And when he left, his father said he'd help me, but he didn't know anything about it either. But he did understand machinery.

"The cleaning was very heavy. We had great big rolling carts to hold the cleaning that came in and we tagged everything, but we had so much, the carts ran over. An Air Force base was not far away and we got a lot of cleaning from the base. I had a high school boy, a big, husky fellow, that would come and clean the filters and oil the machinery and do that sort of thing. Mr. Winter showed him what to do.

"I had two elderly women. They were in their sixties and they would press constantly. One of the ladies was a fanatic religious person, and I'm not against that but she constantly nagged at me because I didn't belong to her Christian church. I was a Methodist. But she would press that press from 8:00 A.M. until 6:00 P.M. or later and tell me off and on, 'You are not a Christian.' They were good workers, good frontier women who never tired.

"We had a very small shop and there wasn't room for the boiler, so the boiler, which made steam for the steam presses, was out in the back, in the open, and of course, it was cold. We get real cold in Alpine. We're in the mountains. And the pipes would freeze at night. So I'd have to go down at 7:00 A.M. and light that old blowtorch and run it up and down the pipes so I could thaw them out, so I could start the boilers and we could have some steam. I cried, and the tears froze on my face. I kept asking, 'Why am I doing this?'

"I had been raised in a very protected home, a protected person, and I kept saying to myself, 'Mother, if you could only see me now.' I never did any of that kind of stuff. I had come out to teach school and this was far and away something else. But I was crazy about my husband, and that was the only business we had. Whatever I had to do, I had to do.

"Before he enlisted, I had to sign papers for him to go into officers' training. So when he came home, I told him that the next time I had to sign the papers, 'I am joining the Marines, and you are staying here.'"

Peg McNamara Slaymaker also worked with aircraft, but in the pilot's seat as a test pilot. She got her pilot's license from the Oakland Airport while she was attending the University of California at Berkeley.

"After I graduated from college, I started working for chemical warfare, and I had just gotten a real good job with them in San Francisco when the war started. So I didn't go into flying right away because I liked my job so much and we had to pay our own way to Sweetwater, Texas, for the Women Airforce Service Pilots (WASP) training. I was sort of afraid that I might not like it or I might not pass. So I didn't go until the eighth class and I was in 43W8.

"I went July 4 and graduated just before Christmas of 1943. The six months' training course was just like the men had to take. We had ground school and flying, and we had to learn how to fly the Air Force way. They were very particular. We went through the primary, basic, and advanced training.

"It was strenuous. There were six of us to a bay. We were in these little cabins. That's where we lived for the six months. We only had two weekends off. We went to Dallas both times. Sweetwater wasn't the greatest place. It was very windy and dirty, hot in the summer and cold in the winter.

"We had civilian men instructors. We were just civil service then, but when we graduated, we were supposedly the equivalent of a second lieutenant. When we graduated, my class was the first one not to go into ferry piloting. They didn't need ferry pilots, so we were sent to training fields. A friend and I were the first women to be sent to the advanced single-engine training field in Selma, Alabama. It was called Craig Field. That was where a lot of the women ran into trouble with the men. Some of the men weren't very nice to the women, but we had a marvelous time. We were assigned to the engineering department, and we were test pilots.

"She and I reported for duty on New Year's Day. No one had told them we were arriving. When we arrived, we had to report to the adjutant general. We told him that we were pilots and that we were going to be on the field. He'd been tilting his chair back and he was so surprised that he tilted it back all the way and he fell right on the floor. He didn't know what to do with us. He said we had to live with the nurses but that we could eat with the nurses or eat with the officers at the Officers' Club. We chose the Officers' Club. We did have a good time."

Opal Braniff Daniels and her family were living in Vallejo, California, during the war. Her husband was working at nearby Mare Island Naval Shipyard, and her two children were in school.

"One day I said, I think I'll go down and apply for a job. I never dreamed that I would get one. I went down to the Mare Island employment office and applied, and in three days, they called me to work. I worked in the master toolroom. We issued tools to the workmen who repaired the ships that came in.

"We had about three days of orientation and very little training. There was a wonderful woman who was head of orientation at the Navy yard. She gave us talks and lectures for our own self-esteem, and that sort of thing. She said, 'No matter what kind of job you do, if you scrub a bathroom, if you do it well, feel happy with yourself.' We had people like me who were totally untrained. We had a lot of black people who were brought in at that time, who were illiterate. She was a very fine person and advanced beyond women's lib at that time.

"Mainly I remember her sense of fairness, wanting women to feel that they were not inferior to any man or any job. At that time, that was unheard of. They needed help badly and women were filling a lot of jobs of various kinds. The Navy yard at that time was a fine place to work because you were treated nice.

"Our bosses were all men. Most of them were kind of terrified. They never employed women. The boss I had in my particular tool-room there, he was a retired sailor. The women could actually wrap him around . . . you could do most anything. He was very kind and I got well acquainted with him and his wife and son.

"In between, when we were not real busy, we all sat behind these great big checkboards that were the size of a sliding glass door and crocheted, knitted. If you didn't have work to do, he didn't care if you sat back there out of sight and did handwork.

"Mostly we worked seven days a week. It was hard with two kids. My husband and I worked different shifts. I worked the swing shift, so I could be there in the morning and until afternoon.

"Sometimes we worked very, very hard. If a ship came in, in need of repairs, we worked like dogs. If they didn't we had it pretty easy."

Early in the war, Margaret Christensen MacLaury was working for the City of New York as an office manager in the civil service department with a good salary. Her Marine Corps husband was sent overseas, and she wanted to do something that was "significant." She looked into nursing programs, but this was before the creation of the Nurse Corps, and nurses' training was three years with summers off. She decided three years was too long and went out to Grumman Aircraft on Long Island to apply for a job.

"I was nicely interviewed but they said, 'We only hire women as secretaries,' so I took a pay cut. I think I went from $42 a week, which was great in those days, to $24 a week just so I could help get those airplanes in the sky. They did hire Rosie the Riveter, but I was trained in administration.

"In connection with that job, I was the vice president's secretary and he was the administrative vice president so I really had a lot to do there in getting people to go to the right places so they wouldn't bother him. But after a while they brought me a bunch of typing to do and I saw red. I complained and said if that's all they had for me to do, I'd go and join the WAVES.

"They said, 'Oh, we didn't know you were unhappy.' I said, 'Look at my training.' They said, 'What was your training?' I said, 'Didn't you look at my application?' They said 'No, we just looked at that big blue hat you were wearing.' That's how things were.

"With my threat to join the WAVES, they said, 'Well, we have an opening. We're losing Bob Dalling over in flight operations. He's a clearance officer and wants to enlist so we'll give you his job.' So I became a clearance officer and flight tester. That means you take on the planes as they come in from the factory. You assign pilots to test them for their first flight and then clear them to the tower, and when they come down again, you get their reports and assign pilots for a check flight. After the planes were tested, I saw that they were delivered to the Navy.

"I learned how to do it by sitting and watching Bob Dalling for about a week. That was my training. It wasn't all that complicated. It was just a responsible job and you had to be on top of it. Anyway, the pilots were such fun. They were wonderful. Nobody gave me any trouble. They just invited me into their little circle.

"They were making little Wildcats when I first came on and the F6S, the Hellcat, was only an experimental model. The engineer who designed it was up testing it and came down. Everyone said, 'Jump, jump.' But he said he was going to bring the plane down. Well, he brought it down. It hit a potato field and he was in a body cast from his knees to his neck. I heard it all on the radio as it was happening.

The plane was in pieces, but the pieces were there. It was the engine that failed, it wasn't the airplane, so that became the F6S.

"I loved the work but my personal life was miserable. I used to think every morning, 'Oh God, there comes the sun, another day.' When the sun went down, I thought, 'There goes another day.' I just put myself to bed at night and I'd get myself up in the morning, so having a place like that to work in was very stimulating. I felt as if I was doing something. That's why I had to be there.

"I did that for about a year, until my husband came home from overseas. They sent him home because he was almost dead with malaria. I was so damn glad to get my husband back. I was not raised to be a career girl. I was just so glad to be able to stay home with my kids after working him through law school."

3

No Ladies Room Here

A t first there were no bathrooms, no breaks, and no lunchrooms, and the workplace was fraught with hazards. As the war months and years wore on, morning and afternoon breaks were established, cafeterias installed, and toilets for women provided. Safety measures required special clothing for all workers as well as a few extra precautions for women. Early in the war, the defense industry's safety record was poor. More people died in industrial accidents than in battle, according to R. H. Bailey's *The Home Front: U.S.A.* (1977). Even as improvements were made, the jobs remained difficult, some extraordinarily so.

Through it all, however, the women were surprisingly uncomplaining. Their patriotic fervor buoyed their spirits. They were motivated by the belief that their hard work would help shorten the war so husbands, sons, and brothers could come home sooner.

Plus, compared to their recent challenge of keeping homes and families afloat during the harsh Depression times, doing men's work was not difficult but provided a welcome livelihood. For professional women, it was a dream fulfilled, even with some accompanying discrimination.

True, some jobs were boring, but the work enabled women to pay for schooling after the war. One air traffic controller was so tense her jaw hurt at the end of the day, but the excitement of dealing with air traffic kept her coming back. A geologist faced haphazard living ar-

rangements as a transient on a seismic crew but stayed with the job
for three and a half years.

Marjorie Cordell Hoskins found it very warm near the cooker ov-
ens at the Morton House Canning Factory in Nebraska City, Nebraska, where they made date pudding to send to the servicemen.
"But none of us seemed to mind it," she said. "There were three of us
women as a rule, and we had a man that helped us, too. We had fun."
In a similar positive spirit, Hoskins thought her twenty-block walk to
and from work every day "was nothing."

Like Hoskins, most women took the hardships and difficulties of
the working conditions in stride. Given the urgent nature of the war
and the sacrifices being made by the men fighting overseas, these
were considered small inconveniences.

*Working conditions for women during the war ranged from dan-
gerous, challenging, and exhilarating, to—boring. Gloria Zamko
Conklin longed for her bosses to offer creative work that matched her
ability. Her colleagues agreed. But with no experience working with
women, many men had a limited approach that kept their expecta-
tions low.*

"I worked at a so-called man's job, one not usually considered a
wartime job. I was one of a number of recent graduates from Cass
Tech High School in Detroit hired by Uncle Sam to work on drafting,
drawing tank parts. The school was exceptional. It focused on what
you wanted to do. It had automotive engineering, aeronautical engineering, electrical engineering. All those things. I found my art training there was even better than at the art school I later attended in
Chicago. With a commercial art background, we had learned lettering
and the use of special pens, using India ink.

"We all wanted to do more than they gave us at work. It was all very boring. We couldn't work on things that were more imaginative. Or more creative. We were all creative people. We were hemmed in with just humdrum—well, it was like working on an assembly line, I suppose.

"I would say that we were probably overpaid for what we did. I'm sure the men who were there were probably 4-F, they were older and more experienced in this kind of thing, and of course they got much more interesting jobs, which I don't blame anybody for. I'm sure that I'd have done the same thing if I were in charge. But it was frustrating. They needed our abilities to do what we were hired for—to be able to do things with a drafting pen and ink and know how to do lettering and tracing and that sort of thing. We were tracing tank parts, exclusively.

"Nevertheless, everybody was happy to do it simply because they were making money. In those days, that wasn't too easy to do. It was important for me, since it gave me my necessary 'nest egg' for art studies in Chicago. Also, I was able to buy fairly expensive clothes while I was working there. The office was in the Fisher Building and I understand the large room in which we worked had been a barbershop. The building had a Saks Fifth Avenue store in it. I didn't usually shop in stores like that, but I did manage to have a very nice wardrobe while I was there. Even so, I saved for my tuition. I lived at home, paid a certain amount for room and board.

"But it was a boring job, sitting at a drafting table for fifty-four hours a week and wishing your boss would give you something more creative to draw. A typical bureaucratic situation."

Women's production records and accomplishments were recognized in newspapers and company newsletters, and occasionally, as in the case of Faiga Fram Duncan, in awards.

> *To produce ninety-three ships in three and a half years, 20,000
> workers at Marinship in Sausalito, California, took very little time
> off—even to be sick, Duncan pointed out. "Absenteeism Aids Adolf,"
> warned the workplace posters. She compared her electrical welding to
> filigree jewelry. Her instructor chose another comparison: "Ladies," he
> said, "welding is like baking biscuits. The more you do it, the better
> you get."*

"I attended a free class in electric arc welding, which involves the
welder fastening steel plates together permanently with a high welding torch. It was an essential shipbuilding process. Only women were
in the class; all but one were wives and mothers.

"We began basic welding—horizontal, vertical, and overhead.
Being left-handed, I had to translate mentally the teacher's right-
handed directions.

"The day after we graduated, we were hired at Marinship as beginning electric arc welders at 95 cents hourly. We did flat or horizontal welding in a large shed. Soon I had my most memorable experience. My supervisor asked me to help a man who was developing a
new method for laying patterns on steel plates. The man was Lucien
Labaudt, a San Francisco artist, working patriotically at the yard. He
was quiet, a bit older than I. I welded as he asked. He received an
'Award of Merit' from the U.S. Maritime Commission, and I also got
the award. Then I heard he had gone with the U.S. Army as an artist.
And the next news was that he had been killed in an air crash, en
route to assignment in India. My award is a keepsake. When one of
my granddaughters saw it as a child, she exclaimed, 'It's Grandma's
medal from the war!'

"Work in the shed palled and I heard that Marinship was going to
let women welders work on the ways, on ship hulls. That involved
climbing like a six-story building, dragging a power line, working at
heights. It was a challenge. I was one of the first women on the hulls.

"Most important was not missing a day of work. It was war production. Once several child-care center children all got the German measles and to keep the women working, a center just for them was improvised.

"I, too, broke out with German measles. I went to work. At the shipyard the rash was so noticeable I returned home. It was only when I got back to work that I got some tragic news. I was asked by a welding classmate, 'Did you hear what happened to Sue? She was killed when a hoister backed her against the wall.' She must not have heard its warning bell.

"Only during our lunch hour, outdoors, did we get to socialize. We couldn't chat in the toilets, as a uniformed woman guard watched. From lunchtime I most remember Bataan Mother, whose name I don't recall. Bataan Mother was older, had married her childhood sweetheart. Her son in the Army was captured when Bataan fell to the Japanese. She didn't know if he was dead or alive. For him, she went into war work. At noon, her husband put his arm around her shoulders. I can still see her anguished face and hear her voice.

"I loved the shipyard activity. I still can't find words for my feeling, watching my ships launched.

"While I didn't experience any discrimination against women in the yard, I did at the Boilermakers Union in San Francisco. We went there one evening to be sworn in as members of Local 6, American Federation of Boilermakers. After the long bus ride I needed to urinate. I asked a woman secretary about the toilet. She said there was none for us, that I should go to a gasoline station two blocks away. After some angry words from me, she consulted an official and opened her spotless bathroom."

Lucille Genz Blanton Teeters became an expert on rivets—all shapes and sizes—and discovered that putting airplanes together was a lot

of hard work. She was at the Consolidated Aircraft factory in Fort Worth, Texas.

"My husband went into the Seabees, and then I took a three-month course learning how to put airplane wings together. They placed us in Fort Worth at the airplane factory there, the B-24s, the bombers. But I had to pull out. My husband was fixing to go overseas and he wanted me to come to Rhode Island to see him before he left, so I went up there for two or three weeks, and when I got back the class had gone off. I had to go back and finish my course. And when they placed us over there at Ranger, Texas, they helped us find a room. We had room mothers and dorms and got up and went to work and everything, real neat.

"I knew some ladies from Coleman and we lived together. I worked the day shift and started in the wing, the wing tip department. Then I got to shoot on that big B-36 that they were bringing out. I got to shoot explosive rivets. When you shoot it, there's a certain kind of tool and then it explodes. We had partners on these wings, and I'd rivet part of one, she'd rivet, and then I'd have to buck on the other side where you couldn't see each other. If you wanted to stop, you tapped. If you didn't, the rivet would go through. Of course, they had men that went by all the time and kept your time sheets, what you were working on, how many hours you spent on this. I worked on the wing tip for a while and then I worked on the wing, they called them the skin, big sheets of aluminum for the wing.

"I enjoyed the work. It was in this big, big building. It was, oh, to walk from one end to the other, I'm going to say it would be a mile. The noise was terrible. And we didn't wear ear protectors. We wore these blue caps so your hair wouldn't get caught in the drill.

"They knew about what position to place you in with a certain group. I feel I was in with a real super group. And you just worked hard. I'd rather shoot rivets than buck them. But this lady who was my partner, she'd prefer to shoot rivets, too. So we'd swap. When you

buck rivets you have a bucking bar, a big old bar, and you hold it in
your hand. It's like a block. If you didn't hold it right it wouldn't buck
right, and the inspector would come around all the time and inspect
this, and if it wasn't right, he'd mark it and you'd have to take it out. If
you drilled that out many times, that hole, you got marks against you.
I don't know what happened if you got too many marks. I don't guess I
got very many. I guess they moved you, transferred you to somewhere
else.

"They called me to the office one day there at Consolidated, and I
thought, what have I done? I got over there and they took my picture
and put it in the little old newspaper, our newspaper. I guess the
mailman had reported I had written a letter to my husband every day
since I'd been in the department, and that I had received about as
many from him. So it was a real sweet write-up. But I was afraid I'd
done something wrong.

"We were off Saturday and Sunday. We did our laundry and our
hair and things like that. But it was mostly hard work.

"One time I got to the end of my rope, I guess, and I took off and
went over to the middle and crawled up in one of those airplanes. I
decided I wanted to see what they looked like. I didn't realize that
they kept up with each worker so much. I went over there and was
climbing up in that, and I was looking this thing over, and then the
foreman came up to me and said, 'You mean you've never seen? Come
here, I'm going to show this to you.' And he got me through, and he
went over that whole plane with me. But I never did leave my place of
work anymore.

"There may have been outside activities, but I didn't go. By the
time you bathed and wrote your letters, bed, and then we got up so
early the next morning. And then our ride comes by and honks and
we ride to work, that's the routine. It was just a routine, just work.

"Two years of work and they called me at work one day and told
me they had a message. I hadn't heard from my husband for a couple
of months, and I thought maybe he's been killed. They called me at

the office. They had a message from the War Department, and I was scared to death—everybody else was, too—saying that he was on his way home. Boy, I threw my toolbox down and I left there and I didn't go back. They begged me not to go. I just thought the war was over. They begged me not to go, and this girlfriend brought my check to me. When he came home, I came home, and then I went back to San Francisco with him. I enjoyed my work at Consolidated but I never went back after that."

Mary Todd Droullard worked both as a coppersmith and a welder under working conditions that she found to be less than idyllic. She also had a unique solution to the problem of using precious shoe ration stamps on work boots.

Droullard started at Associated Shipyard in Seattle, responding to a newspaper ad. Tired of harassment by her boss, she left Associated for Todd Shipyard, also in Seattle, where it became apparent that her sheltered life had inadequately prepared her for the realities of factory working style.

"I didn't want to use shoe stamps for work boots. So I got majorette boots because they didn't require stamps. The boots girls use for twirling. I wore them under my leathers, which weighed about forty pounds.

"Sometimes when you're welding over your head, sparks would fly and burn through your brassiere. I have a lot of scars there.

"I would be working out on the decks in the awful cold and damp, and would often get electrical shocks because of the electric welding. I'd climb up and down the ladders and go down in deep tanks and work down there all by myself in the dark. There'd be a lightbulb hanging on a cord down there. That was kind of scary, working over the engine room, which, if you fell down in one of them you'd really be in a mess.

"When I first started working there I worked as a coppersmith on the British minesweepers, which is what they used copper on, and then they stopped making the BMS and I became a welder.

"The harassment from men stands out mostly in my mind in those years. Always hitting on me. When I became a welder, the same thing. They kept hanging around me and looking and trying to get me to go out with them and all. I was married and had a little girl. I think women in those days were treated pretty shabbily. You got the feeling you wouldn't have that job if you didn't go along with them.

"I didn't say anything to their comments. They'd say, 'Oh, she's sure a goody-goody. She doesn't smoke and doesn't dance. Doesn't do anything.' I got that kind of remark. My mother always sheltered me a lot. I hadn't been out in the working world. This was my first time.

"My husband had asthma and they wouldn't take him in the service, and he was also working at Todd. I remember he would watch me like a hawk. I'd be welding and I'd lift my hood and he'd be watching me. He was a leadman. I never told him about the harassment. I felt like it was my fault, that I must be doing something that made them act like that.

"I also got comments like 'What are you working for, a new fur coat?' Actually I was working for a new house. You couldn't get housing at the time. If you had a child, no one would rent to you. We couldn't find a place. People were coming in droves. We went to housing places and they said, 'Well, you've lived here all your life, you should know places to live.' I went to work to get a house, and also because they had asked all of us to help out.

"The government did provide us with wonderful nursery school care. Just wonderful. They had bright young women, everything set up for children, little beds, little tiny washstands, nap time, and cod liver oil.

"When I quit Todd I went to the department store and got a job as an elevator operator, and they took me right away. But they contacted me later and said the government wouldn't let me quit my job. I couldn't take the elevator job. I could only go back to the shipyard. So I chose to stay home and take care of my little girl."

Sun, sand, the Coast Guard, and drowning victims were Florence Barker Hackel's working environment. She was the first woman life-guard on Chicago Beach, the men having all gone to war, and she worked two summers, in 1943 and 1944.

"I was on the swimming team at South Shore High. They had this test and those of us who were the toughest, who did the best, got on the beaches. The others did the pool. We hit the newspaper once. I was swimming at the South Shore Beach and my sister said, 'Why don't you dive in. This is where I dive.' We both have different diving styles, of course, and I hit a rock and my sister had to save me. It was in the paper. 'Life Guard Saved from Drowning by Sister.'

"But I'm the only—to the best of my knowledge—the only woman lifeguard that year, in the city of Chicago, to save two people at once. Two drunken sailors from the University of Chicago. I pulled them out. I don't know how I did it. You don't know how you do these things. This was at the 63rd Street Beach.

"I had one lecherous man take a picture of me. I have that picture of me sitting up in my den, and now when my kids look at it, they say, 'Wow, Mom, you had good-looking legs.'

"To be on the beach, you had to be able to handle those boats, the boats that are used to go out on Lake Michigan, to rescue people. So you had to spend so many hours on the perch, and then you spent so many hours out there in the water. You push the boat out and sit there. You're way out beyond. I wouldn't have seen one woman I saved if I hadn't been out in the boat because this was a young girl who'd had an appendectomy, and she was in the water and she got more fatigued than she'd anticipated. She was looking a little strange, and she'd slide down and come up and slide down and come up. People drown very quietly. I got her out.

"At the Jackson Park Beach, just over the promontory in the Jackson Park Lagoon, there were Coast Guard guys being trained. Some of them were going to the University of Chicago and having seaworthy stuff done to them there, and they would look over at the lady lifeguards. Then they got to playing around, trying to teach us semaphore. That kind of thing. You might think they would have honored us in the sense that they figured we wore uniforms like them. We had these little white hats, little red jackets, and black suits, and a park district seal on it.

"We'd come out in the morning, and the first thing you'd do is put the flag up, the city flag and the U.S. flag. They looked over at us and saw us doing these things, similar to what they were doing. There was a little ogling, too, of course."

Doris Whitney worked briefly in the office of the Chief of Ordnance in Detroit, where she grew up, and then, also briefly, in Miami at the Naval Supply Depot. Her most vivid recollections are associated with New Orleans and Higgins Aircraft, where they made planes that never flew.

"While I was living in New Orleans, I had met some gambling and horse-racing people and I would go down to Maison Blanche and get my hair done. I'd have on my riding pants and then would go out to the track and exercise the horses—my name was Whirlaway at the time—and I was riding down the street, and I was thinking, 'Jeez, I'm living this indolent life, and the war is going on. I should do something serious.' So I started working for the war effort. In fact, all

during the war, we had a swell time with the servicemen going
through.

"I spent about a month in sheet metal school in New Orleans for
about 50 cents an hour and then went to work drilling and riveting. I
guess I was one of the people who got through the sheet metal class
ahead of time. I was faster than a lot of the country people who came
in to work there, and that's why I got into the drafting department.
I was only seventeen or eighteen. I lied about my age. I didn't go
through eleventh or twelfth grade.

"During the month-long training program for riveting and drilling,
I made a little jewel box for my mother, with rivets, and I stamped her
initials in it. I made a metal funnel for my grandmother and put it in a
package with some lingerie for her, and she said, 'What's this for?' It
was just a joke.

"When I got out of school, I started working at Higgins Aircraft in
New Orleans, drilling and riveting. I got 65 cents an hour. Higgins
boats were very famous during the war, but at the aircraft plant, they
never actually made anything. It was a backup in case they needed
more planes, and in case other factories were bombed. There was a lot
going on, however. It was a whole big aircraft factory and they were
moving stuff around. I remember we had to paint spar with a char-
treuse color. There were a lot of interesting people there.

"One really chubby woman from Texas in overalls kept saying,
'There's one thing you don't hear nowadays, and that's the truth and
meat a-cooking.'

"Then I worked in the toolroom, handing out tools. I loved tools. It
was more interesting than a boring office. A lot of people came in and
out. You'd walk around talking to people.

"We'd go out for lunch and sit on a log out on the bayous and see
the alligators. One day as I rode in, the fog was so heavy we almost
didn't get to work that day.

"The thing that I remember in New Orleans were the restrooms
and drinking fountains; they had them separated for black and white

and men and women and officers and enlisted men. So many different toilets you can't believe it. Sometimes I worked a regular eight-hour shift, but two or three days a week I'd work a ten-hour shift and I remember being sound asleep on my feet. I had my hair in a bandanna and was wearing trousers and walked into the men's toilet and I didn't wake up until I saw a man standing there, peeing. That woke me up in a hurry.

"The buses in New Orleans were also segregated with blacks sitting in back. They stuck a wooden plaque in the back of the seats to divide the bus into front and back, with the whites in front of the plaque and the blacks behind. If a white person wanted a seat and it was empty, he or she could just move this thing back to get a seat.

"I worked in New Orleans from September 1943 until May 1944. Working at Higgins was kind of a carnival atmosphere, what you'd expect in New Orleans, because New Orleans wasn't really a working place. People, of course, worked, but actually one of the reasons I was glad ultimately to leave the place was people drank so much. If anybody was off work you just assumed they had a hangover. But more people showed up during wartime than otherwise."

Phyllis Jack Rohrer graduated from high school in June 1944 and went immediately to work at McChord Air Base near Tacoma, Washington. As a sheet metal worker she repaired airplanes—riveting, drilling, and patching—in a congenial but cold environment.

"It was repair work, not manufacturing new planes. We learned on the job. We were hired one day and on the line the next. I remember having a good time. We weren't under pressure. We all got along. There was no harassment of any kind. I can't remember the names of our bosses now, but I know they were two super men.

"My husband-to-be at that time was in the Air Force. Part of his

training was at Rapid City, South Dakota, and in August he was to
have two weeks leave before he went to England and thought he could
come home. He couldn't, but he was allowed leave in a certain radius.
So I got on a train and went back to Rapid City. I got a leave from
McChord. But then he went overseas, and I returned and continued
working until after the war and they just phased out our jobs.

"I don't remember anything unenjoyable about that job. I enjoyed
the people we worked with. Some were from this area, but I remember
working with three girls that came up from Oregon to work. Two of
them were single at the time, and one of them was from Oregon and
her husband I believe was stationed at Ft. Lewis. I guess we just
thought we were doing our part in the war.

"We were inside one of the great big hangars. In the winter, it
seemed to me the first thing the men had to do was open those hangar
doors, and it was so cold, and working on the cement and hanging on
those ice-cold planes, the fog in the morning. The fog would roll in.

"We wore white coveralls and we'd have to put so much clothes on
under them that we could hardly move. I wore an extra pair of slacks
and I used to wear my flannel pajamas underneath to keep warm.

"One time, the Walla Walla Air Base got behind in their work, and
there were thirteen of us from McChord that went over there to help
them out for about six or seven weeks. We were like six women and
seven men, and the women lived in a hotel in downtown Walla Walla,
one big room, and the men stayed at the air base. One of the girls
from Oregon had a friend that was injured in the war, and they
also have a Veterans Hospital in Walla Walla. We used to go out on
Sunday and visit him and, of course, any of the other men that wished
to be visited. I can remember sitting outside in the sunshine with
them."

*Working on a seismic crew in the Southwest oil country is a gypsy life.
After graduating from Oklahoma University in December 1941, Joy*

Hampton spent three and a half years traveling through Texas, Louisiana, Oklahoma, and Arkansas, the only woman on a crew of ten men, testing for good oil drilling locations.

"I knew how to get along with them. I just became that charming girl who insulted them and giggled. I could throw that line around as good as they could. And we all made the honky-tonks at night. We were transients and people treated us that way. We weren't particularly welcome either. The guys took their families with them. You don't have any social life unless you take it with you.

"We didn't stay in motels. Let me tell you that. If you did, you would be that woman who stayed in motels. I got a room in a private home. One woman told me, 'Now you can fix your own breakfast here, but I'm not fixing breakfast for anybody.' And she fixed it on Sunday and had the hardest old burned-up waffles I ever ate in my life. I just couldn't stand eating those waffles. The men stayed in different homes, too. A lot of people have rooms for rent. A lot of these old maids in Texas wouldn't rent to a woman, they want a man. So I'd go around and they'd have a sign out, and I'd go in and she'd say, 'No, I don't have anything.' And the boys would follow me around and rent up all the rooms behind me.

"The men were deferred for what was considered a defense industry. We got the culls. You could tell just by looking at them.

"The crew itself would go out and get the log, the electric log, made on a recorder, right in the truck, in the field, and then we spent the next day working on it. You look for anomalies, and structures. A structure is a formation below the surface. You must have something before you spend all that money drilling.

"I was called a junior computer. That was my title. I worked on the records and did the geology work. I really enjoyed that. I got to make maps. There was a guy on the crew who didn't like to make maps and I did. We did all the work in an area and submitted all the maps to the client. There were people who employed us, and their responsibility was to keep us working. I was gone three and one half years, from one job to another.

"We had computers and we had special electronic men that ran the records. The electronic gear was all in special trucks. We just moved around. I didn't even have a car. I got along all right with the men. As a woman, you always do more work and get less money. I was kind of ignored. And underpaid. I could have bought a house with the difference in salary, over the years.

"I had a piece of dynamite luggage. They called the boxes flat 50s because they weren't very deep and they carried fifty pounds of dynamite. So my father turned them inside out, because they wouldn't let you on the train with a box that said 'dynamite.' And he hinged two of those boxes together, put a lock on it. I still have it. I carry it around. Everybody on the crew had dynamite luggage."

When Jackie Moxley Romaine was twelve years old, she cut her hair to look like a boy so she could sell magazines. She's been working ever since, including wartime riveting at Curtiss-Wright Aircraft in St. Louis, Missouri, working on troopships in California, and delivering Army trucks out of St. Louis, after she returned from California.

"When my husband was shipped to a Navy base in San Francisco, I went along and got a job in the shipyards, living in Burlingame, California. I was kind of a general flunky. I carried insulation, fiberglass. You itched all over. You had to wear those regular old heavy boots, steel-toed, and a hard hat, heavy clothing. You had to climb the ladders, and then I took a bad fall. My feet went out from under me and I landed on my tailbone. There were ropes and wires and a box where they plugged in the electrical stuff. I lit on this box, right on the tailbone, and I wouldn't go to the doctor or hospital. I came back to Missouri. That ended my career in the shipyard.

"After a while I noticed some trucks being driven by women. I thought, 'I'd like to do that.' So I went to where they were building them and asked in the office, 'Where did you get the girls who are driving these?' And they told me, and I went and got the job. I love driving.

"We drove for United Transport and Commercial Transport delivering what was called 6×6s, jeeps, and 'Ducks' to bases mostly in the Southwest. We traveled in convoys, mostly women, though there was usually one man along as sort of a leader. The trucks were delivered to Army bases.

"I do well remember having to park our vehicle under the direction of a sergeant who was good at yelling and wanted those trucks parked three inches apart and in a straight line and you kept at it until they were.

"We were paid 5 cents a mile and took a bus back home. The company paid our fare.

"I had a problem staying awake on long trips like that. They'd all try to keep me awake. We were traveling in convoys of twelve or thirteen trucks. One time I veered out of my lane, and they pulled the whole convoy over and gave me a good talking to. Walked me around and someone had a thermos of coffee, made me drink coffee. I finally got used to it.

"On one trip to Jerseyville, I turned over one of the 6×6s, pinning me underneath. There were no doors on the driver's side so when I took the ditch to avoid a rear-end collision, I slid out of the door and was pinned under the truck.

"I lay there with both legs up over my face. Lucky for me, most of the weight of the truck was held off of me by the angle of the way it was in the ditch, but it was tight enough that I couldn't move.

"I could see the gasoline dripping, and I thought I was going to die right there. But the whole bunch stopped, and they lifted the thing off of me, and I got right back in and drove again. Somehow they had been messing with the carburetor to get more speed, and they were driving along and stopped suddenly, and I couldn't stop, with this increased speed, so rather than hit the truck in front of me I pulled off to the right and it was full of deep grass, and it didn't look that deep. It flipped over. Scared me."

While her husband was in the front lines with the Army, Althea Bates Gladish was operating several different machines at the Boston Gear Works in Quincy, Massachusetts.

"I'll never forget the night that one of my co-workers reached across her machine to hand a tool to another worker and the front of her uniform caught on a burr on the steel she was working on. Her machine was running and it was only by the quick action of a man working near her that she did not get pulled into the machine and killed, but the men were able to hold her away from the machine, which tore the clothing from her body. Thank God for quick acting and thinking people.

"There were many hazards in those machine shops. One girl caught her hair in the burring machine one night and almost lost her scalp. They shut the machine off. Once a man dropped a gear that was just taken off the cutting machine that had a burr on it and cut the toe right out of his shoe. You had to have your mind on what you were doing every second or some tragedy could occur.

"I traveled many bad snowstorms between Randolph, where I'd always lived, and Quincy. My brother worked there and he transported me back and forth.

"They were making all kinds of gears. I worked on a burring machine, cutting keyholes and gears. We didn't really have any training. If it helped win the war, I am proud of my contribution."

The armed services actively recruited teachers as officer training material. The WAVES were especially after Washington schoolteacher Betty Stuart Hennessey. But her superintendent in Prescott convinced her that her most patriotic duty was to remain in the classroom, since the shortage of teachers was so acute. However, school was not in session during the summer, so like many other teachers throughout the country, Hennessey went to work in a war plant. During the summer of 1943, she took a job in eastern Washington making wing tips for Boeing bombers.

"From eight to five, I ran a drill press and drilled holes in wing tips for the bombers at Brown Industries. It wasn't hard to learn. Nothing to it, really. I had to wear a Plexiglas mask over my face and head protection and the Rosie the Riveter suit—overalls.

"There was a team of three of us. Two women would pick up the sheets of aluminum, and they would fasten them onto a big table, put a template on top of that and secure it, and I would drag this heavy drill press over the sheet and drill the holes. The table was 4×8 feet and about chest high, and the big piece of equipment was on levers that you could move around above the table. Sort of like dental equipment. And then there was this quarter-inch drill on the bottom with a light projecting down onto the aluminum and we just guided it to the holes in the template and drilled.

"It was hard work, six days a week, eight to five, thirty minutes off for lunch, ten minutes for a break in the morning and in the afternoon. There were no chairs in the restroom for fear that we might sit down and tarry too long. There were no chairs anywhere where we could eat our lunch, and fortunately it was summer so we would take our lunches to the north side of the building and sit on the ground.

"We were paid only 50 cents an hour, and somewhere or another the federal government found out about this and forced the company

to pay us retroactively. The money, however, was not the most important point of my going to work that summer. It was kind of a patriotic
duty.

"On the whole, we were very hard working. There were a lot of
middle-aged women. On my team there was a woman I'd say in her
late fifties from one of the Dakotas. And believe me, she knew what
work was. She had come out during the dust bowl days in the late
thirties, and oh, my, what a hard worker she was. I'll never forget her
telling us of her experiences on the farm. There was the young rough-
type woman on this team with me who was very funny. She kept us all
laughing. There was camaraderie.

"I enjoyed going to work every morning. It was so different from
teaching. Also, while it was monotonous work, I realized I wouldn't
have to do it all my life. I looked around, and I thought, oh, how
fortunate could I be, to have had the privilege of an education and be
able to go on and do something beyond it."

4
· ·

Challenges, Triumphs, and Gaffes

O ften what came to mind as women recalled their work during
the war, a half century ago, were the challenges they faced and
overcame, the famous people and historical events they witnessed,
and the tragic and funny incidents that occurred. A tremendous variety of personal and professional experiences confronted the women
during the war.

Several challenges involved trucks. One woman thought she was
volunteering to drive a pickup and found herself behind the wheel of
an eighteen-wheel tractor-trailer. Another was asked to drive a truck
and was afraid to tell her boss she did not have a license to drive
anything.

One woman working as a railroad operator on a Missouri section
of the St. Louis–San Francisco Railroad had to jump aboard freight
trains as they slowed down through the station.

The most satisfying part of a woman machinist's job at a plant in
the Midwest was playing in the company band for fellow workers and
for servicemen in the nearby Veterans Hospital.

*Frances Park Claypool experienced both lighthearted and difficult
moments in her work during the war at two airfields in two different
states. When the war started, she said, "They waved the flag and
wanted the women to take men's jobs, so I stuck my hand out." After*

taking a government test in electronics, Claypool was sent to Duncan Field in San Antonio, Texas, where she was trained to be a flight line electrician. After she graduated, she was sent to Biggs Field in El Paso, where the military feared enemy infiltration.

"They really weren't prepared for invasion. They just had a barbed wire fence on posts. They were always afraid the Germans were going to come in. They were really worried about this. You could walk to Mexico from where we were. They told all the women to get sidearms and to wear them at all times. And those women didn't know how to load a gun, shoot a gun, nothing.

"The word got out that there was a bunch of women over at the fort where they were training the soldiers. So the soldiers decided they'd give the women a good scare one night from the nearby Army base. The women were on guard duty. We had the Norden bombsight on one of the planes there, a B-17. It was top secret at the time and we had to stand guard duty twenty-four hours a day on that. The plane was locked up and turned over to the security force, which was a bunch of women who didn't know what they were doing.

"This night the guys came over to hoot and holler. They made noises, and this woman said, 'Who goes there?' And they wouldn't identify themselves, and she said, 'You identify yourselves or I'll shoot.' And they didn't and she did. He got a whole butt full of twelve-gauge shot in his rear. The commanding officer at the base put out the word: 'There'll be no more horsing around with the women at Biggs Field.'

"There was a guy—we called him shavetail—who was a ninety-day-wonder lieutenant. They're the big lord and master of the whole universe. Anyway, he came in in a P-38, which had dual tanks on it. And he looked at the women sneeringly and said, 'I want my fuel tanks filled to the brim.' He said he'd be back at a certain time. We said, 'Yes, sir,' and we let him go. The commanding officer said, 'None of the tanks will be filled.'

"We had a mountain outside El Paso that was a pretty sharp take-off. They had to climb fast to get over, and if you're overloaded with fuel, you couldn't climb. Well, he came in the next morning, and his tanks were not full. They were probably three-fourths or two-thirds full. He said that wasn't what he wanted, so we asked him to see the commanding officer. He went in and just raised Cain. So they filled his tanks. And the commanding officer came out there and said, 'Now just watch him take off.' We watched him, and he almost didn't get off the ground, and he took the fence with him. Last we saw, he was just barely clearing the mountain and dragging the fenceposts and barbed wire with his wheels, and he couldn't get his wheels up.

"The women did really well. I was really proud of them. Sometimes they didn't know what they were doing, but they were trying, and then they'd ask, and that's important.

"I worked there until they turned it over to the soldiers. Then they released us. You couldn't change jobs during the war without permission. So they gave us our release slips. My husband thought he might be drafted, and my mother lived in California, and I had a little boy, so we thought it would be better if I were near my family for the rest of the war. We went to San Diego and I went to work for Convair there.

"I was the first woman hired at Convair. The general foreman was not going to have any women in his plant. There was no way, and that's the end of that story. The guy who told me about this foreman said, 'He's dynamite. We've got to have women. We know that we're going to have women in here, even if he doesn't think so. So you're on probation. If it works out for you, we'll have a crew of women here in six weeks.'

"And sure enough we did. I worked my tail off. And I never talked to anybody. I outworked the men and they were all mad. I was turning out work, and they were just standing around doing nothing. I was overhauling magnetos, starters, generators, working the lathe and these guys were standing around, going 'Ha, ha' and drinking coffee, and I was doing all their work. So in six weeks they had a crew of women there. Some of the women bucked rivets, some did upholstery, just everything.

"Once they asked for someone to drive a truck. I put my hand up. Drive a pickup truck, no big deal. But it turned out it was an eighteen-wheeler with two 5,000-gallon high-tech gasoline tanks on it. I have an idea I turned pale. I didn't dare say I didn't know how, because I'd have lost my job. I sweat blood. I got up—it was all I could do to get my foot on the fender part, it was so high. I got up there and thought, 'What am I going to do?' and I turned the key on. And I punched the brake. I could hear this whiz. I knew it had air brakes, and I knew it would stop fast. I had to be very careful. I'd never driven anything with air brakes, but I'd heard 'em before.

"I looked down on the floor. There was the gearshift diagram. So I let it run a few minutes, and I studied the thing and found a gear that I thought might pull it. In the meantime, the boss was saying, 'Don't you get near one of those propellers. They cost $25,000 each and if you wreck one, we've had it.'

"Well, how am I going to drive a great big truck like that with two trailers? I didn't know anything about trailers, or towing, or anything. But I held my breath and got by. It was just—after a while I just loved that truck and I could wheel and deal that thing around. Pure luck. Someone was riding on my shoulder. Now, you can't find anything I can't drive. I drove a truck to Alaska with a camper on it, and towed a twenty-two-foot trailer and drove 11,500 miles."

Elanore Bair Kurtz moved to Seattle from her home in the Okanogan Valley shortly after graduating from high school and signed up to work as a riveter for the Boeing Company. Eight months into her job, she fell in love with another Boeing worker, married him, and moved back home when he was shipped off to Alaska.

"An old family friend contacted me and asked if I would try a job with Fish and Game. No woman had ever done it, and nowadays it would be nothing, but then, I was the first woman that had ever been in that position.

"I was working with a program where they were checking to see how many chinook salmon were spawning. The first part of my job was to sit on the dam and there was a fish ladder there, and I recorded every fish that jumped over, every chinook salmon, because there were very few. They expected thousands because they go clear up to the end of the river to spawn. But very few went through, and they never did find out what happened to them.

"When I took the job, I filled out an application, and they asked if I could drive. I wrote yes, because I always knew I would never have to anyway. About a couple of weeks after I was on the job, my boss drove up with this government van with the Fish and Game seal on the side of it, and he said, 'You'll be driving this from now on.'

"I told him my driver's license was expired and I couldn't believe it. He said, 'That's all right. We'll just, tomorrow we'll go to Okanogan and have it renewed.' Then I said, 'Well, I don't know. This is different from anything I've driven.' He said, 'That's okay. You get in it. I'll show you where the gears are.' And he said, 'You follow me until I turn off at the Jergins's place. If you have any problem, just honk your horn.'

"I followed him. I don't think I ever got it out of second. And after I got around the bend, I stopped at this house where some people I knew lived. I called my brother and we practiced that night. I stayed up 'til two in the morning reading all the driving rules.

"The next morning, my boss took me down to Okanogan to take my test, and he said, 'If I vouch for her, can we skip the driving test today, because I really am in a hurry?' And they said, 'But of course.' I know that old guy knew I couldn't drive, I just know it, but I did fine.

"From there on, my job was to drive to a certain point and get out in one of these yellow liferafts and float down the river. I would stop anyplace where there was kind of a riffle and check to see if there was a nest. They showed me how to identify it.

"Then I drew a map of the river at that point. And I didn't find many of them. Then this one other fellow from Iceland, he was over on a scholarship type thing and learning from our government, he would pick up the van and he would meet me about four miles down the river. We kind of leapfrogged that way. It was interesting. As I floated down that river, people from either side would come out. It was like something from outer space to them.

"I think back on it and wonder, how could I have the nerve to do those things. But my mother taught us to be sort of independent, honest, but just try things, and so it wasn't scary at all to me. I enjoyed it."

After her husband enlisted in the Navy in May 1942, Madeline Bart-low Ontis went to work at Mare Island Naval Shipyard, just fifteen miles from her hometown of Napa, California.

"There was a big push on for help. Everybody was expected to do something for the war effort. We went in as classified laborers, and that was the beginning position. The first day, I was assigned to the electric shop. We got on-the-job training. We worked on a bench and made electric boxes for the cables. We put clamps in and soldered the watertight tubes in. There were all sorts of things to do before the cables went out on the ship. We were working on British destroyer escorts. The yard had a contract to do so many of them.

"The floors of the shop were asphalt, it was like the rocky road to Dublin. It was quite primitive. I worked swing shift and there's no place colder on earth than swing shift on Mare Island. We had a small crew, we were called a gang, and everybody was good to us. There were just a few of us to start. I was just a kid. I was skin and bones. There was a lady from Idaho who was older and there was an older man. I say older now, they were probably forty. This one gentleman told her, 'You take care of that kid at lunchtime. She doesn't look as if she gets enough to eat.' They brought something from home. I had more to eat than any two men on Mare Island. The men we had there in that shop couldn't have been nicer.

"I also worked in the toolroom and the supply room and the fellows would come in off the ship and they knew how gullible I was. They asked for a left-handed monkey wrench. Probably today they have left-handed monkey wrenches. With all seriousness, I would search and search and finally I would go ask one of the men in the shop, and they would say, 'Tell them we don't have any left.'

"In the shop, it was like one big family. When you went out to work on the ships, which we did later, you'd work with the other trades. But in our group, we had just the electricians and electricians' helpers. Once I was working out on the ships down at the seawall, and we all had our lunch pails in one area. We kept them pretty much together. Well, these welders thought it was pretty funny and they tap welded those metal lunch boxes to the metal decks of the ship. Just enough that when you reached down to lift them up, they didn't come. That was great fun.

"There was another funny thing when we were working on the ships. They recruited help from all over the United States. We got a lot of Okies and hillbillies. But we also got people from New York, and I was always amazed because there were big shipyards back there. Anyway, one little lady had the layered look before it was fashionable. She wore bib overalls, but she never put the sweaters under the bibs. She put the bib next to her underwear. I think it took her half the shift to go to the bathroom. She never thought to put the sweaters on first and then the bib. But she was a nice little lady.

"I'm a native of Napa and it broke my heart to hear people come and tell how good they had it back home. Now if it had been that good, they would never have left. I had just enough Irish in me to say, 'If you don't like it, I'm sure the train goes the other way.'"

Dena Brugioni Johnson had been married a couple of years when the war broke out and her husband enlisted in the Army. She left their half-completed home and moved in with her parents in Des Moines, Iowa. She got a job at Ford Motor Company working as a machinist, but her most interesting job was not the one she was hired for.

"We were working on farm machinery, on punch presses. There weren't hardly any men left. We didn't get any training. They just put us down there and showed us how to do it, and that was it.

"I joined the CIO union. Everybody that went in that plant, they gave them thirty days. They had to join the union. They paid us just like the men. But at the time, it was kind of piecework. They didn't really pay you by the piece, but they had rates, and they'd time you. There was a time-study man that would time us while we were working and they'd bring the rate in the morning when you'd go on these different jobs. They'd have the rate for you and expect you to make it. They wanted you to work fast.

"They had a band at that time and I played in it. I was one of the girls that played in the band. I played a B-flat sax. It's a very different instrument. It's a straight one, not curved. It looks like a big clarinet. It's real funny how I got to play that. My dad wanted me to play a fiddle and I said, 'I don't know about these. I want to play one instrument.'

"He went down to a place where they hock their instruments, and this instrument had been in a fire, and it hadn't been hurt, just kind of burned up. Well, my dad repaired it all and then he bought it for me. I think he paid $25 for it. Now, they run $500 or $600. So I played in different bands, too, with my dad, and he had his own band. He taught me. My dad taught music.

"When they started this band at Ford, I told my friends and they looked at me kind of funny, and I told them I had something like a sax. They said, 'Well, it probably needs tuning and everything and tabs on it. Bring it over and we'll take a look.' And they silvered it all up for me. Then they said, 'Come on in. We'll try you out.'

"Every Friday we played at noon hour for the workers, and then we played for the Veterans Hospital and different things like that. Every Friday evening, we'd have practice.

"My father was working at the ordnance plant, and when the war was over, they laid everybody off, and he was out of work. Now the band wanted a clarinet player that could play first, and I told them I knew one. They wanted to know who it was and I said it was my dad. They wanted to know how old he was and I said, 'He's fifty-eight years old.' They said they just couldn't hire anybody at that age. See, he had to be one of the employees in order to play in that band.

"So I said, 'Well, next Friday night I'm going to bring him in. I just want you to listen to him play one number.' You know what? The next morning they brought him in the office and he got a job. They gave him a job and he worked there ten years.

"After the war, they called us in the office and they asked us to quit our jobs and give it to our husbands. I told them, no, I'm not going to do it, because I had about three years of seniority, and then my husband would have come in with no seniority, and no job and no work, they'd fire him. Some of the girls did that, and that's what happened. Their husbands lost their jobs. They'd be the last ones in and they'd lose their jobs.

"I was smart enough to keep mine. They didn't make us quit, but they wanted us to do it. The union told us we didn't have to do such a thing. They protected us. There weren't too many that stayed there after the war, at the most maybe twenty-five or thirty out of about a hundred. It was such heavy work that they just kept quitting. When I retired a little over thirty years later, I don't think there were more than three or four women left."

In December 1941, Dolores Kelsey Sorci was living in Boise, Idaho, and was shopping in her local grocery when she heard about the Japanese attack on Hawaii.

"On December 7, the greengrocer, a Chinese fellow, said, 'Did you hear about Pearl Harbor?' He was really elated, of course, because the Japanese had been trampling a lot on the Chinese over there, and he was glad we were going to get into this and help them. So I got real patriotic and thought, 'I'm going down there to town and sign up for work.' So I did, and I didn't hear from them until July. Then the letters started pouring in, all these forms, and I was right in the middle of it. A riveter.

"They gave us basic training, how to cut the sheet metal, how to frame it, how to put the rivets in. I had a girl partner. She and I were in competition. We were kind of the top of the class. They threw everything together so quick. They found an old place that they used as a machine shop at 13th. We graduated in October and were asked which air base we preferred. I chose Hill Air Base in Ogden, Utah. My husband had signed up as a guard there. At that time everybody needed jobs, and my husband was glad to have me working. I was hired at $75 a month—really good pay. My husband signed up ahead of me; he got there two or three months before I did.

"I don't really know what I did. Some little things that went here and there. It just wasn't too interesting to me. It didn't really make much sense. It was all for B-24 airplanes. Hill was a regular air base, a repair base. The planes were coming in to be serviced. They washed the plane down with a hard nozzle, got it all cleaned up, then removed the engine and everything and moved it to the next station and over-hauled it.

"They asked for volunteers to go to tubing and cables and I worked there for a year. Tubing is all the gas lines and oxygen and everything that's in an airplane. It's amazing how many tubes there are along the insides of those walls. That got me completely out of riveting, and I enjoyed it. I had to learn something new.

"If I wanted to order so much tubing for a job, I had to figure it out ahead of time. When you order tubing, it's not like ordering yardage. I had to be really accurate.

"I had a really good boss named Bill, and he and I worked to-gether for about six months. There were women working with me, and that was a problem. We didn't have any men there at that time, and Bill was promoted and he left the department. He said he was turning it over to me, and then I had two black ladies and two other ladies. And one of them said, 'I'm not taking orders from you and I'm not working with those black people.' It was a constant battle. They sent in a boss from another department. He didn't know anything about tubing. He wouldn't ask me, or ask for any advice, didn't want any-thing from me at all. I endured that for a while and then I said, 'I'm going to flight-test.'

"You could request flight testing; if there was an opening they'd take you. It was exciting. I'd get to go to the flight-test hangar. We had an old fellow from Texas named Harry, and he said, 'I don't want any women in my department.' And they said, 'You've got to have women in your department.' So they would take one lady to a crew of five men.

"I just did everything. I pulled a lot of screens in the engine, and installed a lot of spark plugs. You found out how to do that by working with the crew chief and he told you what to do. I think the worst job was pulling the oil screens. The oil would run down your arm to the elbow.

"I did a lot of standing by on the fire bottle. If the engine caught fire, you'd pick up the fire bottle and spray the fire out. You always had to stand by when they were starting the engines, just in case one of them caught fire.

"The fellows would be up to tricks sometimes. They'd take the fire bottle—it had carbon dioxide in it—and they'd run after rats in the hangar and freeze them. Then I'd find the bottles empty in the morning, and I'd have to go get them filled.

"The guys treated me fine. I had an initiation when I started. Someone pried my toolbox open when I just started and took all my tools. Tricks like that. But they were fine.

"We had a captain who flew the thirty seconds over Tokyo—Jack Manch. That guy was six foot seven and he loved B-25s. The captains would take our planes out for a test flight. Manch wore a leather jacket with a big Chinese flag on the back of it and Chinese writing all over the flag. The writing said, 'This man is a friend, give him all the aid you can.'

"There was a little tear down one part. He had it covered with a clear plastic to keep it together, and I asked about the tear. He said, 'That's from when I jumped into the rice paddy.' When they had to abandon those planes in China, they were hiking through those paddy fields, and he was helped by the Chinese.

"Manch was from Virginia, and he was too tall to fly. They weren't going to allow him to fly, but his father knew someone in Washington, and they pulled strings and got him in. He was a good flier, but I would never fly with him. We were near Salt Lake and he would fly over the lake and there was a little island in it with buffalo on it and he just loved to make a run at the buffalo. I said, 'Not going with you.'

"What happened to Jack Manch was—they got the jets in and he was down at the Las Vegas field. He was flying with a young man, and he told the kid to jump and he just rode the plane down. They were in an area where people lived and he didn't want to kill anyone. The engine had flamed out, and he died."

When Naomi Turnbough Campbell served a cup of coffee to a railroad operator who stopped in her mother's restaurant during the war, he told her they needed people to work on the railroad. After graduating from high school in May 1945, she started work as an agent and operator in July near her Dillon, Missouri, home.

"I sold tickets, loaded and unloaded trains, and shipped freight. It was hard work but fun, too. We shipped everything from cream cans to cantaloupes. The cream cans were heavy. Everything we found in the freight room had to be loaded.

"And we handed up train orders. As the train went by, they reached out with their arm and grabbed the orders from a post. Sometimes we had to hand-hold them up and that was even more dangerous. We had to judge the distance from the train, which could be going sixty miles an hour.

"The main job of an operator was the train orders. They told which train was to take the main line and which was to wait on the side track. We got them from the dispatcher. Every train had to get orders because they lost all contact with the dispatcher at the end of a twenty-mile stretch out of the nearest roundhouse. They'd be sitting out there in the middle of nowhere.

"I was proud of working for the railroad. There were only a few other women. The older men who didn't go to war resented me. One agent was cranky and cross and didn't have time to show me anything until he got sick, and then he had time for me. He wanted me to take his place. But the men on the railroad were very good to me, very protective. I never had any problems.

"We worked seven days a week. They were short of help and the trains were busy. You got time off if you asked for it, but I didn't. There were all those troop trains, and the freight. The trains were so packed, people would sit in the aisles on their suitcases.

"I relieved agents and operators along a certain section of the railroad when they wanted time off. The trainmaster would call from central headquarters. Usually they would tell me how long I would be at a certain station. I'd ride on the freight train, in the caboose or the engine. Riding in the caboose was the roughest ride you'd ever want. Terrible.

"For me to get on, they'd just slow down and I'd have my suitcase and my lantern. In those days, the engineer didn't have a phone to the back so they had to guess if I got on. The conductor on the back and the brakeman would try to help me.

"When I took people's places, I'd have to find a place to live. I might be there a couple months. Usually, we had homes where the railroad people stayed. The farthest I'd go would be about 150 miles either way out of Newburg. Some towns were so small, there weren't any laundromats and I had to send my dirty laundry home for my mother to wash and send back. I'd put it in a suitcase, put it on the train, send it home, and she'd return it the same way.

"I couldn't always get meals with the people I stayed with because of rationing. One town, I went door to door asking if I could take meals, and one family said yes. I slept in one place and ate in another. Years later, I went back to this town and looked up the people where I had boarded. When she opened the door, I said, 'You don't know who I am.' She said, 'I sure do. You're Naomi.' After forty years! We had a good visit.

"We didn't have electricity then. We used oil lamps. We had to check the freight cars in the yard during the night to see which ones they brought in. I'd shine my light in the cars and there'd be men sleeping there. I had to tell them to leave. That really dropped off during the war, but right after, these men started riding the rails again. I'd ask them to get out and the minute I walked away, they'd go right back in. This was really scary. And coming to work, walking into that waiting room in the pitch dark, that was scary."

Just before Rita Stangle Reker graduated from high school in 1942, the FBI came to her high school, Immaculate Heart, in Coeur d'Alene, Idaho, to interview people for wartime work. The bureau needed to hire fingerprint technicians and fill other entry-level positions usually held by young men.

"They were looking primarily for someone that would work in the Boise office as a typist. Fortunately, I was a terrible typist, and so they offered me Washington, D.C. I had an aunt who was a nun in Washington, D.C., going to school at the time, so it wasn't just taking off from a little town in Idaho. I thought it was really great. I probably wouldn't have gone if it hadn't been for Sister Clare.

"I think it was six or eight months that we were in school learning. We had to learn to read fingerprints and classify them, and then we would get files and files and files. Acres of criminal prints would come in from a little town or Los Angeles or wherever, and we would classify them and search through the files to see if there were prior records. They had to search everybody that went into the service. They were fingerprinted, and then their prints were searched to see if they had a record. I don't know why.

"At first it was a twenty-four-hour schedule, and I worked from midnight to morning. Then we moved to the National Guard Armory near the Potomac, and that made a big difference because it was so huge. They spread everything out and we worked regular hours.

"One incident still cracks me up when I think of it. Imagine this huge room, and the files were about four feet tall. It was just make-do during the war. We had little stools that were probably a foot high on wheels that we could roll around on. I happened to be standing up and turned the fingerprint card over to read about the man who I was searching, and the charge was there.

"I turned around and I said, 'Gertrude,' because she was quite a distance away, and so was everybody, 'What's sodomy?' And heads turned all over, and a week later I found out what it was, maybe an hour later, and I just died of mortification for about six months. I'd heard the word all my life. It's one of the seven deadly sins or something, but I didn't know people did it or what it was.

"J. Edgar Hoover was strange. He didn't allow black people to work there, so we were never under civil service. We had our own retirement plan because if you were civil service, there were all those quotas. I'm sure he thought women were just one step above blacks.

"J. Edgar Hoover, he told presidents what to do. It was a strange power he had. I knew that he was five feet eight inches tall or something like that. I'm five eight, myself. Yet when I walked into his office and he stood up and shook hands with me, he seemed ten feet tall. It was unbelievable—we were brainwashed into all this, and he was the director and he was very, very, very impressive. We always said that if a directive came down for all of us to walk into the Potomac, I'm sure we all would have.

"While I was there, I was at the Knights of Columbus USO and met a very handsome United States Marine who went overseas. He fought in Okinawa and everything. While he was gone, I happened to run across his print in a separate section where they kept service people's prints, and he was two years younger than he told me he was. I was eighteen.

"But I married him and we had four children and lived happily ever after. I never mentioned that I checked up on him while we were writing to each other. But it really, really killed me because that made him awfully young. In fact, when we married, his mother had to sign for him."

With the title "War Time Sub," Lillian Brooks Crawford was hired as a postal worker at the main post office in St. Louis, Missouri, when she was seventeen years old. She was first hired as a Christmas worker but after the holiday was called for steady employment, which lasted about a year and a half.

"In the winter in this area, when the weather is snowy and bad, I think of the times the airplanes were grounded and all airmail to the servicemen would come to us to be sorted and sent by train. The trucks would bring bags of mail from the airport and we'd have to put everything aside to sort it. Military mail took precedence over everything else. Mail was so important to the servicemen.

"Maybe we'd be an hour into sorting the mail and they would say, the planes are going to take off, gather everything up. So we'd gather everything up and get it back to the plane. We'd send back our tied and sorted bundles with maybe one remaining unsorted one.

"Christmas packages were occasionally not well wrapped, and cakes and lingerie and goodness knows what would fall out. Sometimes you could salvage it, sometimes not.

"We didn't have the breaks that people do now. Only a lunch break. It was the war that brought about morning and afternoon breaks. We could go to the bathroom when we wanted as long as we got someone to take over the machine we were running. When women started into the war plants, that's when the breaks started.

"We made about a dollar an hour, which was good wages then. I took two streetcars to work. I worked twelve midnight to eight. Today, the stores are open twenty-four hours a day and that's the kind of thing we really needed then. Here we were working around the clock and trying to get our shopping done during shopping hours. It wasn't easy, especially since we had to shop pretty much every day, with small iceboxes for storage. Not all of us had refrigerators.

"I left when I was eighteen to get married. My husband's ship came in and we got married and went to Philadelphia and I couldn't get a leave of absence, so I just quit!"

Gretchen de Boer Courtleigh's first job was as a monorail operator at Higgins Aircraft in New Orleans, Louisiana. She dropped out of college to take the job.

"The monorail is an overhead crane. I was in this little cage, or car, hanging from the ceiling on two rails. The whole object was to put things on this hook attached to the car that I could move about the plant. I worked there for a long time, and I learned to operate the hook, but they seldom ever put anything on it. So all day long, I'd go up and down on my monorail. If you didn't line up properly on the rails, your little car would tumble down into this bottomless pit, where they were building airplanes.

"My friend Doris worked in the engineers' department and I could go overhead and wave to her. In fact, that's about all I did was visit a lot. I was trying to remember things, and my husband asked what we made. I don't know exactly because it didn't mean a thing to me. I was seventeen or eighteen and it was an awful lot of money. I'm sure we got the minimum wage, whatever it was, and I do remember working Saturdays and Sundays because you got double time and overtime for doing the same thing.

"I used to go to work with the *Daily Worker*. I just thought it was smart to do that. I was playing communist, socialist, really. We didn't know what communists were. I would buy the *Daily Worker* and kind of tuck it about so that people could see it. I didn't really know anything about it other than it was a piece of show.

"At the plant, we made C-47s, which was a huge cargo plane, and they finally got one put together and it was on the ground floor of the factory and they were going to have a big ceremony the next day, and I knocked a ladder onto the plane. I was very suspect because of my *Daily Worker* paper.

"But nothing happened. They just kind of gathered about and said, 'Is this sabotage? Did you do it? What did you do? Why did you knock the ladder on the plane?' Well, I didn't see the ladder and my monorail truck knocked it over on the plane. It didn't really hurt the plane that much, but they couldn't have the ceremony the next day. That was my big experience at Higgins Aircraft."

ElvaRene Daughhetee Plimpton was teaching in Texas in 1944 when a friend left Texas for Portland, Oregon, with her serviceman husband. Plimpton accepted her friend's invitation to join them in Portland and get a job in the shipyard. Plimpton was particularly eager to earn money so she could pay her father back for some recent surgery and for her college education.

"I got on the graveyard shift as a welder. The graveyard paid much more. I worked at the Commercial Iron Works. I got a room of my own in a boardinghouse and then got a place in the temporary wartime housing, living with another girl.

"I was treated well by the men at the Iron Works. But I had a very strange experience with some of the women. I grew up on a farm, and all our lives my parents emphasized the importance of education. My mother graduated from college in 1914. We were always told to treat everyone equal, and we did. As a matter of fact, my father was instrumental in making sure the farmworkers' children got some good education.

"But when I got to the shipyard, there were some racial problems. For some reason, our records were left open and people could see whatever you'd been doing. People discovered that I had been a teacher, so I got the nickname of 'Teach' from the black girls. Because I had an education and most of them didn't, they kind of ganged up on me, and they were going to get me.

"I would go up the stairs to the lunchroom, and they would sit there whittling with their knives out, long switchblade knives. I was told they were going to get me. My leadman told me I should pack a gun. I wrote my father for a pistol my brother had given me, and he told me to come home! I didn't. I simply made an effort to become very friendly with the black girls and they left me alone. I had never done anything to antagonize them, but they had that feeling of resentment.

"I had to quit soon, because my eyes are poor, and sometimes when your hood is up and someone strikes an arc, the pain from the light is very great. So I went up to Hoquiam, Washington, where I had an aunt and worked at Boeing as a riveter. I started as a bucker, then got to riveting.

"I had a serious eye injury on that job. There's a spring that should be screwed on the riveting gun, but the man near me was in a hurry and he hadn't done that. I was bucking for him, and he touched the trigger and the trigger flew out and broke my glasses, my regular glasses because safety glasses hadn't arrived yet, and I had to go to the hospital with pieces of glass in my eye.

"Whenever a telegram came to the shop, it became so quiet you could hear a pin drop. The shop is so noisy, with riveting, hammering, but when anyone came to the door with one of those telegrams, everything would go quiet. One day my name was called and of course I thought of my brother, but it was some friends wanting me to come to Portland. Another time when the whole plant got quiet, of course, was when they announced that Roosevelt had died."

Before the war started, Jane-Ellen Washburn Bartholomew was a reporter in Santa Cruz, California, first with the Santa Cruz News *and then the* Santa Cruz Sentinel. *She had moved further north and was working for the* Santa Rosa Press Democrat *when the Pearl Harbor attack occurred.*

"I was sports editor. I believe I was the first female sports editor west of the Mississippi. There weren't many men in those days. I knew sports pretty well. I mean, I was always interested in everything, but football was my downfall. But I worked it out by going to the coach after each game and he would explain to me what they were doing, and it worked out very nicely. I covered myself pretty well.

"Six months later I went to the *Oakland Tribune* as a reporter, taking the place of a man. I was treated real well. There were three women on the staff, and I guess a lot of anemic men. I never felt different. I felt accepted.

"It was exciting, really exciting. I met the ship in 1945 that brought back prisoners, American prisoners who had been in Philippine camps. They were people captured from the Philippines and then sent to Japan after the long march that they had in the Philippines.

"They were blind from malnutrition. Later they regained their sight, but seeing them come off the ships was really traumatic.

"I was the first one to interview so many that hadn't been heard from for three years. I remember one captain, I can't remember his name, but his fingers were big bulbs at the end of each finger. They had pulled his nails from his hands so many times in torture. It was very moving."

5

. . . .

Mentor or Tormentor?

O ne of the first questions that arises about women working side
by side with men in offices and factories where they previously
were excluded is, "How were you treated by your colleagues and
superiors?"

An almost equal number of women were treated with respect and
offered assistance as those who encountered discrimination, proposi-
tions, catcalls, or derogatory remarks. For every woman who was told
she must sleep with her boss or lose her job, there was one who met a
supportive boss or co-worker.

The women with positive experiences felt they were treated with
the same respect men would give their daughters or wives, saying
they never thought twice about being a woman in the workplace.
However, some women who continued working after the war were
jarred by the change in attitude toward them, from one of acceptance
to much greater resistance as they became much more of a minority
and were viewed as taking jobs that rightfully belonged to men.

The negative encounters with men ranged from practical jokes
undermining women's work, to much more vicious vocational sabotage, to catcalls and whistles, to outright sexual bribery: put out or
lose your job.

For the most part, women accepted the practical jokes and whistles and winks as part of what was to be expected in the workplace,
rarely thinking about reporting the behavior or taking it seriously.

However, beyond winks and unpleasant remarks, most women did not hesitate to confront objectionable behavior. Their solutions to harassment included threatening the men with the tools at hand or telling their superiors.

As far as husbands' attitudes were concerned, most were supportive and many worked alongside their wives or in the same region. They were glad for the extra money and pleased with their wives' work. Occasionally, this wasn't the case and the husbands resisted their wives' work.

Inka Sanna Benton of San Rafael, California, encountered friendly, kind men in two places she worked during the war, with the exception involving someone from outside her place of employment. A native of Poland, Benton came to the United States in 1940 after enduring two months of German occupation she says she would rather forget. While completing the architecture training she began in Europe, Benton was offered a job at Steuben Glass in New York City. She and a male architect worked side by side for two and a half years designing all the glass for this exclusive crystal store. She left the job to pursue her studies further.

"By then, I had decided to go back to school and get my master's in architecture, and Harvard was opening up a place for women for the first time. I applied and was accepted, but I knew I had about nine months to wait, so I went to work in an architecture office because I thought it would help me. I applied in an office that was the most old-fashioned place I've been to—especially after Steuben Glass. When I came in, I don't think I saw anybody that was younger than fifty.

"I was shown to my desk and it was a high, very large, stand-up desk that I was too short for. They looked around and found an apple box so I could reach the drawings by standing on it. They were doing work for the City of New York, designing hospitals. In the old days, the drawings had to be kept so they had to be drawn on linen. A very special technique. You take the linen—it has a very smooth covering, it is blue and called drafting linen—and you are given the original drawings that I would lay on my table and put out that piece of transparent drafting linen and copy it. That was my job. Nothing creative, but difficult. You had to know how to do good drafting because it was quite tricky.

"I was the only woman with about a dozen men. They were older, between forty and sixty, and the boss was older than that. They were sort of nice to me but, of course, they saw me as a young girl who has the whole world open for her. One day when the inspector for the hospital came in—he was not employed by the company—to check on the work, he said to me, 'Hello, young lady, what do you think you are doing?' And I said, 'As you can see, I'm making a copy of this hospital design on linen.' He said, 'You're doing very nicely but I will give you some advice. It would be much better, I think, if you stuck to kitchens and gardens. Much easier for you, young lady.'

"I was really upset by that. But that was in the days, after all, in 1943, and there were very few women in architecture. As far as the men I worked with there, we were so far apart we hardly talked. We really were living in another world. I was a young woman determined to get ahead. I think they were really people who just had a job. I don't think they thought of me being in the same profession as they were. I've got to say they were impressed when they learned that I had been given a scholarship to Harvard. On the whole, they went out of their way to be nice to me.

"When I quit, they prepared a lovely farewell drawing, showing me walking through the gates of Harvard, carrying my rolled-up scrolls for drafting and other equipment, and they wrote a nice limerick about me. I thought this showed they thought highly of me."

On the other side of the country, at an oil refinery in Martinez, California, Sally Boyce Davis found one co-worker particularly helpful in
her work testing gasoline products. With a husband overseas and a
mother-in-law available to care for her baby, Davis was looking for
work when a friend told her about the refinery.

"Jobs were easy to get—at least that one was. I walked in there cold,
with no background, and they didn't blink an eye. Just, when can you
come? It was wonderful. I wish it had been like that the rest of my
life.

"It was all women working in the department. As you came in—
you didn't all come in at once—when I came in they gave me to
someone who had been there a while and she took me through the
paces of each test, which I now have forgotten. But as she did her
work that night and every night for that week, I would stand by and
write down everything she wrote down and she would describe to me
what she was writing down and why. And she'd show me the steps of
the test.

"Then the second week they put me on one machine and I would
just work that every evening for my shift. I just kept doing that same
test but on different jugs of gasoline. None of them were marked
except by numbers. But at the end, they all went out to different
companies: Richfield, Mobil, Associated, all of them. It was all out of
one vat. I always thought that was really weird.

"There was a great sense of camaraderie. At lunch break, we all
went together. It was fun. We were all young.

"I guess you'd call what I was doing manual work. It wasn't anything that took great intellectual ability. They taught you how to do
these tests, and how to put down the answers and hand it on. Someone
else made the decisions. In this little department where I was, there

were eight women on each shift. Women had taken over all these jobs. There was one man, a 4-F, who was fairly young. He was like a man Friday. He did everything. He filled in where other people weren't able to do things. You could always call on him. He seemed to know about it all, and if things were too heavy for us, he'd help."

During her work as a shipfitter's helper at South Boston Naval Dry Dock in Massachusetts, Julie Raymond Elliott was treated like a younger sister by most co-workers and given advice by her boss on how to respond to sexual advances by other men. Elliott was eighteen years old and newly married to an Air Force lieutenant bombardier who was stationed overseas when she began her war work at the Boston Navy Yard in Charlestown, transferring six months later to South Boston Naval Dry Dock.

"I worked with a lot of nice people and men that were—at the time I thought they were old guys—they were probably forty or so. They treated me like their little baby. They used to pick me up every day and I would squeeze into a car with maybe four or five guys. They'd take me to work. They were very good to me. 'Gotta get our girl, get her to work,' they'd say.

"It seems to me I worked night shifts because it helped kill the time and I'd have time to go visit my mother during the day or my sister, and then at 3:00 P.M. to go to work. One week I worked seventy-two hours, and I went home that night and slept the whole night and the whole next day, I was so tired.

"Sometimes you had some problems with men that were fresh to the girls, young girls. Of course, you're kind of naive at that age, and the boss I had said to me that any time any of these guys gives you a hard time, you strike an arc. If you've ever been around welding, when you strike an arc you know you can get a flash that can be very painful. So he more or less taught me the ropes. He was a man in his thirties, and he'd say, 'Don't take any stuff from these guys.' There were some men that thought some of these girls are fast and loose, and there were some girls like that. But he said, 'If you want their respect, don't let them talk like that to you.' He was a good guy to do that.

"One time, my boss let me do shipfitting and he said that I knew how to do this, and he gave me a helper. I did it for maybe a week. It was a matter of hammering wedges into a U-shaped steel piece to hold down the girders. Then somebody would tack it. At the time I was doing that, he had the construction officers come through, and he bragged, here is my lady shipfitter.

"I did it for a week with no pay raise. We thought we were making a lot of money, but it's like peanuts today. And then I said, 'I don't want to do that anymore, Johnny.' It was hard work. So I went back to doing my shipfitter's-helper work.

"A lot of the girls I hung around with had husbands in the service. I lost my husband over there in Romania when they bombed those oil fields. He was killed May 5, 1944. He'd enlisted before we married, but I can't remember the reason that he didn't go for six months. So we had six months together before he left. Then he was killed about a year and a half later. So I was a widow when I was twenty. It was a sad time for me. A lot of the people there were helpful to me at the time.

"I think I worked there through the whole war. When President Roosevelt died, I was working there and that's where I got the news that he had died. We saw prisoners come in—they kept them there in prison barracks—German prisoners."

Not all women, however, experienced the same hospitality and graciousness from their co-workers. For some, it took time to be accepted. After graduating from Stanford University in 1941 and completing a year of graduate work at Claremont College, also in California,

Alison Ely Campbell moved back to Portland, Oregon, to spend a
year with her family. Knowing she would be there only a year and
feeling the pressures of the war, she decided to join the war effort and
landed a job in the Progress Department of Kaiser Shipyard, typing
and tabulating numbers. "Terribly boring," she said. "My education,
of course, didn't count for anything." Campbell learned of an open-
ing in the assembly bays tracking the welding and was accepted for
the position, but the department manager delayed sending her to the
assembly, putting her to work typing in the field office for a couple of
months.

"I kept asking when they were going to send me down to the job I had
asked for. I finally learned that they had found another woman to take
a similar job so I wouldn't be the lone, first woman to join this crew
of men.

"The all-male crew met us with cold, stony stares. The foreman,
whose job was to train us, took us around and showed us each our
'territory,' told us briefly what to do, and gave us each a huge book
filled with drawings of every section that went on the ship. Period.
End of training.

"War industries worked under the cost plus program in those
days. The shipyards and other war industries drew money from the
government based on the amount of work performed during a certain
period. The Progress Department tracked the welding, and as work
was completed, the company could draw the government funds. The
job I asked for was reporting welding done in the assembly bays.

"To keep track of what was done on each section being assembled,
we had to be able to recognize the pieces from the book, where the
welding seams were, how much was done, and when the piece was
finished. At first, the pieces all looked alike, but my colleague Helen
and I would put our heads together in the ladies room and figure out
what they were and which ones were sections being assembled in our
respective bays.

"Meanwhile, the guys obviously had made a pact not to talk to us—to freeze us out. But we were friendly, doing the job, and after a couple of weeks, they not only thawed out but actually enjoyed us and we enjoyed them.

"Helen and I soon learned to read the diagrams and recognize the parts coming through our own bays. I found it fascinating to see the whole operation. Eventually, I knew all the parts to an oil tanker and had an opportunity to go over a ship under construction on the ways.

"I saw lots of the women welders at work, as well as the men. The winter of '43 was unusually cold and nasty. The rain and snow and wind blowing through the assembly bays were bitterly cold. Water would settle and freeze in the areas of the sections that were enclosed by beams. Many days I saw women kneeling on the ice to weld when there wasn't a man welding in sight. Helen and I used to comment about it. These were tough ladies and really earned their pay. I have thought about how it must have been for them, when the war was over, to receive their pink slips and lose their economic independence or take low-paying jobs."

For geologist Dorothy Henderson Smith, the limitations placed on her because she was a woman were a more subtle form of harassment and discrimination but frustrating all the same. After graduating from Oklahoma University in 1943, Smith got a job with Carter Oil Company in Tulsa for a year before moving to Oklahoma City, where she worked for Magnolia Oil Company for the rest of the war.

"I was running samples, which means you take samples of the cuttings that come up from the well, you wash and dry them, then you put them under a microscope and look at them and make a log of what you've seen about the different lithologies and different colors. Then you describe the lithology. When it's all over, you have a complete log of the well.

"I did kick up my heels, which means I'd go in and ask if there was something else I could do because I was tired of doing that. Nothing came of it.

"The only thing I didn't do that the men did was they would go out on the well site and 'sit on the well,' as we call it, and stay there until the well's drilled and run samples out there. They wouldn't let me do that because I was a woman.

"They were wonderful to me but since I was a woman I couldn't drive a company car. That was discrimination. But they couldn't have been nicer, otherwise. I was the first woman geologist that Magnolia had ever hired, and they didn't know what to do with me. I don't blame them because they didn't know what to do with a woman geologist. I was a woman first and a geologist second. I was very careful not to learn how to type because you become a clerk if you can spell all those hard words, and I didn't go to school for four years to learn to type."

Needing funds for graduate school, Patricia Herbert Cody got a job during the war as an electrician at Electric Boat Company in Connecticut for a year. She faced her share of negative attitudes from men at the plant.

"I was an apprentice electrician, so I worked with a master electrician. They had a company union at that time and he got a journeyman's wage and since I was an apprentice, I got an apprentice's wage. He was a very solemn—umm—jerk from a rural community who had the hots for me. At the same time, he was a religious soul, so he didn't bother me too much. The attitude of the men toward the women was totally exploitative—what would you expect? And women never got to where they would be journeymen instead of apprentices.

"Training for the job was simply working with this guy. It wasn't that difficult. Our responsibility was the sound system in the submarines. This was very primitive technology by today's standards, but we did all these boxes so that officers, or the crew for that matter, could punch a button and talk to the captain or whatever. I was very much in favor of the war because I wanted to defeat Fascism and when we finished the sound system, we had to test the whole thing. Instead of just saying, 'Testing, one, two,' I would give little talks about how important it was for the war effort, and now I realize I was just nineteen years old and terribly naive.

"It was a huge shipyard. The wind swept up the river and I worked the swing shift. It was like a factory. There were lots of men there, deferred because of critical industry needs. Most of them were married.

"In one way, of course, I hated working there because it was mind numbing. We couldn't do the wiring until the welders had welded the boxes in place, and with only two welders for a ship, there were hours of just sitting around, waiting. But my first interest was my career and I needed the money for tuition. At this job, there was always this constant, *constant* sexual harassment by these assholes. These guys were always propositioning you and making remarks, so I was just crazy to get to New York, where I planned to get my master's in economics at Columbia University."

Bosses could be equally difficult as co-workers, but with their advances they presented the added threat of job loss if women refused to do what they asked. For Florence Stoll Protte, the threat was more than implied at her job at Ametorp Company in St. Louis, Missouri, where she was inspecting engines. The Navy took over American Can

Company during the war to make torpedoes, hence the name Ame-
torp. After the war, the factory reverted to American Can, which it is
today. The men who worked for American Can Company were bosses
primarily over the machines, and other men were hired as inspection
bosses.

"I had been working there, oh, I guess about six months at the very
most, when my boss, a big fat slob who chewed tobacco, said I had to
sleep with him. No way. I wouldn't have slept with him if he were the
last man on earth. Besides, I didn't need anyone to sleep with. I had
been married for just six months. And he said, you do that or lose
your job.

"Fortunately, the men who worked on the machines were bosses
from American Can, and Pappy Stewart was a boss on the machine in
my department. I went up and said to Pappy—he was a straight
guy— 'Well, you're not going to have me as inspector around any
longer. I'm going to be fired.'

"And he said, 'What are you talking about?' And I said, 'Well,
John wants me to sleep with him and I won't do it and he's going to get
me fired because he just tore up two tickets.'

"These were 'scrap' tickets, meaning the equipment was to be
scrapped. There was a sleeve on the torpedo and the women's hands
could fit down there with the micrometers. The men had to use a stem.
We got a more accurate reading. I knew this particular torpedo didn't
measure up right, and I put two scrap tickets in there and he tore
them up.

"Pappy said, 'Oh, no you're not going to get fired. I'll mark 'em. I
know where to mark 'em.' And he went and checked them and
marked them so they'd go through and that torpedo came back and
when it was tested it blew open and Pappy Stewart went up and told
the whole story to the supervisors and I didn't get fired but neither did
John. Pappy told him never to walk through the department again.

"Those American Can Company men were longtime employees of

the company and were good machine shop men. I worked there almost two years, but I got sick and had to quit."

At her job in the machine shop at the Watertown Arsenal just outside Boston, Phyllis Kenney Skinner made her stance clearly known to the men—including her boss—early on.

"When I first got to the Arsenal, they put me on a drill. We were making guns for the Army and Navy. The first thing I recall is that I was on a worm that was used on a sixteen-inch gun on the big warships. A worm feeds the gun as it rolls up and down or side to side.

"From there, I went on to a multiple drill and after that to a big boring mill. I worked with a man then because the materials were so heavy that they needed two people. I was a tomboy. I always have been. I still am. I'm over seventy now. I enjoyed working like that. When I was growing up, I was my father's flunky, I guess you'd call it, because my brothers were so much older. Married and gone off. I was the next one to help.

"I stood up to the boss one time. He put his arm around my shoulders and I said, 'Take it down, please.' He said, 'What's the matter with you?' And I said, 'You'll see if you don't take it off.'

"A lot of them wanted to pat you and all this. We were new to that. I picked up this worm that I was talking about and I swung it, and to this day I don't know how I did it. It weighed seventy pounds. And I said, 'I'll take your head right off your shoulders if you don't take your arm off me.'

"I wasn't that type of girl to begin with. Very shy, and I was raised very strictly and he stepped back in a hurry. The men all were looking at him and me, and I said, 'This is to let any of you know that I'm not that type of person.' And from then on, I was Miss Kenney. They bowed and scraped and when I went to the tool bin or whatever, I was well treated.

"I worked there about a year and a half, and my intended was overseas at the time. When he came home, I quit.

"We wore coveralls, and a hair net and a cap to keep our hair under at all times. We looked like the wrath of God. But we had to do it to keep our hair away from these spinning things. Some girls fought it, but they realized they could lose their scalp otherwise.

"When I went in to work, I was dressed as a lady and changed into my uniform and then when I left, I was dressed as a lady. I stayed long enough to get my face on and high heels and hose so that even the guard at the gate said, 'Miss Kenney, you sure don't look like a factory worker.'"

Before she was even assigned to her job, Eva Schifferle Diamond had trouble with her superiors. She had undergone two months of training in Santa Monica, California, to become an air traffic controller and toward the last week of class was invited to a party at a local country club to celebrate.

"There was a group of Navy air traffic controllers being trained at the same time, and the man in charge of training the fifteen of us women apparently offered me to a commander or a lieutenant commander for the evening and I was to go to the party. I had to go to the party, and I took one of the enlisted men with me because I had a sense that something was up but I had no idea the repercussions would be so great. I was asked to leave. I went down to Venice Beach and spent the evening, and then about two days later when they handed out the assignments about where we were to go, I didn't even get my last choice. And I qualified for number one choice.

"I went to the top man and said, 'How could you do this?' And he said, 'You know, you shouldn't even have come to ask me. You have a lot to learn about the world. You have to learn to play the game.' I was twenty-one. So I knew where I stood. They sent me to Burbank. I looked about seventeen. The man in charge there wouldn't believe I'd graduated from college and he was very abusive, and they gave me the worst shifts—at night when there were no planes flying—and the only way I could make my way was to be better and faster than anybody else.

"It was very hard at first, because each area has its own code and I didn't know the codes. That's what he was holding against me. Then after I got fast, I was all right. He accepted me. He seemed very old, but I suppose he was forty-five or fifty.

"I lived in Glendale and worked in Burbank. I worked in the center, not the tower; I didn't have much experience in the tower because I didn't play the game. Then an offer came up to go to San Diego, and I was very happy to go. We were working with Army and Navy people, and I was young, and I lived with three other women. My parents, who were afraid to have me go into the Navy or Army, never knew that I had to get a streetcar at one o'clock in the morning to walk ten blocks to where I lived.

"I stayed until my father became terribly upset that I wasn't going back to the Bay Area, so he went to the—my father had a great deal of charm and I loved him dearly—head of the Civil Aeronautics Administration in this region and told him my mother was dying, which was absolutely untrue, and so he transferred me to Oakland.

"There were six women controllers—most of them had pilots' licenses—and they tended to have what you would call a more traditional education than the men who worked there. And the younger men who worked there were afraid of being drafted so they didn't want it proven that women could handle the job as well as they could. So they made it hard for us. If there was a lull, we had to clean up the place, and you weren't allowed to read during a lull, and we were given the worst shifts. I didn't like the way they treated women and I decided I wanted to get a job where there were only women, to work for a woman. I really wanted out.

"But I couldn't get out because if I got out it would prove that I could be replaced and if I could be replaced—they wanted to prove that they needed everybody—if they let someone go that meant that nobody was needed. I needed a release and they wouldn't give me one. I couldn't get another job without a release.

"Then something happened and they did let me go after that. This was one of the larger disgraces. I went to work about 7:30 on a Sunday morning and there was a flight plan for General Bradley. He was coming all the way from Kentucky and they were going to have him met, they said, at Hamilton Field by a brass band. So they wanted reports sooner. This started early. This was going on all day. Progress reports on where he was. This was my line that day.

"Also Hamilton Field wanted to know—usually they didn't go to this much trouble—but they wanted to know all across the country so they could be all set up. So they reported every half hour. It was a beautiful day, so weather was no problem. The pilot started calling in and I'd get a report from the radio. He was estimating San Francisco at 14:30. Just before this happened, they emphasized that you weren't supposed to have any loose conversation. Just relay the information on the time, and so on. I kept having the radio call the pilot and ask, 'Where are you going?', and they said 'San Francisco' every time.

"I kept calling 'San Francisco' over to Hamilton Field and then I couldn't get in touch with them. The pilot tuned out. I kept saying 'San Francisco,' so they piled all the brass band and motorcycles and I guess they got across the Golden Gate Bridge and when Bradley landed at Hamilton, there was nobody there to meet him.

"So the next day when I got to work there were, and I'm not exaggerating, there were twenty Air Force people with all their badges, from the top on down, waiting for me in the director's office. I was very young. I looked like sort of a twit, dippy girl, and I came in and they were waiting for me. And they had the recorder, and it said

'San Francisco,' and I kept saying, 'check destination,' and the pilot kept calling in 'San Francisco.' It had passed through my mind that it should have been Hamilton Field and that's why I kept calling radio to check destination. But they had to nail it on someone down the line and I was that person.

"They signed my release within days. I'd been trying everything I knew for six to eight months. So I left air traffic control. I had already talked to the Red Cross. I thought I could work in hospital service. So that's what I did. I worked for women. I did social work."

While repairing aileron rudders at McClellan Air Force Base in Sacramento, California, Stella Vanderlinden Alway and her female co-workers encountered resentment by the men. Alway had transferred to California from her home in Kansas, where she had worked in sheet metal and other jobs at Independence Air Base.

"The men would give you dirty looks, or if you made a mistake they wouldn't try to help you. There was sexual involvement, too. Either you 'came across' or else. That was an old-time thing. Maybe there were those that did, but they didn't stick it out very long. I was one who said no. I was working on a rudder one night that the inspector was inspecting as the whistle was blowing, and the next morning there was a red tag on it. Someone had deliberately damaged it and they had to do that for spite. No one ever admitted that they did it.

"I asked the boss what it was all about and he said that was the way I left it. I knew that was wrong, so I found the inspector and he came down and told the boss that I had not done it and the boss had to believe the inspector. I feel it was resentment someone had against me.

"There wasn't much time for entertainment, with long hours and overtime. I liked the work that I was doing. I didn't like the way the men treated us. Even the bosses were inconsiderate. We had one boss who just seemed to like to irritate women. It was his hobby. Some of the crew chiefs were the same way. They had a dislike of women and did everything they could to make you quit. It could have been more pleasant if the men had been more considerate. I never asked any of them to take over any of my jobs. I was capable of doing anything they gave me.

"I had a mechanics rating and they were going to put me out on the line in the cold. I couldn't see them doing that, when they let people who hadn't worked as long as I had stay inside. I asked not to be put on the line, but they said, 'No, you gotta go.'

"It wasn't just that it was cold. You had to get up in the airplane, and there were times you had to lay belly to belly or butt to butt with the men, if you were in a tight place trying to buck rivets. Well, I just didn't like that. I went in and told the boss I didn't particularly like that. He said, 'Well, you can go down to first aid and tell them you don't feel good.' I said, 'That's not telling the truth.' He said that that was one way to get out of it.

"Well, rather than laying belly to belly with the men, I did go down to first aid, and, of course, right away, they threw the book at me. That's when I came back inside and they gave me the work no one else would do. There was one man who had poor eyesight I guess, and he kept messing up and they'd give me his mistakes to do over. I didn't think that was fair. I asked why they didn't give it back to him. They said he didn't see well enough. But then they'd turn around and give him another job that he'd mess up again. And then they'd give it to me. This went on for a couple years or more."

While most husbands were supportive of their wives' work during the war, and many worked with their wives or at nearby plants, occasionally a man couldn't understand why his wife would want to get in

*grubby clothes and work around dangerous machines in a dirty fac-
tory. This was the case with Kay Kane Whitney, who knew from the
start that she would have to conceal her job from her husband, who
was in training at Camp Campbell, Kentucky. She moved back home
with her parents in Boston.*

"I had been working before we were married, but he didn't particularly want me to go to work. But I told him I wanted to help out my
country. So I went to work in the Boston Navy Yard in Charlestown,
but I didn't tell him I was working as a welder.

"I took a crash three-week course. We had a week on horizontal, a
week on vertical, and a week on overhead. This made us experienced
welders! When I think of it now, I have the horrors. I actually did the
welding well, but I had to pick up a lot of it myself because what we
didn't learn was far more than what we did learn in those pathetic
three weeks. But they were in such a horrible rush for everything. It
was fun. I loved it. And they loved the fact that I was putting something over on someone. Because if he had ever known that I was
working on welding, he'd have had a fit.

"He came up to Boston on surprise orders before shipping out and
was in the kitchen visiting with my mother when I came trudging up
the backstairs in my filthy saddle shoes, lunch pail, men's socks and
workpants, red-and-black wool lumberjack shirt over a full set of gray
wool underwear, and an Italian laborer-type bandanna covering my
entire head, and he said, 'What the hell is *that*?!'

"I said, 'Well, ha, ha. I changed my career.' He was wild. He said,
'You get out of there. That's disgraceful.' He didn't like the way I
looked. You had to have your hair tied up and you wore a welder's
helmet. I enjoyed it. It was liberation. This was 1942 and 1943.
Women just didn't—the only jobs that women had were teachers, or
nurses, or work as a scrubwoman during the graveyard shift so you
could get the kids off in the morning and then go to sleep.

"We were working on landing barges, welding the 'ashcans,' the depth bombs. That's what I worked on mostly. We were just welding everything, except the really technical stuff. Every once in a while we were put on the great big stuff, and we'd weld the great big sheets together for the ships that carried the supplies.

"It was a wild place. They put on recordings at noontime. We had a lunch break, and everyone would dance, and the best dancer of all was a big, husky black guy who had lost his right leg. He would be out there jitterbugging, and the girls were fighting to dance with him, because he was such a marvelous dancer. One leg and a crutch. And there were so many wild romances, unhappy romances. So many girls with husbands overseas, and they'd give in to the feelings of the moment.

"It was bitter cold, right on the Atlantic, on the waterfront. You had to wear three or four layers of clothing just to survive the day. When you were welding, you had to work out in the open because the fumes were toxic, but every once in a while you'd have a girl, mostly the girls because they were weaker, they'd try to get in a corner and weld and you'd hear a crash and the girl had toppled over. She would be trying to get a little heat, but the fumes would get her.

"I only lasted about a year over there. But I loved it. I joined my husband and we went down South, and I worked as a medical secretary in an Army hospital in Jackson, Mississippi. My husband was killed in the service in 1948. We were married five and a half years and only lived together about ten months.

"I absolutely felt after that welding job that I could do anything. You also learned how to take care of yourself. You learned from other people that you didn't suffer in silence. You learned a lot of things.

"Once when we were in North Carolina, we had an interesting thing happen. A black sergeant was coming down to report to work down there, a New York kid. He got on the bus, going out of Greenville, and he just plunked his stuff down right inside the door and the bus driver said, 'Where do you think you're going?' And the guy said where he was going, I forget the name of the place. The driver said,

'Not sitting there, you don't.' And the guy said, 'I paid my fare. I'll sit anywhere I want.' He wouldn't get off, he absolutely wouldn't get off.

"The bus driver went in and he got three or four other bus drivers, and they pulled the guy off the bus. They beat him up and hung him from a light pole. I'd never have known about it but the guy next door was a Greyhound bus driver and he came home at noontime. He was pale green, and he said to his wife, 'We're getting the hell out of here.' There wasn't one line in the paper. That was 1942."

6

. . . .

Coping with the Basics

Not only were wartime jobs unfamiliar and demanding, women had to cope with inadequate housing, limited transportation, heavy industrial clothing, long grocery lines, child-care arrangements, and rationed goods.

When families arrived at their defense industry destinations, they found various solutions to the housing shortage. People opened their homes and rented furnished rooms to newcomers. Trailer camps, even tent towns, sprang up. Some housing units were hastily built to accommodate men and women, dormitory style. The National Housing Authority initiated housing construction for defense workers, though it never quite satisfied the need and offered varying degrees of comfort.

But from this adversity came friendship. Occasionally, hosts and guests in private homes became like family. Margaret Furey Walsh worked first as an electric welder in the Boston Navy Yard and then as a gas welder at Curtiss-Wright Aircraft in Buffalo, New York. She was especially well treated by her host family. They soon became "aunt" and "uncle" to her and her husband and provided meals, although the initial arrangement was room only. Before long, "aunt" was doing laundry as well.

Getting to work often proved difficult with gas rationing, limited train and bus travel, and poor connections. Some women who had their own cars were not always confident of the autos' reliability. Where shipyards and factories provided transportation, their workers' burdens were eased considerably.

Clothing, too, required accommodation. Most women reported it was the first time they wore slacks or steel-toed boots. They all disliked the bandannas and snoods required for safety. To cater to this new worker, customized coveralls were available in department stores, though many women visited their local Army surplus for their outfits or borrowed something from a male member of the family. Some women created their own personalization with emblems and colorful scarves.

Not being able to meet some of their more basic needs required one more level of coping for women taking on men's jobs during the war, but as with most other difficulties, they managed to keep a sense of humor.

By wartime housing standards, Loretha Tabler Bradley lived in luxury. When she came home each day from rebuilding torpedo engines at Keyport, Washington, she was greeted with Pacific Ocean views and Washington's green hills. The Navy housing did, however, provide her with an initial challenge.

"The houses were heated by coal. A big coal furnace was set centrally in the house. I had never even built a bonfire before. I felt like a pioneer, learning how to build a coal fire and bank it at night. But I learned. It kept the house warm all night, and in the morning you just had to shake it.

"The housing was in a beautiful setting. Everything's so green in Washington, and they kept the lawns mowed all the time. It was on a hill and looked out over the water. You had to furnish the houses and could actually get furniture from a central place. They had electric stoves, no washer and dryer, but I sent the laundry out. Drying the clothes was the biggest problem, with all the rain. We had to dry them all through the house. It was a three-bedroom house with a living room and huge kitchen with dining area. We were really very comfortable.

"I worked on the repair of torpedo engines; they had either been on submarines, ships, or airplanes and had to be torn down. Frequently we would rebuild them, put new parts in, whatever, adjust them. Training was, you might say, on the job. It was our job to repair them. Then the engines were dropped in the water, tested, and put back where they were supposed to go.

"Anybody could get those jobs. They were crying for people. I had gone there hoping to be near my husband, and I stayed while he went overseas. I got the job because I thought it might be kind of fun instead of just sitting there with the kids, among strangers. My thought was, hey, I'm helping. Not only is my husband out there, but I'm helping too. I'm very proud of that. I never dreamed I would be doing such a thing as working on those engines. It was an experience I'm proud of, and it was a fun time.

"Once we got some captured torpedoes from the Japanese and that caused quite a bit of excitement, to see how they were put together and how they worked.

"I had never been out of California to live—and there were a lot of Scandinavian people living there, and I thought I was in another world, and it was a really lovely experience. I enjoyed every minute of it. I met many wonderful people there.

"There was a nursery right at the housing project. Different mothers would walk the kids up the hill. I didn't have a car. Then we'd take the bus and go to work and pick them up in the evening. I have a son and a daughter.

"I remember one time a girlfriend and I went down into a submarine. The sailors that came in, they would throw the torpedoes into the shops and wouldn't have anything to do while they were being repaired. One of them told us, 'Hey, come over to the dock. We could go over and go down into a submarine.' He told us what time to come over and it was lunchtime.

"We went in there, and oh, it was horrible. It was so close, and to think they lived in such close quarters. But I remember that time maybe because it was lunchtime, and I was hungry, and they were serving pork chops. They gave each of us a plate with the meal. We couldn't get meat as civilians—or not much—those were the most delicious things I've ever had. But I never wanted to go down in one of those things again."

Housing problems were often solved by families joining forces and living together. Rose Judge Toomey and her eight-month-old daughter moved back to Toomey's family home, where her sister and brother also lived. In Toomey's case, this also solved her child-care needs while she worked in the Boston Navy Yard in Charlestown, Massachusetts, as a sheet metal worker. Even with those details taken care of, Toomey faced troubled times during the war.

"I had to work, definitely. To get to the Navy yard, I had a forty-minute trip. I walked eight blocks to the bus, which took me to the train that then went right into the shipyard.

"I worked from seven to three so I could get things done during the day, and my sister came home from working at the telephone company and would take over, so it wasn't too much for my mother.

"The war took a great toll on me. I couldn't understand all the fighting, all the killing. At the Navy yard they discharged me because of poor attendance. I worked less than a year. The war effort demanded that we give full strength and I just couldn't do it. What was going on, the headlines and all. I had a nervous breakdown. I couldn't comprehend the war. What I should have done is not read the papers.

"When they discharged me it was a big deal. I had to wait and see the commander, go down to his office, and I remember the time of the year. He was dressed in white with the gold and everything, and he read me down about keeping up with my work. They actually fired me. What was difficult was that my husband's father passed away about that time.

"My husband was in the European war. He went in as an infantry person. He went into the Signal Corps and ended up as a photographer. He took the Army pictures. He took Eisenhower. He was in the same unit as Audie Murphy—the most decorated person.

"When we went to pick Bill up when he came home from the war, we went to the station, my little girl was almost three, and all she knew about him was the picture with him in the Army hat and uniform. She just leaped out of my arms, broke away from my grip, and ran to the first soldier, who was a lieutenant. My husband was a sergeant. And the soldier said to me, 'I wish I was coming home to this.'

"We had a hard time finding a place to live. We finally ended up in a neighboring city called Chelsea, a poor area, in an apartment, difficult to keep heated. Big spaces. I wasn't too happy there."

The unemployment office did Goldie Shamchoian Deckwa a favor when they said her unemployment benefits would be canceled unless she took a test to work in the Navy shipyard. The shipyard paid much better than the canneries and packing plants in her hometown— Fresno, California. Much to her surprise, she passed the test and was told to go to the labor board at Mare Island Naval Shipyard in the San Francisco Bay Area.

"I didn't even know where it was. I was told to take a physical, which cost a whole $5. I didn't have a car, so I took the Greyhound bus. I was one of seven girls, but by this time, I was the only one. I was devastated to be alone.

"I got to Vallejo, and they gave me all kinds of tests all over again, and when it was time to close up shop, they asked where I was staying. I said I was going to downtown Vallejo to one of the hotels and get myself a room. They looked at me and thought, 'This country bumpkin.'

"They felt so sorry for me. They called the hotel and found the one thing that might be available. They said there was a woman whose husband was out to sea, and I could sleep in her room, but if he came in from sea, I'd have to sleep in the lobby in a chair. He didn't come in, and I slept in one of the two single beds in the room. With this complete stranger. It was a nightmare. But the lady was nice, and I feel like I'm a nice person, also.

"We went out to dinner and we shared the room that night, and the next day I went back to the labor board for more testing. The one thing they promised me was they would not hire a single lady unless they had rooms. But they called me anyway, my tests were so good, I guess. They called me before they called the locals.

"There was a USO in Vallejo that catered to ladies and you could have cooking privileges, and a cot and showers and so forth. And they would look for a place for you to stay. They found a place with a Navy chief and his wife. A man at work (I'd started working) helped me move, and the Navy chief's wife said, 'I'm sorry, you can't stay. You've got boys visiting you and so on.' This was just a man who was helping me move!

"So I went back to the USO and said I had to leave. They found a place with room and board. We'd stay in one house and go to the other one for meals. They treated me like their daughter. It was a good spot. The owners of the two houses were from Texas, and they'd been recruited to come up and help provide housing. There was no laundry. We had to scrub our clothes on a washboard, including the uniforms we wore to work—overalls. Wash and starch our clothes. We had to use shoe ration stamps for the steel-toed boots we wore to work, which meant we didn't have ration stamps left for dress shoes.

"I finally did get an apartment in the wartime housing project, a studio apartment, where I had to cook on a kerosene stove.

"My job was to sharpen tools. Starting out, I'd sharpen on a machine that would sharpen drill presses and it was controlled mechanically and I had no problems with that. Then they had me sharpening little drills, half-inch, three-quarters, by hand, and I got very good at that. I felt all along I was doing my job to help the war effort. By the time I was through, I was a third class machinist."

The day Liz Arnold was to marry her new fiancé, he was shipped overseas with the Signal Corps. They met at the USO at Hamilton Army Air Field in Novato, California, where he was playing drums with a band. When he discovered she could sing, he invited her to join the band as a singer.

"The minute Harold went overseas, I went down to the Federal Building to see if I could get in the WAVES or WACs, or whatever, but my vision was not good enough to be in the armed services. They suggested I go up to Benicia and take a job at the arsenal. They had clerical jobs for people with two or three years of college.

"I met a really nice gal in the employment office up there who ended up being my roommate. We shared a furnished room in Martinez and went back and forth on the ferry.

"The room was in an old Victorian on G Street where the water lapped up outside the window. It was lovely, even if it was old and almost tumbling down. Our landlady had inherited this big old house and was taking in roomers because of the war. There was a community kitchen and she furnished lunch. She made the same lunch for us every living day; it was Spam and lettuce and mayonnaise on Wonderbread. And an apple. Every day.

"Once when we were filling the bathtub for our bath, her little boy looked in and ran down to tell his mother that we were filling the tub. She only wanted us to use about three or four inches of water.

"At the arsenal we were given very explicit testing of all sorts—fingerprints by the FBI, tight security. We were typing and sending out shipments of munitions to the various trains. We worked in a small office, no windows, four desks and filing cabinets on all walls.

"You know the way freight cars come through with all those letters and numbers on the sides? Florence and I had to memorize alternate numbers. Each night we had to put them in different files, and the files had to be locked with a combination lock.

"I had no idea what a really great memory I had in those days. It was amazing. Only the supervisor of the office knew which file was going to be sent out to which freight car system at which time. We had all the munitions for Rock Island, Illinois, and for Fort Dix, and Camp Stoneman. It was extremely precise work and we didn't dare make a mistake. We made $29 a week, and paid $10, which we split, $5 each, for room and board."

With a chemistry degree from the University of Arkansas, Fern Stephens Brooks applied for jobs in a couple of regions of the country, choosing a position with the Continental Oil Refining Laboratory in Oklahoma because it was closest to home. She started as an analytical chemist in late February 1943, examining various petroleum products at different stages of the refining process to ensure they met the government's strict wartime standards. But she did not stay in Oklahoma long.

"I worked there five or six weeks before my high school sweetheart came home from the war. He had been in the Pacific for three and a half years, on a heavy cruiser. He was in all those South Pacific battles. He only had a few days for leave, so if we were going to get married, we had to do it right away. We got married there in Ponca

City, where I was working. There were no members of our family, only two or three people that I worked with.

"When he went to the Coast, I went as far as Oklahoma City with him on the train. We had to sit on our suitcases all the way, it was that crowded. I went back and worked until September. By that time, he had been assigned to an oil tanker. He was on an oil tanker and I was sampling the oil! I decided to join him in California because he had some time before he actually went to sea. So I quit my job.

"Another interesting train ride. I didn't have a seat until the next state or so. The restrooms included a kind of lounge, so I sat in there until I was able to get a seat. For a day, probably.

"When I got to San Francisco, I looked all over for a job. First we had a room, a miserable room, and then we got a room with kitchen privileges in a big old three-story house in San Francisco. There were three or four different groups of people that had rooms there. We shared refrigerator space, and fortunately our room was on the first floor, handy to the kitchen. We had a table in our room and could take our food back in there to eat it. And here I am, a bride.

"After a few weeks, my husband left on the tanker and I got a job near Vallejo at the Union Oil Company, doing exactly what I'd been doing in Oklahoma. One thing we worked on went into trinitrotoluene, which is TNT. We did a lot of aviation gasoline, too. I worked there until April of 1944.

"My husband wanted to get off the tanker and go into submarine duty, so that meant going to New London, Connecticut, to submarine school. I quit my job—again—and we rode a train—again—all the way. But it wasn't one long stretch. We stopped to see family in Arizona and Arkansas.

"When he went to submarine school, again I was looking for a job, and I wound up working at the Electric Boat Company, as an electrician's helper. Actually, I was more of an electrician's helper's helper. The helper was a woman. We climbed all around the submarines under construction, checking the wiring and the telephones. We didn't do much. I carried a screwdriver around.

"My husband finished submarine school and was assigned to a boat that had been built there. I hadn't worked on it. They went out to sea for brief periods and then they finally went out to the Pacific. I was pregnant and went home to my folks in Arkansas and sat out the rest of the war there."

During the war, Margaret Schroeder Gibson took a leave of absence from teaching elementary school but ended up working in the same field. After completing an eight-week course at St. Louis University in International Morse Code, Gibson was hired to teach the code to students at Scott Field. The classroom was a large Quonset hut with no air-conditioning and very little heat. She lived at home and found various ways to get to her job, which rotated among three shifts.

"I would take the streetcar to a certain place in St. Louis, in a steel smelting area that was a very bad place. You had to walk from the streetcar up steps to the top of a viaduct. It was rather scary. I'd do that one week, and the next week I'd drive.

"Coming home at three in the morning, one time, I got a flat tire. I was all alone and it was a Sunday night, going through East St. Louis. It's a depressed area, noted for its crime. There was nothing to do but get out and change it myself. I was frightened out of my wits. I had a bumper jack and put it up on that, changed my own tire, and went on home. It was the first and last time I ever did that.

"Another thing I will always remember is coming home one afternoon, again, all alone, and I hit a rooster—a beautiful big red rooster—I didn't know what to do. I was afraid the owner would come out and scold me. I jumped out of the car, threw the rooster in the trunk of the car, and drove off. I wanted to get out of there so fast— there I was, a hit-and-run driver.

"The men were very helpful, very cooperative. They liked women instructors, especially when they were understanding. I wouldn't say they were all interested in learning, but they were threatened with going into the infantry, and they didn't want that. If they were unhappy, they could unload on me, and they couldn't very well do that with a GI instructor. A lot of them wanted to talk about their families and conditions at the field.

"The men were from all walks of life and different ages. Some were eighteen, some in their thirties. There were a number of artists, and they would draw little caricatures of me, or write little messages to me under a picture they had drawn. These were things I appreciated. I kept some of them."

Patricia Teeling Lapp met her future husband in a Chicago suburb in the summer of '42. By autumn they were both separately studying Morse code in Chicago. By then, he was in the Air Force, training to be a radio operator/mechanic. Lapp, a civilian, was learning to be a weather observer and communicator for the Civil Aeronautics Administration.

"As long as we were going around talking in Morse code all the time, we thought it would be a good idea to get married. But two or three days after the ceremony, I was assigned to an emergency airfield at Lone Rock (population 500) near Spring Green, a bit west of Madison, Wisconsin.

"The newest hired and with the least seniority, I worked mostly from midnight to 8:00 A.M. interspersed by a few 4:00 P.M.–to–midnight shifts. To get from town to the airfield, I bought an old Model A Ford from a farmer, and, for 'protection' during those long nights alone, I borrowed my landlord's Irish setter. This car, which I'd bought for $50, had a flat tire almost every other day.

"It seemed in those days instead of buying a new tire when you had a flat, the cheap route was to patch the tube and put a 'boot' inside to cover up the hole in the tire. A very fragile solution. Also there was the leaky radiator. With those 40 degree below zero nights they were having that winter of 1943, the radiator would freeze and boil, which meant that with the dog sitting bolt upright beside me in the passenger seat, many mornings the two of us would be driving back to town in a cloud of alcohol fumes.

"Sometimes my husband would have a day and a half off and he'd come out from Chicago to join me. He'd sleep on the floor while I worked my night shift. We'd have a few wide-awake hours together before sleep overcame me and it was time for him to catch his train.

"I rented a room in the town banker's home, but I ate all my meals in the dining room of the only hotel in town. The waitress would ask what I would like for dinner and I'd say, 'What do you have in the icebox?' And I'd choose something from her list.

"It was lonely out at the airfield so I was glad to have the dog with me. Except for one thing that he did. He'd fall asleep on the bare floor of this building about the size of a small rural school. When he got into a really deep sleep, he began to dream. His legs would go into spasms and suddenly, out of the deep silence, one of those little office chairs on wheels would fly across the room without any warning. It used to scare the daylights out of me.

"I had to monitor the radio constantly for pilots calling in for weather information. Some of this information I 'created.' Every hour I had to go outside and do weather observations, which I put into code and entered in sequence on the teletype. Also this station had a dit-dah (a beep) that was going out over the airwaves—something like a black line on the highway to guide pilots. Heaven forbid, they should land! We were just an emergency airfield and we had a lot of snow. We did have little lights outlining the field just in case.

"One midnight shift, I saw a light, a car coming up this little road to the station turn into our driveway. I said, 'Oh, God,' but the dog slept through the whole thing. This guy comes up the steps. He was the county sheriff and he said, 'I always come out here to scare the airport girls.'

"I came out for my shift one frozen winter night just before midnight to relieve the four-to-midnight person. For some reason the station manager, who only worked days, was there and it took me just a few minutes to realize he was drunk. For no reason, he became verbally abusive. I may have carried myself in kind of an independent manner in those days and this may have offended him, although I only saw him one day a month when I had a day shift. But it's possible from where he stood that I wasn't showing enough humility or something. Many of these station chiefs were retired from the Navy or Marines.

"Well, he became increasingly abusive and there I stood in my sheepskin coat, snowboots, with my dog companion and carrying my lunch for the midnight shift. At some point I just said, 'Listen, you can just take your old job.' The dog and I walked out into the frozen night. I went home and went to sleep.

"The next morning I called Chicago headquarters to explain what happened. But the manager had already been in touch with them and had made it sound as if it was I who had become abusive! Fortunately, the man I was relieving that night had been standing right there and heard the whole thing. He was a nice former U.S. Marine. He agreed to defend me at the hearing. That's how I came to be reinstated to another emergency airfield at Hobart, Indiana. But soon the exposure to the bitter cold and the strange shifts took their toll and I was able to leave the service with a medical discharge so it wasn't a terrible mark on my record with the Civil Aeronautics Administration."

Geraldine Collogan Richey traveled on a bus from Cardon, Iowa, to Oakland, California, to join her Coast Guard husband, just out of boot camp. Both assumed he would be there for a while, but within two weeks of her arrival, he was sent to Long Island, New York, to

diesel school. Richey found herself working for one of the very trans-
portation systems that were so overloaded.

"There I was, all by myself, and I didn't know a soul, but I had gotten
a job just before he left at the Kresge dime store selling Christmas
cards. We knew he would only be gone about three months to school,
and of course, I just went out on a shoestring. I had to have a job to
live. After the Christmas season, I decided that surely I could find a
job that paid more.

"There was an ad in the newspaper for conductorettes. I got on the
electric trains right away that went across the Bay Bridge. There were
also women conductors on the streetcars in Oakland.

"I liked my job very much. The uniform was sort of a steel blue, a
skirt, a coat or a jacket. We were supposed to wear white shirtwaist
blouses. We even had a cap, just like the conductors, with our number
on it. And we had to wear the change makers, or change belts, where
you click to make the right change.

"The train went by where the people would be getting off shipyards and jobs. People pulled each other down, or crowded or shoved,
and were just so frantic to get on the trains, to get home or to get to
work. I'd never seen that behavior before.

"We got trained on the job. It really wasn't that much. You mainly
had to know how to make change, and you had to keep track of every
trip across the bridge so the toll could be paid later.

"When my husband's schooling was over, he was put on a patrol
boat in San Francisco Bay, patrolling the bay and escorting ships
through the mines. We had an apartment in Oakland.

"We were well accepted by co-workers and bosses, and the public
respected us. I didn't hear any slurs or anything like that. I worked
almost up to the time I had a baby. I did keep wearing my uniforms
and there were a lot of people when I quit couldn't believe I was
really pregnant.

"They wanted me to come back, but the thought of having a babysitter, and in a place where we had no relatives, or anybody that we knew—I just opted to stay home. By that time, if you were a service-man's wife and weren't working, you could get—I think—$50 a month, and $20 or $25 for a child. But I was able to save enough money. We really got along beautifully until he was discharged be-cause we just watched it.

"We had to live on ration stamps for sugar and for canned milk for formula. My husband was a great lover of hamburger, and I had lived on a farm my whole life and had never eaten a hamburger. We had our own meat, but we didn't make it into hamburger. So he bought a food grinder, just one that you crank with your hands, and we would buy a roast with the least ration points, and he'd grind it so we could have hamburger, or make it into a meatloaf or something.

"We grew up in the Midwest where everybody wasn't that wealthy or anything, and we knew how to conserve, and either do without or with less. That was my first experience of seeing domestic rabbits in meat markets, and they had no ration points on them, you could buy them."

Lucille Gray Rogers was delighted when an opportunity opened up that allowed her to earn good money, keep her house, and hold her husband's job for his return.

"My husband worked as a clerk in our post office here in Scottsburg, Indiana. When he was called into the service, the postmaster asked me to take the exam and if I passed, he would let me work in my husband's place. I passed and went to work in July of '42. I waited on customers, selling stamps and taking money orders. I also sorted mail for the carriers.

"I walked to work since we didn't have a car, but the postmaster was kind and thoughtful, and on really cold, rainy days, he would come in his car and pick me up to keep me from walking in bad weather.

"A lady came in and lived with me who took care of my sixteen-month-old son. She lived with us for her room and board and I think I gave her $5 a week. That doesn't sound like anything, but back then that was. There were people who needed work and were glad to get it.

"I have no idea what I would have done if this didn't come up. My father and mother lived on a farm about twelve miles from here, and I suppose if worse came to worst, I could have taken my child and gone home, but I didn't want to do that because I wanted to keep the house and everything, so when the war was over we could have the family life we had before it all happened.

"I enjoyed meeting the public and had never had a job where I would meet the public. Everybody who came in would ask about your husband and you'd find out about everyone that was in service and how they were doing and this sort of thing. It was really interesting to me.

"Of course, we had lots of packages that were mailed overseas, and, really, there was a lot of work to it, but it was rewarding because you knew you were helping the servicemen by getting their mail to them.

"One thing was very sad. When I worked there, the mail came by train. There was a man who worked there that would go to the train and get the mail and bring in all these big bags of mail to the post office. He also was the man that usually went with the Army people to tell them that their sons had been killed or injured in the service. The Army people would come to the post office, apparently because we had all the addresses, and this man would go with them. Even though you didn't know all the people, it was sad to know that something had happened to one of their loved ones.

"My husband got home the latter part of October 1945 and he took a month off before he started work. I kept on working. When he was ready to go back to work, I came home. For a while I missed it, but I knew from the very beginning that that's what was going to happen."

Commuting for seventeen-year-old Gwen Porter Palmer meant rubbing shoulders in her greasy uniform with stylish office-bound workers, a scene still fresh in her mind. She went to Los Angeles to find work at North American Douglas Aircraft, only to discover they did not hire people under eighteen years of age.

"I saw this sign at the Standard service station: 'Women wanted.' They referred me to a training station in Inglewood, and I applied. I can still hear Mr. Donnelly, the manager, who interviewed me, saying, 'You know, you have to be eighteen,' and I told him I could do anything an eighteen-year-old can. I convinced him and went into training, a ten-day training session. I became a service station attendant, a grease monkey. I could repack the wheel bearings, the whole thing.

"It was a totally new experience. I weighed about 110 pounds. I had long hair and wore it in a snood because I had to keep it from getting in my way, and snoods were popular. We had a special coverall type of uniform with long sleeves, buttoned in front, kind of a slate blue.

"The red Pacific Electric bus used to go from El Segundo and Manhattan into downtown LA and usually I would take that bus, and it was so funny to get on that bus. I wore bright red fingernail polish to hide the grease underneath, and I'd get on that bus, and I'd be greasy from having worked. You couldn't help but be greasy and sometimes had grease in your hair, which I couldn't take care of until I got home, and here were these people all dressed to the nines going into downtown Los Angeles.

"I had so many funny experiences. One fellow came in with this huge tire for me to change. It looked as if it had come off an airplane, and I said, 'Absolutely not. You take that back and have one of the guys at the base change that. I'm not about to do it. I can't.' In those days, to break the seal on a tire you had to jump on it. They didn't have all those wonderful tools you have today. He took the tire back. They had done it as a joke. I was kind of a cute little kid.

"I sold batteries and installed them, and tires, I switched tires. One time I had a car up on the hoist and I had flushed the engine with the flushing oil and I had this bucket hanging underneath to collect the oil. The bucket was so full that when I lifted it down I had all this warm oil going down the front of me.

"Leo Carillo—the actor, remember him?—came into the station twice. He had a yacht and was on his way down to it. He had a station wagon with big steer horns in front. He chatted with me while I was filling the tank and servicing his car. At that time gasoline was 20 cents a gallon, 19 cents for regular, and you couldn't get gasoline without your gas ration stamps. I told him how much it was and asked for the stamps and he said, 'I gave it to you.' And I said, 'I'm sorry, sir, you didn't,' and he said, 'I know I did.' And I said, 'Well, I don't have it.' Then I remembered he had opened a stick of gum, and we looked in the trash, and he had thrown away the stamps with the gum wrapper.

"People were pretty surprised when I came out—and the type of service we gave them was great. We even had a little dustpan and brush to sweep out under the driver's seat. Wiped off the headlights, got the windows. Once I was doing the windshield on the rider's side, and this guy gets out and closed the door while I had my hand in the hinged part of the door. I said, 'Excuse me, sir, my hand is in the door.' He just about died.

"I was the only woman in the station. I had to open the station in the morning and stick each tank and measure it with a wooden stick and record what each tank held. The valve oil had such a delicious smell. I tapped the valve oil with my finger and tasted it and it was just awful, although it smelled wonderful. It smelled like banana oil.

"I had to do the banking down in Manhattan Beach. They didn't want me to go back to school. They offered me the management position. But I told them I had to go back to school and finish. It was a summer job.

"It wasn't too long ago I saw someone packing front wheel bearings the old-fashioned way. And I thought, Gosh, that takes me back! You put the gob of grease in the palm of your hand, and then take the thing in your right hand and tap it into the grease, going around in it. It's all saturated with grease."

Attracting admiration and attention on the ferry run between San Francisco and Oakland were Marge Young Altschuler and her three companions. They wore black leather pants and jackets—not particularly unusual. But to the jacket backs, they sewed green V's for victory, and riding across the San Francisco Bay to work, they sang songs, encouraging other riders to join in.

"When we went to apply for the job—we went to the Kaiser Shipyard in Richmond—we were all women who had jobs in San Francisco. We wore suits and hats the way they do in San Francisco. We weren't out of work and scrounging around. We were making good money. Our motivation was mainly patriotic. Everyone was doing his share and we wanted to do ours. They tossed us from one to the other because we were pretty good-looking young gals in those days. Finally, they said, 'Okay, come back.'

"We had to go to school over there for two weeks to be welders. We were told where to buy leathers, so we did that, but we added the V for victory. It was cold, we went over at midnight and came back in the morning. We wore jeans and heavy flannel shirts and then our leathers over that and our steel-toed boots and our turbans, black turbans. We looked like four spooks. But we had to wear this stuff back and forth on the ferry because we started out when they first started with women, and there were no lockers for us. We had to go through muck and mud to get to the school.

"We were there at the beginning of the war and the men were not used to having women around. That first day they didn't have enough hoods for us in the training, so we took turns. We went into this little place, like where you keep cattle and stuff, and we had this welding hood and they said, 'We'll take you one at a time in there.' We didn't know you couldn't see through these hoods except when welding, which, of course, we weren't doing yet. And we would stand there looking through the hoods, not seeing anything and groping around with our hands. This is how dumb we were.

"The men were not used to having women around, and I'd be working on some metal, steel, in the pipe shop, and they would come up and tap my shoulder. They wanted to see what we looked like and sounded like and all that. I would have to lift my hood up—they work on a hinge that goes up and down. The man in charge called me in on the carpet and said, 'You've got to stop flirting with these men,' and I got so shook and I said, 'Listen, I quit a good job to come here, and I can't help it if these guys are tapping me on the shoulder and I have to take my hood off to see who it is. It might be someone giving me some orders.' After I explained it, he understood."

While women in factories struggled with weighty leathers, bandannas, and steel-toed boots, Mary Jo Davis Owens worked with a different kind of clothing hazard—the too-large, leftover movie usher uniform of her male predecessor.

"There was a chain of movie houses in St. Louis, Missouri, that showed first-run musicals and dramas out of Hollywood in their heyday. To staff the larger houses with the remaining men, they staffed the smaller houses like the Missouri Theatre with women usherettes.

"They must have thought it was only temporary, because they didn't order uniforms for us and we had to make do with the same ones the men wore. My friend and I were the only ones tall enough to wear the 'greatcoat' with all the gold braid.

"They kept two guys to assign us to our stations, and they tried many rookie pranks on us just to let us know who was boss. The favorite was to send the newest one to the other show down the street to get the curtain keys!

"Between movies, the manager would go on stage and take pledges from the audience for the purchase of war bonds. We would run up and down the aisles to get the signed pledges. Then a few days after they were issued, we traveled around the city to deliver them. Complete in our uniforms, in hot weather, no air-conditioning on those streetcars. Our manager was an old vaudevillian, and he just ate up getting up there on the stage at the intermission and selling those war bonds.

"We got our big break in show business whenever there was a horror show coming the following week. When the previews were being shown, we took turns lying in the loge boxes and screaming for effect.

"I remember losing things and having to disturb people around the spot, going down with the little flashlight looking on the floor. It was different then. People didn't go to the show at the beginning always, but would go when they wanted to and come out whenever they wanted. Once in a great while, when it was crowded, we'd have people behind the ramps. They had these velvet cords. We had to release the people in line one at a time, just as one or two came out. There were people who believed in starting at the beginning, and then it would be a larger group coming out. Sometimes it took two of us to keep the crowd from pushing through.

"There were some really graphic movies. I remember seeing pictures of Okinawa or Guadalcanal and things like that. They were very vivid. But all those old musicals and everything like that, those were our favorites.

"We developed quite a camaraderie, we usherettes, and went to the USO together. Once we brought back four or five servicemen for Thanksgiving dinner at one of our mothers' houses.

"My sister, Betty Davis Kubik, worked as a doorman at the Missouri Theatre and actually became assistant to the treasurer of the theatre.

"We must have impressed the industry pretty well, because one of the large shows downtown put in a complete staff of girls after the war. There was one difference. They were all so smartly dressed in their tailored uniforms. What a comparison. Well, we tried to look as smart as we could and everything, but you had to pull the coat over and tighten the belt."

7

. . . .

Women's Ingenuity

Having women enter a male environment often provided a new perspective to the tasks at hand—a feminine touch in some cases or another set of eyes in others. Not having worked in these offices or factories before, women were not bound by the conventional procedures. Coming fresh to the work, they questioned the way things were being done in a way that men who had been on the job no longer could, having long ago accepted the status quo. Being temporary in most cases, some women felt freer to introduce innovation.

Women's dedication to the work was fierce—stronger than with many of their male counterparts, due to the need to prove themselves and determination to work at least as hard as the soldiers overseas.

Working at Douglas Aircraft in Santa Monica, California, in the 1950s, Bill Smith said he was impressed by his female co-workers who stayed on after the war. "The women were so much more professional. They had more patience, they seemed to take more pride in their work," he said. One woman particularly stood out in Smith's memory. "She was our model. Everybody tried to meet her quality, and it just couldn't be done," he recalled. "When I was a younger person, I was a perfectionist. I thought I could do anything better than anybody. But no matter how hard I could try, I couldn't do as good work as she could."

As Dorothy Martschinsky Comstock said about her work at North American Aviation in Kansas City, Missouri, "Learning to be a riveter was simple for me; I crochet a lot and work with my hands a lot. It was

real easy for me." Many women compared their work in the factories
to other tasks they knew—like sewing—and applied those skills to
their jobs. Like Comstock, several welders from different parts of the
country found welding particularly similar to stitchery.

Some women brought a cheerfulness to the workplace that added
a new element. While taking the work itself seriously, they also were
able to have fun with what they were doing and often drew the men
into their gaiety.

*Harriet Pinchbeck Carpenter found a job at a small machine shop in
Bridgeport, Connecticut, after she and her husband abandoned their
real estate endeavors in favor of defense jobs. This was one of several
machinist jobs she held during the war.*

"They were making aluminum three-inch-long bushings for Bellanca
Aircraft in California. They could taper—I remember the job—up to
three-thousandths of an inch. Now, that's a lot of taper when you work
in a machine shop. But they had to be concentric with the center.

"The foreman had to make a special holder to hold the bushing on
the lathe. That's called an arbor. It had to be made by the toolmaker,
the right size, and then annealed, and then done again, and I followed
them around and watched them do it. He says, 'Where are you going?'
I said, 'I'm going to watch you.' Well, the average woman would have
stayed at her machine, just waiting.

"I went to watch to see what he was doing, which I think makes a
difference for any employee anywhere, any job. So they came to me
and I was turning those down on the lathe. That's the expression:
turning them down. The foreman stood. This time I was on days. The
contracts were getting caught up from the government. He looked at
me and said, 'You're turning those down at one cut.' I said, 'Yes.' I

said, 'They taper, but measure them, and they are concentric.' And he replied, 'And they said it couldn't be done.'

"I had one more job before I left there to go with the employment service, working on a special bolt they had, a small job, maybe a dozen of them. But they were hard. They had to be threaded. I scrapped a few and I apologized. The foreman said, 'Mrs. Carpenter, don't worry.' He said, 'You're doing so much better a job than we've been doing on those bolts. Don't worry about it.'

"I really enjoyed it, the small shop, because I could pick out a job, and the men were very nice to work with. They were always nice to the few women who were there. There were three or four of us women on nights.

"Lots of times we shared things during the war. In the summer, they let the men go out just a few minutes early to go to where the market was open all night and get a lot of corn. It was fresh in. Butter was rationed, but I had some butter stamps I could spare, and we all shared, and they roasted corn over the annealing fire. It was fun."

When Lorraine Gaylord Moscow came home to New York from Northwestern University in 1942, her mother told her that a man down the street said the Ford Instrument Company was starting to think about hiring women. Fresh from college with a degree in economics, Moscow followed her mother's suggestion.

"I'll never forget it. It was March 2, a Sunday, they worked seven days a week. I had to wait about four hours and the next thing I knew, yes, I was hired. I was the first woman hired as a mathematician. This is Hannibal Ford, they were doing what was then the beginning of computers on shipboards.

"The idea was you had to decide what the speed of the plane is, the target, the pitch of the board, and so you used three-dimensional geometry for this. Now that original Mark One that I worked on is part of the museum there at the *Intrepid* off 42nd Street in Manhattan Harbor.

"It was a small instrument that was on the decks that was to compute all this at once. If you were trying to shoot down a plane, you had to know the speed of the plane, the arc of the bullet, and of course the pitch of the ship and the speed of the ship. I worked on that and that's where I met my first husband.

"I walked in there and I was the only woman. One man said, 'She's going to put up drapes?' I'll never forget that. They didn't know what to make of me. I was twenty-two. This one man came up to me and shook his finger at me and said, 'You are not to listen to anybody else here but me.' I said, 'All right.' About two months later, he shook his finger at me and said, 'Now, we're going on our honeymoon in July.' And he became the father of my four children. But in the meantime, I was making the very high salary of $19 a week.

"I learned to read blueprints there, and then I went to Gibbs and Cox Naval Architects and tripled my salary. They're down on 14th Street. There were, I guess, sixteen floors in the building. There were all male telephone operators, male secretaries, and male elevator operators. So I had to go down my fourteen floors and walk across the street for a ladies room. They finally did get a couple of other women.

"I was up in this huge drafting room and there were 250 men in the room and I was asked to sit there at the drafting table and do ordering for the ships. The first thing I had to order were urinals and pea jackets, and I thought they were connected! It wasn't until I asked the man next to me at the drafting table about it that I discovered my error—and did my face turn red!"

Polly Ann Stinnett Workman excelled as a welder at the Stockton-Pollock Navy Yard in California, despite her family's skepticism. She worked there for three years, mostly on hospital ships, commuting forty-eight miles from her home in Sacramento to the shipyards in Stockton.

"At the time of the war's outbreak, I was married. I didn't work. My husband got his greetings. I don't know why I took to welding. I was sort of a tomboy. I have four brothers and everything they did, I had to do as well or better. I think the reason I did it was that we were driving down the street and I saw a welder welding in a shop and I said, 'I think I'd like to do that.'

"My husband laughed. I'd never worked. I went home and told my mother—we were staying with her—and she just laughed. The next day I went into Sacramento—that's where I took my training—and signed up and did beautifully. I went every day, and of course it just shocked everybody because they didn't think I'd be able to take it.

"When we went from Sacramento to Stockton to take our test, I rode with a woman and man from the welding school. I was very shy, scared to death. I said, 'You go first,' and they did. Each one came out and said, 'Oh, I made it, I made it.' And they were hired as trainees.

"I went in and did, I think they called it a guided bend test, and the instructor came in and jerked it out and threw it in the barrel, and I thought, 'Oh, my God, I can't even pass the test.' Then he said, 'Try this, do a vertical,' and I did, and he came in and said, 'Come on in the office.' I thought, 'I'm going to be embarrassed; I'm not going to get the job.' And he said, 'You passed, what shift do you want?'

"I told him I wanted to work on the graveyard shift because I'd be riding with my friends and he said, 'Okay,' and he filled out my slip. He handed it to me—this is how dumb I was—it said, 'Welder, Jr.' I thought welder, junior. I thought, that's terrible. He said, 'You'll be working with all men and all welders. There'll be no trainees where you'll be working.' I don't know how I got around to asking what the jr. was, but he said, 'Now, you're a journeyman welder.'

"I went outside and was too embarrassed to tell these people that I had made it better than they had. They asked if I passed, and I said yes. We got in the car and went back to the school. Earlier, the instructor had said to me, 'If you don't make journeyman welder, I'm going to clobber you good.' So when we got back he said, 'Well, how'd you guys do?' And they said, 'Oh, we passed, we passed.' And he said, 'Where's yours, Polly?' Finally, I gave it to him, and he said, 'Oh, I knew you'd make journeyman.' Those two people got so mad at me they wouldn't let me ride with them. I had to hunt another ride. I learned an awful lot. I was nineteen, going on twelve.

"I was the only woman welder on the graveyard shift. I was welding fifty-foot walls in the hull of the ship. The working conditions were wonderful. As far as I'm concerned, it was the best job I've ever had. It gave me a sense of accomplishment.

"When I went in, they were working on a cost plus job, and the first night I was there the supervisor took me around to get me on a crew, and nobody wanted me because I was a woman. They'd say, 'We have all we need.' Finally, the supervisor said to the leadman, 'This is your welder.'

"They tried every way in the world to show me up. They put me on a cost plus job, working out in the rain, on a big tunnel they had contracted. Cost plus meant they had a certain time to do it in, and you had to do real good. They put me on there hoping I'd flub up, which would be especially bad on a cost plus job. But I didn't, and from then on I just did real great.

"The tunnel was part of a ship. This was in January, which is the worst. We had to wear those heavy leather pants and jackets, and it was so cold you just darn near froze to death. When he put me on that job, I was terrified. There was all this loud noise, the shipwrights, the chippers, people dropping hammers and dropping metal, this was really terrifying to me but I didn't let them know it. I was nineteen and had never worked before, and he said, 'Do this.'

"They didn't tell me anything. You'd have to wash the slag off to make the perfect bead and I had the perfect bead. I did perfect work. It's kind of like embroidery.

"One time I remember they needed some welding done in a big spot that was a hard place to get to. I was the smallest one on the crew. It was off the deck about three or four feet down, and the lead-man held my feet while I welded upside down. It was on a ship that had come in and had some sailors on it. So I went out there with a portable welder and worked on that for two or three days. I was very proud of that. They brought me sandwiches. They were great to me.

"By the time the war was over, I was kind of tired of the work. You're young, and you don't want to do the same thing all your life. They didn't lay me off. I quit. My brother was managing a ranch and needed some help."

Another Californian who took quickly to welding was Mary Entwistle Poole of Tiburon. Before the Japanese attack on Pearl Harbor, Poole taught in a little country high school near Sacramento. Believing that teaching seemed "rather irrelevant" with the war going on, Poole answered an appeal for workers to help at Marinship in Sausalito, California. First, she enrolled in a welding school for four days at San Rafael High School.

"After a disastrous beginning, I finally caught on. I went there the first day and proceeded to get my rod stuck. You operate with a welding rod that's more than a foot long and this is attached to an electrical stinger. The heat from the electricity melts the rod and also melts a little bit of the steel plate that you weld on, and the two are supposed to form a bond. Well, I just got my rod stuck and I had to call the instructor.

"He said, 'Well, the first day, this happens all the time. It'll be okay.' The second day the same thing happened and the third day the same thing happened and I didn't want to come back. I thought, I guess I'm not made for this. The fourth day all the things seemed to fall in place and I was welding, welding. The instructor came by and said, 'You know, I almost told you not to come back yesterday.' I said, 'Well, I almost didn't come back.'

"I've always told people that he taught me a great lesson that all teachers should learn—that you never give up on anyone. He didn't give up on me and the fourth day said, 'You know, you can do welding fine. You can go down to the yard.' There was further training there.

"I worked all three shifts by the time I'd been there three years, from July of '42 until August of '45. I started out on the day shift. I became leadman on that, which meant I had a crew. It varied from ten to fifteen. That happened because the fellow who was the boss of the first crew of women found out I had been a teacher. He came to me one day and said, 'You've been a teacher, haven't you?' I told him yes. He said, 'How would you like to run this?' I said, 'What do you mean, run it? I'm not even a journeyman welder yet.' He said, 'That doesn't matter. You know what I want to do? I want to get away from here. I want to get down to the other end of the yard and never see any of these women again.'

"I said, 'Well, if they don't object, I don't object.' So I became a welder leadman with very little knowledge. I didn't know what I was doing.

"They were in such a hurry to get the ships built that they had you welding long before you were a really good welder but you didn't do anything that would have caused danger to the ships, glass welding and that kind of thing, until we got pretty good. I worked there about a year and then discovered that the people who worked the graveyard shift just as welders, not leadmen, worked an hour less than the day shift and got paid much more an hour and I thought, why am I doing this? Here I've got all these worries about who has disappeared and all that kind of stuff, so I went on the graveyard shift.

"The only reason welding was a man's job is that men had always done it. There was no reason in the world why a woman couldn't be just as good a welder as a man anytime. In fact, I would say if I had to take a position on the question, I'd say that women probably made better welders, possibly because of their hands. Their skill. Sewing and all the things that you do when you're a housewife, playing the piano, maybe. All of those things help you in welding. Dexterity.

"I think that also they were more conscientious. They might not be now, but they were then. I would say that I didn't know any men welders who were any better than the women.

"It was fun. I really enjoyed the job. I was a good welder and had no regrets about anything I ever did. I don't think anybody ever found any fault with my welding, which was a great source of pride. If you're a teacher, you might do a good job but hardly anybody ever notices. How do you tell the difference between a good one and a bad one? But you can easily tell the good welders from the bad ones. It's right there in front of you. You can see it, the foreman can see it, everybody else can see it. It was the first time I'd ever done anything like that. I could see that I was doing a good job. I'm very proud of it. People say I brag about it. Well, why not?"

A third welder, this one in the Midwest, was also a school teacher when the war broke out and wanted to switch to war work to help the country. After her fiancé was drafted in the spring of 1942, Winifred Shaw Johnson finished the school year at a school in rural Nebraska and moved to Wichita, Kansas, where she lived with her aunt and uncle while welding for the Boeing Company.

"Lots of people were flocking to Wichita because Wichita had three different aircraft factories. They had Cessna, Beechcraft, and Boeing, so they were capable of hiring many, many people, which of course they did.

"It seems like I trained for a good part of the summer. I worked at Cessna first, for maybe three or four weeks, and then I moved to Boeing. I was an AA welder, which means I was supposed to be good. If you passed a certain test, you had to weld a certain thing together and then it was judged or evaluated, then you became an AA welder. It meant that I got more money and that I could wear that on my badge.

"I worked on the Stearman training plane. That was a little bi-wing plane they used early. I was making a whole section of the tail. I had to assemble all the metal and put it in the jig and weld it up, and I made two of those a night.

"We had to wear uniforms and we had to have our hair under control. Some girls just couldn't stand that and they'd have their hair out, and girls who worked around the drill presses, invariably they'd get their hair tangled up in that drill and lose part of their scalp and a few things.

"Of course, a lot of the girls were riveters, and they had to learn to keep these rivets in their mouth, and invariably somebody would swallow a mouthful.

"It was a very noisy and hot place to work. It was atrocious, just atrocious. We had to take salt pills all the time. Wichita, Kansas, can be desperately hot. And there was absolutely no air-conditioning out in the factory. We were warned that when we went to get a drink of water, to take a salt pill so we wouldn't dehydrate. They were right there by the drinking fountain.

"I know people who would come out of the air-conditioned offices and maybe have to get some information out in the plant and they would just about die. They couldn't wait 'til they got back to their office. You had to be kind of tough to go through with it. I was slaving over a hot welding torch on top of that, so to help me forget how miserable I was, I would sing.

"I had my goggles down and nobody could hear what I was singing, and I didn't care if they did or didn't, but it was one way to pass the time because the noise was atrocious anyway. You kind of felt like you were in a world of your own, behind those dark glasses. All you could see was your welding puddle of metal, so I'd sit there and sing.

"When people asked me what I did when my husband was away at war, I told them, 'Well, don't you know? I was Winnie the Warbling Welder from Wichita.'"

It was a male co-worker who noticed that Caryl "Jeri" Johnson McIntire's work was different from that of the men. In 1943, McIntire was working for the USO when she saw an ad for "War Work—Welders Needed Immediately." Despite advice from several friends not to become a welder, McIntire signed up for a week's training class in welding at Boston Navy Yard and then requested the 11:00 P.M. to 7:00 A.M. night shift when the call went out for welders on that shift.

"To this day, I don't understand why people were telling me not to sign up for welding, as I have never regretted one minute of my experience. They seemed to think it wasn't the thing for a girl to do.

"I loved it from the first day, I just loved it. There was such satisfaction. It was a challenge. I had no idea what I was getting into but the training was very thorough and it didn't matter that I was female. The fellows were just great with us.

"In the huge building where I was assigned, the shipfitters and their helpers would lay out the steel bulkheads on the day shift so the welders could work on them during the later shifts. This was flat "on-the-deck" welding, but I liked vertical welding the best.

"One sheet metal worker I worked for would lay work out for me because he was on days, and the next morning he'd be coming in as I'd be leaving. He'd look at it, and he'd say, 'I could tell a woman did this because it's got a woman's touch.' There was sort of a neatness

Above: Mildred "Hut" Ferree is seen at the controls of a North American AT-6, in WASP training at Avenger Field, Sweetwater, Texas.
Official Army photo.

Left: Margaret Berry, right, and her bucker, Donna Holley, dressed Donna's niece as a riveter, like them.

Above: Patricia Lapp interviews women pilots for the Douglas Aircraft *Airview News,* a weekly paper.
Courtesy: Douglas Aircraft Company.

Right: Maggie Gee was the first Chinese American female pilot, and joined other WASP trainees at Sweetwater, Texas.
Official WASP photo.

Florence Hackel, perched above Lake Michigan on a Chicago beach, scans the horizon for swimmers in distress.

Weather Bureau employee Virginia Denmark relies on the helium-filled balloon to supply weather information.
Photographer: Arthur Witman, staff photographer, St. Louis Post-Dispatch.

The ones in aprons are the sailors at Mare Island Naval Base.
Goldie Deckwa and her friend on the YMCA tea party
committee enlisted their help.

Eila Weisman, in the middle, reaches for traffic information, listening
to airline radio operators relaying information in the Chicago area.

Above: Eva Diamond, on a day away from her job as air traffic controller in Burbank, California.

Right: Rose Toomey and husband, PFC William Toomey, are in Everett, Massachusetts, while he is on leave. She is a sheet metal worker in the Boston Navy Yard.

Cecile Barbash, purchasing agent for the U.S. Army Corps of Engineers, receives an award for improving requisition forms. Lt. Manfre, left, presents the award and her supervisor, Oscar E. Meddaugh, looks on.
Official U.S. Army photo.

Helen Steffes is ready for third base with the Rockford Peaches.
Photographer: Millie Deegan.

Left: Margaret Walsh, an electric welder in the Boston Navy Yard, is seen with her husband in Buffalo, New York.

Below: Rose Ann "Tex" Barbarite majored in electrical engineering and became an engineering aide at RCA in Manhattan, often doing repair work on recording equipment.
RCA photo. Courtesy: Thomson Consumer Electronics.

Above: Margaret Berry returns to work as a riveter, on the B-29, in 1993. This time she is a volunteer, restoring old planes for the Museum of Flight in Seattle, Washington.
Photographer: Jack E. Ballard.

Right: Velva Davis is ready for her job as gear inspector at Pratt & Whitney, where aircraft engines are manufactured.
Photographer: Henry R. Davis.

Joyce Holloway, center, flanked by her husband, William H. Webb (left), a day or two before he took off for Army basic training, and her brother, John Leslie Taylor, home on leave from Navy boot camp. *Photographer: Myrtle Taylor.*

Gladys Ehlmann helps Emerson Electric Boat Company with the
United States War Bond Drive. She is a punch press operator.
Courtesy of Emerson Electric Company.

Above: Mildred "Hut" Ferree appeared in this photo of fellow pilots the day she met her future husband, Lt. Col. Charles Ferree, USMC. Pilots in the picture are (left to right) Grace P. Jones, Mildred Feree, Beverly Cangiamila (deceased), Carla H. Horowitz, Barry V. Smith, and Nancy U. Foran.
Official Army Air Force photo.

Left: Lunch pail packed, Cecilia Kutna is off to work at the New York Shipyard in Camden, New Jersey, where she works on aircraft carrier superstructures.
Photographer: Betty Jane Rutherford.

Above: Margaret Beezley has a
reunion with the kind of plane
she worked on during the war
—a B-24 on view at Boeing Field
in Seattle, Spring 1993.
Photographer: Ted Jagers.

Right: Betty Davis Kubik joined
her sister, Mary Jo Owens, as
usherette in the Missouri Theatre
in St. Louis. They inherited the
men's uniforms, cinching the
belts to make them fit.
Photographer: Joseph A. Kubik.

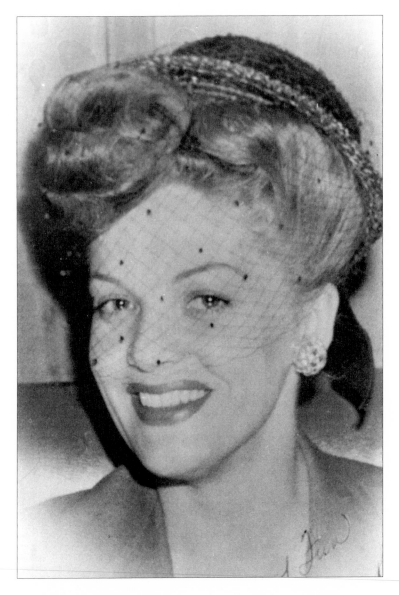

True to San Francisco tradition in the 1940s, Marge Altschuler wore hat and gloves when she applied for a job at Kaiser Shipyard in Richmond, California. It was the last time she wore them to work!

Ruth Fritz relaxes for a minute before going to her job as riveter at the Glenn L. Martin plant in Middle River, Maryland.

about it, I guess. Maybe because a woman sewing would be satisfied with her stitch. That's the way that I felt. It was all in the wrist.

"I liked the vertical welding because it was more challenging and so rewarding to see the neat bead exposed once I removed the slag. Slag is the residue that forms over the welded bead as the welding is in progress and then you can flake it off. It can be hot. I had many burnt holes in various shirts and was glad to learn the Army and Navy stores were selling leather welding jackets.

"A shipfitter's helper was killed on the day shift when a load of bulkhead steel broke loose from the overhead crane and fell on her. I often worked that area after that and always had a sense of un-easiness whenever the crane passed overhead, even though the operator would signal. All of us were really uptight that night, but we just had to keep going. The day before there had been a lot on the news about how critical a certain battle was. We all had such a patriotic spirit in us, we just felt that her death was terrible but the work had to get out. That schedule had to be met or that ship wouldn't be launched.

"We followed the news closely when we were working inside. We weren't really supposed to have a radio in there. It was the foreman who had it because he had two boys in the service. At break time or lunchtime we all sort of gathered around. It was usually on the hour so that's when the news came on.

"We were pretty much on the honor system once assigned a job, as the yard could not find enough supervisory people due to the manpower shortage. We felt very important. It made us feel they had confidence in us and it gave us more confidence in ourselves."

Joan Ascher Cardon's sense of humor and artistic abilities helped brighten Hazeltine Electronics in Little Neck, Long Island, where she worked from November 1942 to June 1943. Cardon was almost nine-

*teen when she quit college in 1941 and took a three-month evening
course in drafting.*

"We were working on the beginnings of radar. I was hired as the first
female in the drafting department, which was staffed mostly by young
boys right out of technical high school. We were a small department
and this was mostly in the laboratory. They hadn't even gone into
production; they were building models under contract. The radar sets
were for airplanes flying off the carriers and the radar sets would be
on the carriers themselves.

"We had very close ties with the British—we were getting together on this. The head of the department was an old-line German
who still had a bit of an accent. He was skeptical that a female could
do the work; I felt he was very uncomfortable with me. But he had a
good sense of humor. One of the peculiarities was that when we did
drawings, we were supposed to stamp them ourselves. We had three
categories of stamps. One was secret, one was restricted, and one was
confidential.

"I remember asking him, 'How am I going to tell the difference?'
'Secret,' he said, 'means only the people in this country working on it
and the Germans know about it. Confidential means only the people
in this country working on it and the Germans know about it—the
Germans know about it, have used it, and have discarded it.' They
didn't use restricted.

"I remember one thing. We were drawing to one thirty-second of
an inch accuracy and our lighting wasn't very good. I started to com-
plain about that and he was at a loss as to what to do. Finally, I had to
go to an eye doctor. I was seeing double. The doctor told me not to use
my eyes! He gave me some exercises. On my way to work with the
defense workers out on the Long Island train I was doing my eye
exercises, and everybody thought I was crazy.

"Very shortly after I had been there, they needed somebody down
in the lab with the engineers to make the first drawings from the

actual model. I was asked to do that and I suspect I might have been asked because I had a good memory and could draw accurately. I didn't know a damn thing about this—it wasn't my field at all.

"I got to know the young engineers and they were practically having nervous breakdowns because they wanted to be in uniforms. In New York, everyone who was healthy was in uniform. A lot of them wanted to join up and they couldn't because they were frozen in the job. So they were always feeling depressed. We all had to bring our lunch and I remember organizing a baseball team to cheer them up, and also going down to the waterside and socializing there and having lunch there. We'd play games—word games—anything to relieve them.

"I decided in May there really wasn't much point in my keeping this up. It wasn't going to do me any good after the war. I'd also been training as a nurse's aide. But when I decided to leave, I found out I was also frozen in the job. It took me a month while I was still working at Hazeltine Electronics to get permission from the Navy to leave the job and go back to school—but not go to another job."

Near the end of the Depression, the local Board of Education near Schenectady, New York, decided that no married woman should have a job. Marie Templeton Westcott was one of three teachers who were let go. She was staying at home, starting to write, when her son brought a note home from high school asking any mother with children over fifteen to take an electricity course sponsored by General Electric so they could work in the company's test department.

"To make a long story short, I worked for GE all during the war. This was in Clifton Park.

"There were a lot of housewives who took that course. They hadn't been studying or things like that. There was another young woman who, with me, was at the top of the class. The woman who was hiring came to interview us and she gave us a ticket and said, 'Don't stand in line; give these tickets at the door,' because there were a lot of out-in-the-country people coming to get a job.

"We were put on a woman's job for two weeks. Then we were put on a man's job with the warning that when the men came back, we'd have to go back on a woman's job, and it happened that way. I liked the job quite well because we were building things and I learned to read blueprints.

"We had factory hours. I had to get there by 7:00 A.M. To do that, I got up at 5:00. There was a special bus. I didn't get back until after 4:00 P.M.

"I started the job and at first I was just putting screws in a machine. But I'd watch the other women with their blueprints—I had time in between when there was no work for me. The boss brought around a job. I was sitting there, I didn't have anything to do right then, and I told him, 'I think I can do it.' He looked at me in surprise. 'Well,' he said. 'Try it.' From then on, I was building things from blueprints. I always loved to make things. I used to embroider. Even after I retired from teaching, I started to paint.

"We were making push buttons, like buttons that are on the dashboard of a car, and they ran engines. There were all kinds that were ordered. I can't name them because I don't know what they fit on.

"I'll tell you one instance of my contribution. There was one thing we were building. It had a flat plate on the bottom, maybe seven inches long and three inches wide, and the left side was the part you had to build. But on the end of that flat side, it was open. There was one screw and the blueprint didn't have the number of the screw on it. At the bottom, it said the number was on another blueprint for that screw, just that one screw. I couldn't understand why it wasn't on that first one.

"So I had a little trouble getting that other blueprint, but I found it and a flathead screw had to go in it. But I saw other women working on the same thing and they put a roundhead screw on it. I asked my son—who took mechanical engineering in college—if it was okay to put in the roundhead. He said, 'No, they want that flat for something they slide into there.' So I made mine with a flathead. And I went to the boss and told him. He paid no attention to us. They had an inspector there, too, who sat down all day. She was sitting and testing those things.

"On my way through a room that was off the main working space, I saw all these things that were sent back and I wondered what they were. As I said, I had told the boss and he paid no attention. But later on, he came down the aisle toward me and with him was the brigade from the Office of the Army or the Navy, whatever it was, that was in Schenectady. He said, 'Marie, where did you find the number for that last screw?' I told him about the two blueprints. So all those roundhead screws had to be replaced.

"Most of the women were very nice. But one man didn't take to us. When we first went in his department, the young man—he hadn't been drafted yet—was angry that women were in the men's department. He said, 'Get the women the hell out of here!' Guess what? He couldn't be drafted. He had lung trouble. But he didn't know it then.

"I stayed the whole time during the war. When the war was over and the men came back, we had to go back on women's jobs. At first I was angry. We were laid off for a while and then went back, and I had to take a test from a woman, fixing blocks in the right places with my hands. I was insulted. The woman who started with me, she kept on, but she was doing office work instead of in the factory.

"I quit GE and went back to teaching, which was better because eventually I got a better retirement."

As a Texas rancher, Hallie Crawford Stillwell was accustomed to strenuous physical labor and the company of men. Like many ranchers and farmers, her husband, Roy, was deferred from serving in the armed forces because agriculture was an essential industry. But her older son was not exempt, and neither were the cowboys and ranchhands that helped out on the Alpine, Texas, property.

"My husband and my younger son and I ran the ranch. We were shorthanded, so we had to tighten our belts and do our own work. It kept us pretty busy. We had to ride from sunup to sundown and tend our own stock. It wasn't easy. But maybe it was good for us. We have 22,000 acres, but we're small ranch people. This is a big country out here. It's rough. It's isolated. You have to be a certain kind of person to stand it. We had about 1,000 mother cows, and that doesn't count the extra steers, bulls, calves, and all that. Nothing came easy. We're a long ways from the railroads and from town. Have to go a long ways to get mail—forty-six miles to Marathon, the closest town.

"We had three cowboys, and we always kept some Mexicans. I think ranch people were allowed a little more gasoline, so gas rationing didn't fall so hard on us. But we were all restricted. I don't think anybody felt free of it, and people accepted it gracefully.

"I had ridden by the side of my husband, always, so it wasn't too new to me. It wasn't something I had to learn, because I was already aware of what had to be done and had learned the skills of taking care of the cattle.

"As far as housework is concerned, the cowboys were just as good as I was. We shared all the housework. And the cowboys were good cooks. They were used to rustling for themselves. They didn't depend on a woman. They didn't depend on me or they'd have been in bad shape.

"Everything was harder in the war.

"I've done things not too many women have done. Branding the cattle, doctoring them. We have the screwworms that every calf that is born has to be doctored for. Tending to the cattle, just general ranch work. We did everything on horseback back then. Now we have a jeep. But there are some things I have cowboys ride for. These vehicles can't go up to the top of mountains and down in deep canyons.

"One time, I can't remember why, but I attempted to go down the back side of the mountain. I got about halfway down the mountain and it was perpendicular. Boulders, no trail. I got halfway down and my horse refused to go any further. So there I was. Suspended. I couldn't go back and the horse refused to go forward. I got behind him and put my hands on his rump and pushed him down that mountain. That's about the worst predicament I ever got into. I was about ten miles from home, and I had to make it. Out in the wilderness if a fog comes in, you can't tell by directions and you can't see anything. It's pretty bad, and I've been caught in those.

"Another time during the war, our son Guy had gone ahead of us to the Fourth of July celebration in Marathon. As we got ready to leave, we realized Guy had not loaded the butane bottle—a 200-gallon container—to take into town to get it filled up. We depended on our butane. So my husband and I attempted to load this empty bottle, and it was too heavy. We tried to figure out how we would load it into the truck. We rolled it to a dump and backed the truck up to the dump. Then we rolled it, both of us pushing, up into the bed of the truck.

"Well, we just looked at one another and said, 'What will we do if they take Guy into the service?' We had already given up our older son, and Guy had been deferred. We depended on him to do all the heavy chores. You can imagine how we felt, how helpless. We just looked at one another thinking we were doomed if they took Guy.

"We drove to town and told the man we needed our gas bottle filled. He came over to fill it up and found that it was full! Then my husband and I looked at one another and laughed a little. We had loaded a full bottle! We felt real proud of ourselves and weren't as old as we thought."

8

. . . .

From Shy to Sure

Standing up to men who challenged their ability to do the job, working in situations bordering on hostile, meeting tough production standards imposed by wartime exigencies, climbing heights, carrying heavy equipment, getting grubby and sweaty and cold and weary—these are ingredients that produce change. And many women working during the war were changed. They talk about a transformation brought by those years that gave them a new and lasting self-esteem, greater self-confidence resulting in unexpected rewards, and knowledge that widened their horizons and led them to activities that made life fuller: teaching, painting, writing, social work, raising plums. Audrey Ward Norman sums it up: "I was shy and quiet before the war. I don't know what I might have done if I hadn't had that job, but it certainly made all the difference in the world to me."

Jennette Hyman Nuttall found herself sixty feet in the air, in the cab of a crane, clinging to the ceiling of an aircraft plant. Getting up there was one thing, getting down another. But once she mastered the descent, she was able to use her crane operating skills in her next job in a shipyard. Nuttall started in Phoenix, Arizona.

"My cousin and I went to the Alcoa plant to look for a job in 1942. The openings they had were for crane operators. At first, they put us on forklifts, and we did very well on them, and then they decided that we could graduate, so to speak, to crane operators. The cranes ran on two rails about sixty feet up in the air. I remember when I tried to get up there, all they had was a lean-to ladder from the ground up to the rails. You had to climb up that ladder and then into the cab of the crane. The first time, they had somebody with you, watching you, and I was scared to death going up, but once I got up there and stepped into the crane, they had one of the foremen up there with me, and he showed me how to run it.

"There was another female operator with me, and they called her 'Boots.' She was a real cowgirl. I learned how to operate the crane, and the foreman went down. I said to Boots, 'You know, I will never, never be able to do this. I'll have to run a crane on the ground.' She said, 'Don't. Force yourself to do it.' Then the buzzer rang, and she said, 'My shift is up. I've got to go.' So she left me up there. It was only a practice crane. I wasn't allowed to carry anything yet.

"Finally I wanted to come down, so I moved the crane over to the ladder and then I started blowing the horn, because no way was I going to step out of that crane onto that ladder. I just kept blowing the horn, and a couple men came over and I said, 'I'm afraid to get down off of this crane.' One of them climbed up and into the cab, and the other one stood on the rung below me, and they were holding onto me and the one in the cab was holding onto me, and I finally got my foot out of the crane and this guy down below put my foot on the rung. I wasn't able to look down. Finally, I got the other foot down, and this guy put my hands on the rung, and this is the way I came down the ladder. Each one was holding a hand and bringing it down, or a leg, and bringing it down to the next rung.

"I finally got down and I said, 'I'm never going to go up there. As long as I live, I'll never go up there.' But he said to me, 'It's always difficult the first time.' He said, 'Don't say you won't. Make yourself.' I was young, I was eighteen or nineteen. You're more reckless then and more daring. The next day I came back in and I went up again, and it took me a few days. Then I loved it. I just loved it.

"We carried these big metal racks, I would say at least twenty feet long, in the shape of a U. Long tubes. I would have to pick this whole rack up when they finished filling it and carry it over and pile it up on top of the other racks. You really had to learn what you were doing because if you didn't get the rack right on top of the rack below it, you could topple this thing over. You had to be very exact. I was very, very careful.

"After about a year, I went back to Boston where I'd lived before, and I went down to the Boston Navy Yard at Charlestown and applied for a crane operator's job there. They asked me what experience I had and they told me they didn't have women operating cranes. I said I had all this experience and they said they would give me a chance. As a result, I found out they had two other women crane operators that they weren't even aware of.

"I remember one time they needed a crane operator inside one of the buildings, and I went in there. When the men in there saw a woman up in the crane, they threw down their hats, their gloves, and would not work. They were afraid to work under a woman. I said to my rigger—he's the one that directs the crane operator exactly what to do—'What do you want me to do?' The rigger said, 'You stay there. You can operate the crane and they're going to have to learn to live with you. If they don't want to work, they can walk off the job.' He just stood his ground.

"They kind of hassled me. When I'd come by with the crane, they would act as though they were afraid I was going to drop something on them. They didn't give me a real hard time, but I thought it was funny the way they were acting. It took about a week to convince them I could really do the job. After that they'd come in and—in fact, they were a nuisance because they talked to me so much that I would be blowing the horn for them to get out of the way, and they would just move at a slow pace. But they trusted me that much. When I had to leave, they sincerely didn't want me to go in the worst way because they had gotten used to me and they felt good with me there.

"Of course, you weren't constantly busy, and at that time my brother was in the Air Force overseas. He was a tail gunner. We used to have a contest to see who could write the longest letter. I used to write him every day. I think I wrote the longest one and it was twenty-five pages, each side, so it was fifty pages. Also at the time, I wrote a song for his squadron, and it was published in the *Navy Yard News*. I also wrote a poem for the flag raising on Iwo Jima.

"The jobs I had during the war made me realize that I was a little bit more daring than I thought I was. I had to climb so high; I was not naturally an athletic person, but I didn't have any fear after the first time. It gave me a lot of confidence when it came to something like that. It showed me I could hold a very responsible position, which it was. I was carrying hundreds of tons of material over people. It did a lot for me in that respect.

"I love talking about those days. I'm sorry it had to be wartime, but at that time I was young and reckless, and we did all kinds of crazy things. The job was always very exciting to me. It was even more exciting after I left it, because it was so rare. I never met another person who was a crane operator. And I show my grandchildren, 'See that crane, way, way up there? Grandma used to run a crane like that during the war.' Most of the grandmothers were welders and things like that."

Frances McCormick King was in charge of the laboratory at the National Folding Box Company in New Haven, Connecticut, where she took the place of a young man who went to war. The company manufactured boxes for packaging food, and her laboratory tested materials to ensure they were pure. Her tenure was short.

"One day I went to my boss, because it didn't seem as if I had much to do. I would get things done by noon. I told him I would like to know more about the papermaking process. I thought I could understand better what I was doing. He just sort of smiled at me indulgently. If he didn't say it, he meant, 'Little girl, don't bother your head.'

"That turned me off completely. The other thing that bothered me was the response they gave me when I asked about the man whom I replaced. I felt I must be missing something, since I had so much time on my hands. They said he used to go out and sit in his car in the afternoon and listen to the ball game on the radio. I was full of enthusiasm and I wanted to learn more about the process and the head of the lab kind of laughed at me.

"I had already applied elsewhere, including Whitney Blake, the cable maker. They called me and I knew I wanted to get out of the job I was in. So after about two months at the box company, I moved to Whitney Blake in Hamden, Connecticut, where I had the great fortune to work for a man who explained everything to me, who helped me in every way, and was a perfect role model, mentor, whatever. He was the cable development engineer.

"So I was able to do a lot because I had him to fall back on. I didn't have the depth of engineering knowledge that I should have had. I had about six weeks of physics and electricity. He was extremely helpful, and I found the men in the factory extremely helpful. I remember the first time I had to go out and tell a man who had been working on a machine for thirty years what to do, and I thought, 'This isn't going to go over very well.' Here I was, twenty-one years old. But it was fine. I generally found I got respect from these people and didn't have a problem, which was very nice, since sometimes I would be a little afraid of the situation. But they were extremely helpful. We had black men working in the factory. They were the best as far as getting things out of the way and generally making things accessible.

"We were designing wire cable, which, of course, I had never thought about. It was pretty much a hands-on job, running samples. We worked from requests from customers for particular things, and many requests were from the government, so we were working with specifications to develop a wire that would meet their needs and also writing up standards, which the factory then used in making the product. Much of it was for the Signal Corps. They needed a lot of field wire, telephone wire, and they made wire for airplanes and multicable wire.

"We also worked on trying out new products and developing new products as well. We got a Big E (for excellence) award and had a big banquet to celebrate that, and it was pretty exciting.

"It was interesting because I was tossed into something that I never even knew existed before. There was so much to learn and so much to do. It was sad with the war and all, but on a day-to-day basis, there was always a lot going on and you felt you had to accomplish a lot, which did keep it interesting. That feeling of accomplishment was especially important during the war. I was certainly involved in things that I knew absolutely nothing about beforehand and would not have been involved with otherwise."

From her home in Perry, Arkansas, Nova Lee McGhee Holbrook heard about the work available in California shipyards. As wartime production got under way, she and her husband headed out to the Kaiser Shipyard in Richmond, California, where they both were hired.

"They offered me office work, but I said, 'I want to be a welder.' They said, 'It's going to be dirty.' 'I can wash it off,' I said. I went down and took a welder's test, flat, vertical, and overhead, and passed, so there I was, a journeyman welder. I wore leather coveralls and leather jacket and gloves, a welder's cap, and used a welder's hood. The hood had three glasses to see through, the panel with one white glass, then a dark green glass, then another white glass. We were constantly scraping the slag off them. We wore hard-toe shoes and hard hats when in the yard. The padded welder's cap was worn under the hood and often to and from work, as we felt proud to be seen with them on. If a lady wore a welder's cap in transportation, everyone knew you were a welder. It was hard work, but believe me, the people noticed us.

"I welded down in the hatches, boiler room, and everywhere else that the men did. It was a pleasure to be assigned to weld on a bulkhead.

"I carried a rod pot, stinger, small hammer, wire brush, welding rods, and most of the time a long lead on my shoulders for hooking up to the machine while climbing tall ladders from one deck to another. I worked right with the men doing the same jobs, and I enjoyed every bit of it.

"My husband and I lived in San Francisco during those years, and we had the same hours. He worked as a pipe fitter in Yard Three. We rode the ferry across the Bay for about six months, then bought a car and drove across the Bay Bridge, which was so beautiful. But all the time we were there, San Francisco was under a dimout, and we never did see it as it really is.

"I had one very bad flash burn during this time but got over it and went back as soon as I could see again. No one can explain how much those burns hurt, but they are very painful.

"Sometimes people would steal your lead. The lead is a very heavy electric cord, coated and heavy, and you roll them up and carry them on your shoulder. And maybe you've got one running from your machine down to another deck and also up to another deck, maybe three leads, and somebody would go up and get your middle lead, and you're down below working. Then if your light goes out and you can't weld, you know that somebody took one of your leads. They took them because they couldn't find enough of them, and just took yours.

"I quit when my husband went in the service and I left with him. They said you couldn't quit, but I just walked out. A year or so later I wrote and asked for my wages and told them I would send my key to my locker and my badge and everything, and they sent me some papers to have notarized and they sent my check and I sent them the key.

"I was raised in a small town and went all through school in that town and didn't get to go to college because my folks didn't have the money. So when I went out to the shipyards, it gave me courage to go on and do better things. To meet the public. When I came home, I worked in a café in Perry and met the public there. And then I got a job interviewing for a new clinic in the county and went house-to-house interviewing. The man who hired me said it would only be a three-month job. When the three months were up, he said, 'I've been interviewing seven people doing this, and I've picked two of them to stay, and you're one of them.' So I worked for the Rural Area Health Care Clinic doing research work and then as a receptionist and bookkeeper. No one would ever have believed I was a welder and went home with black on my face and hands and wore leather clothes when they met me at work in white.

"I will never regret my two years or more in the shipyards. It gave me a good start in life and how to work at anything you wanted to do. I learned to do other jobs, too. I decided if I could learn to weld like a man, I could do anything it took to make a living."

Maggie Gee was a seventeen-year-old freshman at the University of California at Berkeley when the Japanese attacked Pearl Harbor. She quit school and got a job as a draftsperson at Mare Island Naval Shipyard. Her mother took a job as a burner-welder at the Oakland Shipyard. But Gee was more interested in the air than the sea, having been attracted to flying since she was a young girl and spent many days watching planes fly out of Oakland Airport. Through her determination, she became the first Chinese American female pilot in World War II, a member of the Women Airforce Service Pilots (WASP).

"I wanted to learn to fly, and I cashed in war bonds to learn. I went to Minden, Nevada, with hopes of getting into the WASP. WASP recruiters signed me up and I went to Sweetwater, Texas, for six months of training.

"We had the same training that the men had. It was very rigorous. We weren't supposed to have any romantic affairs, of course. We were trained by men. All the Army personnel were married, but the instructors were civilians. They were about my age. Some were good, some would harass you. They were somewhat envious because they were 4-F and they had wanted to be in the Air Force. But a lot of them were wonderful. We see some of them still. Some of the women married some of them.

"The training was vigorous and it was good. It was exciting. We went through our basic training. We were busy all day, going to ground school. We were confined to post. We became service pilots. I went to Las Vegas and worked as an instructor. I had the opportunity of flying a couple of mock gunnery missions in a B-17. That was exciting.

"Once one of the women didn't have her safety belt on one day and they were doing acrobatics. She fell out of the plane. But that was okay. We always wore parachutes.

"It was a very short period of my life. The big thing is that it did give me that self-confidence. I'd led a sheltered life, had hardly been out of the state. I grew up in the Depression. My generation was fascinated with flying. And I had the opportunity to do it."

Cecilia Null Kutna swept the decks of a pocket battleship and hauled scrap metal to dumpsters as one of the first twelve women working on the ships in the New York Shipyard at Camden, New Jersey. In her spare time, she went to school for shipfitters right in the yard, where she learned to read blueprints and other skills to qualify her as a third class shipfitter. She went to work as a grinder in the superstructure of aircraft carriers.

"After three or four months, I got promoted to actually building the ship's watertight collarplates, lining up decks and stringers. Then three weeks later, I was promoted to second class shipfitter—as high as a woman could go. I was a straightener and straightened decks, bulkheads, and hatches. After the welders finished, their heat had warped the metal. I had a woman for a heater who heated the metal along the stiffeners and I followed, squirting water on the hot spots. That actually moved the deck we were sitting on, on our little wooden benches. I had a water tank and 50 to 100 feet of air and water hose.

"Sometimes I had to have antifreeze in my tank. It was 2 degrees below zero with a wind blowing. Hey, it was cold there. We used to toast our sandwiches at lunchtime by putting them against the wall, or bulkhead it's called. It was bulkhead 44 because that was special treated steel and it was heated. It had to be heated to be welded. So they had heaters on there all the time, and we'd toast our sandwiches on it. It was also very hot in summer.

"For that I got $1.12 an hour. But I loved it because I was helping do my part to win the war and bring our men home victorious.

"Lunchtime was only fifteen minutes but we took more time. We were down in what they call a trigger pit—it's got something to do with the launching—and there the men used to shoot craps, and I used to loan them $5 and collect $6.

"When VE day came, I stood on the top deck of an aircraft carrier and cried for joy as the tugboats went up and down the river blasting their horns. Soon after that, in May 1945, I was laid off. I worked on many ships. I often wished I was back again in New York Ship. I had a special feeling as I watched each ship grow from the keel to a big ship with guns, radar, and men. A little city in itself. I had tears in my eyes as I watched them slide down the ways when they were launched. It was hard work but I loved it.

"Building the battleships and aircraft carriers gave me a lot of confidence for later years, and I found out I could do anything I wanted if I wanted to do it hard enough.

"From the shipyard, I went to Budd's and I did bomb fuses. That was on Hunting Park Avenue in Philadelphia. That lasted about a month. Then they put me in shop welding. Not that I'm bragging, but every employer I have had has always figured, 'Gee, she has that background, I'll teach her something else.' So really, I know how to run a lathe, a milling machine, a shaper, everything like that."

When Nancy Baker Wise enrolled at Northwestern University in Evanston, Illinois, in 1939, the campus was full of discussion about whether the country should be sending men to fight in Europe. By 1941, that was a moot point. Wise graduated in 1943 with a degree in English composition.

"My first job was with the Office of War Information in Chicago. I wrote spot announcements for radio stations, plugging war bonds and asking people to save grease and donate blood. The office would have preferred hiring men, but since they were in short supply, they took women.

"I left that job for a position at Swift and Company meatpackers, also in Chicago, where I worked in the Agricultural Research Department. This had been a man's job. The department hired graduates of agricultural colleges who were ex-farmers or ranchers and knew the subjects they were writing about—like chicken diseases and crop cultivation. The information was presented in institutional ads run in farm weeklies throughout the country—full-page affairs that were written under the Swift and Company name. They also produced brochures on these subjects.

"When my co-worker, Beverly, and I turned up in this department, you can imagine the disdain with which we were received. What in the world could two urban young women possibly know about cattle diseases and the use of fertilizer? The men who were there, family men old enough to be deferred, were patronizing. Obviously, we read up on the subjects before writing about them, and we managed to satisfy the department head. I learned a lot about coccidiosis.

"The higher-ranking men at Swift were able to have lunch in the company restaurant, while the lower clerks were relegated to the cafeteria. The food was very good in the restaurant—and there was no problem with meat supply! Among dozens of tables in the restaurant was one table in the far corner of the room reserved for the few management women who qualified for this privilege, and for secretaries to the president and officers. Beverly and I were grudgingly admitted to this corner.

"All my life I had been handicapped by shyness. It was hard for me to speak out in class, to do interviews for journalism assignments, and to encounter new situations. But after working at Swift and Company, convincing my colleagues I could do the work, and talking about story ideas with my boss, I began to lose some of that shyness.

"Beverly and I made some business trips to meet people in agriculture departments at universities. That experience representing Swift gave me confidence. One assignment was to talk to high school classes about nutrition and shopping, and that helped develop a self-assurance I used in a later career—teaching."

Before the war started, while she was in high school in Missouri, Audrey Ward Norman worked at the post exchange at Jefferson Barracks. When the United States joined the fighting, Norman quit the PX and high school and worked for four years at American Can Company in St. Louis, which had been converted to a torpedo factory. Norman worked in a large wire cage.

"I was right in the middle of the plant. I did bookkeeping. All the machines and everything were around me. My job was to record who took out what tools, who brought them back—the tools to repair the machines.

"We had no fans, no air-conditioning, and with the machinery going and all the drilling, the air was absolutely blue. All the time. The building was three stories high and with nothing but glass up around the edges of the top; it was very noisy.

"One thing I remember was that because of the food shortages we were rationed on meat, and I looked forward to Tuesdays because that's the day we could have meat. The rest of the days we got scrambled eggs or something like that in the cafeteria.

"Also, I don't smoke, but they rationed cigarettes, so once a week, when they sold them, I was everybody's friend because I'd get cigarettes for them.

"One of the bad things I remember is that they were horsing around one day—to put out fires they had buckets of sand around— and they were horsing around near me and I could see them and they threw the sand at each other and it went into the machinery itself and that machine was shut down for several days because of that. The management came around and wanted to know if there were any eyewitnesses, and I said, 'Oh, absolutely not; I never saw a thing.' I didn't know what those guys might do.

"It was all men. I was the only woman. Some of the men treated me as if I were a queen and some of them treated me like a whore. I mean, they said that to my face. My husband was overseas in the Navy at the time. And one man had come back from a concentration camp, and evidently his wife had been running around on him and what not, and he couldn't have a good word for me whatsoever. I think he was brain damaged because he would call me everything in the book. To my face. He would walk up to me for no rhyme or reason. Just because I was there and my husband was overseas—he thought I had no business working out there with all those men. That I was only out there for one reason.

"Those four years had considerable impact on my life. I was so shy before I ever started this thing that I wouldn't even go first in the door of one of those buildings with a group of people. I'd always tail along at the back of a group. I couldn't step forward and be in front for any reason. After four years in there, I have been forward ever since. I love people. I love being around people, and I've been all over the United States.

"I'm still doing volunteer work. I'm doing income tax for senior citizens, for disabled and the poor. I'm doing it for free. After I finished working for the federal government and then the state, I went into my own business as an income tax consultant and did that for thirty years.

"Those four years definitely gave me everything I needed to tell myself that I could handle it, no matter what. If I could do that, I could do anything. I could handle it—bring it on. That was my attitude. Dealing with the men was what did it. The good people and the bad people both.

"On top of that, at the same time I was working in the factory, I had the chance to go to night school and I was getting a higher education, which also helped my self-esteem.

"I've had a wonderful life—I'm sixty-eight years old now and when I look back there's a few things I regret, but the majority of my life has been upbeat—and I really credit it to quitting school and going in and taking that job. I really don't know what I would have done otherwise, but I certainly wouldn't have been out in the public eye."

The summer of '43 offered experiences to June Fine Roberts that brought her out of her bashful mode. Always reticent and self-conscious, her job at a box factory, and dancing with the USO servicemen, changed the quiet girl from rural eastern Oregon to a person who surprises people when she says she was shy.

"Working at the box factory reinforced my confidence that I was as good a worker as any of the other women there. My brother-in-law was the millwright for the factory—a wooden box factory—and suggested I might want to work there. I did. Anything to earn money. I'd been working since I was thirteen, babysitting, herding sheep, cleaning houses, anything I could get.

"I bought these lightweight denim shirts and I had some old dark blue slacks that my mother had made, and I put calamine lotion on my face because I still had acne, although I had started taking thyroid my freshman year at college. I put the lotion on my face and that awful-tasting stuff on my lips that tastes like camphor, no lipstick, no makeup, and skinned my hair back. I looked like the spook of the West.

"It was hard work. I had to operate this machine in which you balanced a bundle of wooden cleats—they were about two feet long—you yanked this handle down that put the wire around them and stomped with your foot at the same time. I remember once setting it up on the cart that we loaded them on, and it was just the right height, and I sat one right on my nipple, through my bra. I tell you I just nearly went through the roof. I guess I turned perfectly white because the lady who worked on the next spot said, 'Listen, why don't you take a break.'

"Another job I had was called tailing off. The saws where they would cut a long 2×4—long pieces of timber, or short—would have a sawyer on one end and that was always a man, and you'd be on the other end, receiving whatever it was that was coming out and then you'd have to pile it, stack it, whatever. It was nine hours a day, with a half hour for lunch. Saturdays 'til noon. It was hard but fun.

"Nineteen forty-three was a very exciting time in Lakeview. It was just crawling with servicemen. They were on maneuvers in the desert. The local ladies there started a USO. My half sister would go and play the piano and they would take food there. The servicemen were at the dances and so forth. I was always very shy, and it was a very good experience for me. People always laugh when I say how shy I was. I don't believe if you're terribly shy that you ever completely outgrow it. What happened that summer that was very good for me was not only that I was treated as if I was as good a worker as anybody else, but also I went to the dances, which were frequent, and I had my hair curled and I had on some lipstick. I didn't have calamine lotion and one time at the USO, my sawing partner, when I was tailing off the saws, he didn't know me."

Gertrude Clark Beavers was a teacher before the war, so it was a logical next step for her to teach a classroom full of Air Force men at the air base in Lincoln, Nebraska, preparing them for overseas duty. The subjects were new to her: recognizing enemy airplanes and U.S. planes, repairing a plane's electrical system, soldering, reading technical orders, and solving mechanical problems that might develop during warfare. The courses, with fifteen or twenty Air Force men in each, lasted eight days, with a different topic taught each day.

"I have often wondered how many pilots lost their lives because of such hurried and short preparation. Imagine, if you can, a downed pilot remembering the exact stitches to use and having the material to repair a torn wing on a plane, or needing to solder a broken part and having the proper equipment to do so. This instruction was no doubt useful at bases, but not in the open fields. I always felt the courses were much too short and hurried, but of course, this was wartime.

"At the beginning, my classes for the soldiers started at 11:00 P.M. and lasted until 7:00 A.M. After trying this for several months, it was decided that it was almost impossible to keep the soldiers alert and able to learn at these hours, so I was shifted to the hours of 7:00 A.M. until 3:00 P.M.

"I was about to go to sleep myself. I had two children and wasn't getting a lot of sleep. But you had to keep the men awake, because if one of the big shots came in, that was too bad. They took all the chairs out of the classrooms except one room. There was one class where they had to use books. So in that one they had chairs. Otherwise, they had to stand, and that was pretty tiresome.

"I was insecure about teaching something I had just learned myself. I went through school in six weeks. I was insecure. It was very hurried instruction.

"There were only a few women instructors at the base, and we worked side by side with the Air Force instructors. After a rape at the base involving a civilian worker, the women instructors were removed from the classrooms. I don't think it was an instructor. I didn't know the person. I'd been teaching about a year before this happened.

"I was then transferred to the supply room in mechanics at the base. Here I checked out supplies to the soldiers as they worked on plane repair. I was the only woman in the hangar with many soldiers working on plane repair but was always treated with respect.

"This experience increased my self-confidence. It gave me self-reliance because I had to support my family for the two and a half years that my husband was in the hospital. He was first in Utah, then Springfield, Missouri, then Battle Creek, Michigan. As one hospital was closed, they would move him to another one.

"I got a nice recommendation from the Air Force when I left. The school remained in Lincoln for about two years and then was transferred to Oklahoma. I was offered a transfer but due to my family, I declined. I went to Western Electric in Lincoln, where the work was secret, but we assumed the electric coils the company made had something to do with wartime communication. I stayed with this company until the close of the war, when Western Electric moved to Omaha. Again I was offered a transfer, but I preferred to move to Edgar, Nebraska, to teach in the public school, which I did for twenty-three more years."

Winifred E. Tanges worked a milk route with her mother for two summers in New York State. Finding men during the war to drive a milk route for her father's company was difficult. The job was not prestigious, she said, and the men proved untrustworthy and didn't maintain regular schedules or handle bill collections reliably. Occasionally, they just walked off, confident they could find work elsewhere. So Tanges and her mother filled in.

"I'm not a feminist, but I'm an ardent independent person, and that job, along with the extraordinary independent spirit my mother passed on to me, made me feel the equal of any man.

"Daddy had built up his milk business from Nyack, New York, to two routes in Hempstead, Long Island. Mother and I managed the old route, while Daddy built up the new one.

"We had to go to the plant—my Dad's partner's plant—and load up our trucks there with our milk cans. High-necked bottles. We'd leave there about one or two in the morning.

"The thing I remember about delivering milk those two summers was just about dawn when the sky is getting pink and rosy and the birds are beginning to sing, and you can just begin to make out each other in the light, we would stop for breakfast, because we had done most of the route. Ordinarily, breakfast would not be the big meal of the day except when we were delivering milk. We would always go to this one diner. And they'd see us and call out, 'Here come the milkmen!'

"We delivered to at least 200 customers, and they would be scattered; they wouldn't be just right next to each other because we were a small outfit just beginning. We were fighting competition, like Borden's and other large companies. As a matter of fact, Dad built this company up to the biggest independent in Nassau County. We named it Crestwood Dairy.

"Since my mother and I were the boss's wife and daughter, the other men treated us well. The customers loved us. They all thought it was great, the two women, mother and daughter, delivering milk. We wore slacks. They had little insulated boxes for putting the milk in, and we worked from a route list that told us where to put the milk. Sometimes we would go into the house and put it in the refrigerator. We would also deliver eggs and butter, but we had to make sure we got the ration coupons for the butter. Watch out for the dog, if there was one—the route book had it all. Everything was laid out in the route book.

"We had to pick up the empty bottles and take them back to the milk plant, unload them at the pasteurizing plant, then take them back to our garage. Somewhere or other we had to roll forty-gallon milk cans full of milk onto the truck and take it to the pasteurizing plant. Unload the truck—nobody helped us. It was our job. Our route finished about 5:00 or 6:00 A.M. and then we'd have that big break-fast. We'd take our time—a half hour!

"Out on the road, Mother and I would reminisce about the time I saved her life. One time when we were out in a storm, raining hard, we were getting the milk out. Mother started to get out of the truck, and for some reason, I said, 'Mother, wait. Just stop.' And she did. How we discovered this, I don't know, but there was a broken power line in a puddle of water, right next to the truck. I don't know whether I saw it or if it was a premonition, or what. A man came along an hour later and was killed.

"I think the health problems I have today are the result of the heavy laboring I did as a young woman. I try to tell the youngsters today that they may think themselves equal to men, but there are certain things girls should not do. But the job also reinforced the feeling that I was the equal of any man. That's why I think my three marriages failed. I thought I was their equal, if not better. I have a feeling that I send out vibrations and that my attitude, that I was unaware of, says to them, 'Don't mess with me because I'm just as good as you and I can be just as tough.' I probably worked harder all my life than they have."

9

· ·

Hey, I Want This Job

When the war ended, factories and shipyards devoted to war-time manufacturing shut down immediately, some in midshift. Workers were out of employment within hours, days—at the most, weeks. For those operations serving the peacetime economy, most jobs were turned over to returning veterans, leaving women out of work or relegated to clerical or lower-paying, lesser-status positions. Similarly, many women were shut out of professional jobs they held during the war, forced to reassess their career plans, or, in some cases, abandon them for other choices.

This abrupt change in circumstances was a jolt for many women, bordering on insulting. For several years, they had proven they could successfully perform work formerly considered too difficult, dangerous, or complex for women, and now they were loathe to leave. Not only did they resist the loss of managerial posts or high-paying factory jobs, they resented the reduction in pay. For many, that was the greater penalty.

Having unloaded construction tiles at a lumberyard as a high school senior in Mapleton, Minnesota, and fed a crusher at a hemp plant a year later, Vera-Mae Widmer Fredrickson was employed as a punch press operator at Honeywell in Minneapolis, Minnesota, toward the end of the war. She had worked her way up to that position.

"At first, I was put on a bunch of jobs that were women's jobs because I had fantastic hand-eye coordination, but these jobs were boring beyond belief and they wouldn't let me work at my own pace because then I'd be a wage buster.

"Finally, they put me on a punch press, which is a big machine that punches metal, and I just loved that. It was very noisy. You had to wear ear plugs. It was a man's job because you handle this big weight. It was physically demanding. I felt I had more control, however, in what I was doing than in other jobs. It was very tiring. When you're adjusting to punch the hole for the bomb sight, you just sit there and adjust and adjust and adjust the tension. Oh, it was maddening.

"I was happy in that job, but I got boosted because the guys came back from the service. It was 1945. The guy came back to my specific job. It was union and the punch press was a man's job and had always been. They put me on the extraordinarily tedious job of putting labels on switches and adjusting screws, which women were supposed to be good at, and I quit. I was furious. I went to the union about it, too. Didn't do a bit of good. They said, 'Boys from the service, you know.'

"I went to work as a waitress. After that, my jobs were traditional female jobs because they were available. Overnight, those jobs that were men's jobs vanished. We women talked about it, some of us. Some were just passing time, waiting for their boyfriends or husbands to come home. Or some were being patriotic, and making more money than they'd ever made in their lives.

"But some felt like I did. I'd always wanted men's jobs. I'd been resentful that the word was that women could be secretaries, nurses, that jazz."

Wilhelmina "Mina" Eckey Terry was similarly frustrated by the return of the man whose job she filled in the personnel office of the Campbell Soup Company in Camden, New Jersey. Terry had not set out to work in personnel. With a degree in home economics from a small Quaker college in Indiana, Eckey's dream was to work in a test kitchen for a food manufacturer, developing new recipes and products. But product development stopped once the war began. She relocated to New Jersey to be near her mother-in-law and started out in Campbell's employment division recruiting laborers for the tomato harvest.

"I would go to mothers' clubs and the Italian clubs, the Polish clubs, to try to persuade women, and to the high schools to persuade high school kids, to work during the summer processing tomatoes.

"We always managed to get enough labor. This was unskilled labor so you were attracting people who didn't have high skills. A great many housewives who had never worked outside the home came to work for that season. It was a short season—about six weeks. That's where I started, and then I worked in the employment division for the rest of the year, interviewing for factory jobs.

"Then I was promoted to do interviews for office and technical jobs, which meant a new locale for me. I moved to the general offices—a whole square block of offices. That was what I was doing until the end of the war in 1945. I really enjoyed it because I became acquainted with the entire manufacturing process. I had to know something about every department, and it got me in contact with all the department heads, because I had to learn about the job I was filling so I knew what to look for.

"I enjoyed the variety, the different contacts with all kinds of people. At that point, I was fresh off the farm. I had never experienced the industrial process. I found it fascinating. I still do.

"But starting at that job was probably the hardest thing I ever faced at Campbell's. When I was promoted, they were firing the man who had the job. He was tall, handsome, really stunning, but he was all talk and very little do. The company told him on Friday night that that was the end and in the meantime, they told me they were promoting me to that job. As I took his place on the following Monday morning, I had to sort of run the gauntlet down this block-square of general offices with every eye on me. It was really dreadful.

"At the end of the war, I had mixed feelings about the men coming back from the war. I knew when the man who had my job came back, he would want it back. On the other hand, my husband was one of those men returning.

"Still, I was upset when I lost that job. The company had definitely stated that any employee who worked there before the war would find his job waiting for him when he returned. There was no federal law at that time that said that, but it was company policy, and I certainly respected it.

"However, the job had evolved a great deal within the company, just in the period I was there. The man I replaced had worked in the employment division. That's where I started out. He was under the employment manager. I went into the office of technical employment and was more or less my own department head. Of course, he wanted his job back. The office manager with whom I worked closely said he was very sorry but this was the way it was; they had offered the man other jobs but he didn't want them.

"There really wasn't much I could say. They vaguely offered me another job, said they'd find something, somewhere in the company. But I really couldn't see what it was going to be and I didn't like the vagueness of their offer so I became determined to look for another job. I was very annoyed and quit.

"I found a new job easily with a hosiery finishing company as personnel director. The company was just starting up and they were remodeling an older building and starting a second plant in the Philadelphia area. I went in on the ground floor and did all the hiring for the whole company. I felt triumphant that I could get a job that probably wasn't any better but at least sounded better because I had the title of 'personnel director' and could go back and tell them that.

"A little postscript here: the man who wanted his job back at Campbell's and got it, was let go not too much later because the job had, indeed, changed. They wanted a college graduate, which he was not and I was. By that time, I had moved on to different things—moved away—and I didn't really pay much attention to it. I heard about it from friends who were still working at the company."

With two daughters to support due to a recent marital separation, San Franciscan Cecile Zilberman Barbash needed a job in 1941, even before the United States declared war. A perceptive acquaintance came along at the right time.

"I had never worked before but my daughter Barbara was friendly with the daughter of a captain, they were in school together. He knew I was separated. This was in August and he said to me, 'I know you and your husband are separated and I want you to know that there's a war coming on and if you like, I can put you in touch so you can be appointed to civil service but you have to take a typing course or something in order to pass.' So I registered in business school and took a course in typing and passed. The test wasn't very hard to pass and that's how I got appointed.

"When I was in line to get appointed to the civil service, there was a big long line of people, and the person that interviewed me for the job was a former maid of mine. She was nice about it. I got appointed as a purchasing agent for the Port Quartermaster in San Francisco. The War Relocation Authority was under that office and that's where I started working.

"My job was to purchase materials for the relocation camps. The camps were in different states. The Japanese could only take a few things with them, so their valuables were put in warehouses in San Francisco. And the warehouse people were stealing from them like mad. I consulted a lawyer because I was very embarrassed about it, and he told me as long as I was working for the government, I couldn't do anything about it but I should keep a record of what was going on. So I did testify in the 1980s when they were making reparations.

"My daughter Sally was in tears over the relocation. She lost her best friend. They lived just a couple of doors away from us. It was wrong, very wrong. Of course, just a couple of years ago, they were making the reparations and the government admitted it was wrong, but then the damage was done.

"But I couldn't take that war relocation. I stayed with that about six months and then asked to be transferred, and I was transferred to the Corps of Engineers. There I purchased construction materials for bridges and other projects, and all the materials for the Pacific Theater headquarters, including MacArthur's palace.

"You had to have three bids, you had to have requisitions. I just learned on the job but I got pretty good at it. I could open the bids. It had to be the lowest bidder. Some things you couldn't negotiate. There were also open negotiations. Because of my judgment and being able to locate things, one of my bosses once said, 'I don't know how she does it; I don't know how she finds things.' It's persistence. It was from my own experience as a woman who bought for my household.

"I used to get nasty notes thrown on my desk from the other people, because I was popular. There was a lot of jealousy because I was getting all the big requisitions. I'd get real nasty notes. Once, I looked up and a man was at my desk, shorter than me. He said, 'I just had to see what was behind the voice.' We got to be friends after that.

"You had to be careful that you were not being bribed. The salesmen could be very aggressive. They would offer to take me out, and they would offer me a commission if I would throw the business their way. You had to watch your step all the time. There were many millions of dollars involved.

"MacArthur had requisitions for gold and silver. He had gold-plated doorknobs and sterling silver service. Plates with gold rims and the military insignia. Very elegant furniture. Everything the best. That was also a scandal. Millions of dollars. When the requisition came in, I had to fill it.

"I was constantly being propositioned by the merchants to come and work for them. But I was afraid. I had two children. I thought, no, I'm set here and when the war's over, they're not going to have any more use for me anyway. I had to work and I thought I had more security with the government than with one of those companies.

"After World War II was over, they were dismissing people. I got a notice on my check in 1945 that I was to be terminated. I could figure by what was happening, I knew there was another war coming. It was my own intuition. So I went up to talk to the major in charge, I guess to have an interview with him, and I said, 'You know you made a mistake in dismissing people because there's another war coming.' He looked at me but he didn't say anything. I was let go on the condition that I be hired back in another war. A couple years later, I got the job back for Korea.

"Afterward, I heard from his office staff that he said, 'How the hell did she know that?' I worked through that war but when the Vietnam War came along, I just couldn't take it. See, originally my parents were pacifists. I was sent to a Quaker boarding school in Bucks County, Pennsylvania, just to get away from New York during the First World War. That's why I couldn't take it. I knew the wars were wrong."

Marna Angell Cohen was newly married in 1942 and a recent college graduate. She and her husband were living in Bridgeport, Connecticut, where he was an engineer with General Electric. In addition to needing a job, Cohen felt drawn by patriotism when she applied for a job with the same company.

"The sense then was, 'We're stepping forward to replace the men that have to go to the front' kind of attitude, and nobody sort of questioned whether women could do these things or not.

"At the job, my memory is that the women felt rather cocky and pleased with themselves. The men either didn't pay any attention or thought, 'What are all those pretty little things doing running around here?'

"We were making searchlights for the Navy. As a stock chaser, I was responsible for seeing that all the parts that went into the searchlights were at hand when the people doing the assemblies needed them. I had to find the lightbulbs or castings or whatever. People would scream at me and I would have to arrange for transfers from other parts of the factory or from outside suppliers and be sure that everything was available. It sounds like a clerical job, but in fact it meant a lot of on-the-spot checking, so I was out on the factory floor a lot, being sure things were running smoothly and noting when supplies and parts were getting low and then chasing them. It was a lot of problem solving and actual visual checking as well as clerical work.

"One thing I keep remembering, which continues to give me a chuckle every time I see a reference to it, although it's not something I was directly involved in, but the designers came down and set up the lathes during the day, and the people on the floor found this really slowed them down. So the night shift would reposition the lathes and rework them to turn out the parts to specifications, and they felt they could always do it much better than those well-educated guys up in the front office that didn't really know what was going on. So they would break down the setup, revise it the way they wanted to, and then before they went off from work, fix it again, put it back the way the engineers said it ought to be.

"The company started laying off the women because the men were coming back, which I resented. I had to leave. I was angry. I had really enjoyed the work. I felt they were much cruder in those days than they would be today. They simply said, we can get men now, so goodbye. I was laid off right away.

"I think that was when it really hit me that they perceived this as men's work. I felt that it was fair for men coming back to get their jobs back. That I would have understood. But I was not asked to leave because a particular person who had worked there was returning. This was just that they preferred to have men, and now that there wasn't the need for us, we were sort of brushed aside, and that did make me angry. I felt I had done a good job. It was like there was no recognition. Okay, now, we're through with you."

As the war started heating up, Eleanor Boysen Morgan already owned an airplane, a Fairchild 24, and was working on getting her commercial pilot's license, which was a requirement for being paid to fly. Once she obtained her license, she began teaching flying.

"I was gaily teaching flying. There were a lot of schools there. I was teaching in Lone Pine or Manzanita or something. Then Jacqueline Cochran came along and she thought that women would fly. She invited about thirty women who had quite a bit of flying time. At this point, I had 300 or 500 hours.

"We went down to Houston, Texas, and we trained on everything the Army had. We spent about four months there. At this point, most of us could outfly our instructors. Out of thirty, twenty of us graduated.

"We drew straws about which bases you would get. We started picking up airplanes from the local factories and delivering them to the fields so the men could be relieved of the duty.

"Of course, there was a lot of prejudice. It was the jerk who was telling his girlfriend how absolutely wonderful he was and suddenly someone five foot two walks out of a bomber. The instructors were supportive. It was mostly the men, the inadequate men, who were a problem. I think the prejudice you have now of women flying is, do they have the strength? It doesn't take a lot of strength to fly an airplane.

"In our group, we were kept secret for six months. They were afraid that there was a lot of opposition to women. Can't fly during your period. What do you do if you get pregnant? They kept it quiet until we graduated. During our training, it didn't happen to me, but one girl, you'd land at a field, because we flew across the country, you'd land at an airport and they'd think you'd stolen the plane. One girl, they got her out of jail.

"About two years later, they threw all the girls out. The war-weary men could come home. All the girls were upset about that. So a lot of girls did a lot of flying things. I had bought an Army plane because they sold these Army planes for nothing. By this time, I was a really good pilot. I could fly anything the Army had.

"I started flying the men, or anybody, in from Palm Springs to Los Angeles. We would have a lot of fun dressing up as feminine as you could with the full skirt, but they had to go with you. They said, this is your pilot, and the passengers would grit their teeth and go with us. That was about the end of my flying career.

"Just after the war, I went to New York. I went to Pan Am and said I wanted a job teaching instruments, and they about fell on the floor. They said, don't you want to be a stewardess?

"No, I didn't want to be a stewardess and then asked about being on the crew. They said no, what if the plane went down in the desert? The men and women would be there together. This was the Dark Ages. I could have been a very good instrument instructor."

Although Alice Dickie Perry was not a welder before World War II, her exposure to it evoked such a fondness that she sought to continue welding after the war's end. In the mid 1940s, that was not possible.

Perry was a nursery school teacher in Marin County, California, when the war broke out.

"I happened to attend a meeting of the Voorhees Committee, which was trying to get more nursery schools going for women who would be working in the shipyards. During the meeting, I thought to myself, 'I have no children, so I should work in the shipyards so women who *do* have children could be at home or in a nursery school with children as long as possible.' I went into the shipyards with that motivation. I was in the shipyards for three years. Two years in Richmond, California, as a shipfitter and one year in Marin as a welder.

"As a shipfitter, one of my jobs was to place brackets in the hold of the ship. As I held them in place, the welder would weld them securely into position. I particularly enjoyed this job because the welder, who was a black man, would sing as we went from bracket to bracket!

"I think we were all enjoying ourselves. I didn't have any feeling of any depression about what we were doing. We were all very excited, tired, and so on. Then I went onto a Marinship ship. I made the change because they were hiring on the swing shift and I could make more money and I could also learn to be a welder. I didn't feel that what I was learning as a shipfitter was anything I could do in the future.

"I went to welding school on site at the Marinship yard—I think it was about two weeks—and then actually one was qualified as a so-called journeyman.

"I had one experience as a welder I'll never forget. A Liberty ship had been damaged at sea. It came to Marinship yard for repair. I was sent with one other person (who rowed the boat) out to the ship. I welded a crack on the outside of the hull. It was fascinating. That was thrilling!

"I was the last woman to quit other than the women who came to clean Marinship. Literally. I mean, I looked around and there was nobody. I was the last, at least of my shift. I didn't go to the office and say 'Are you sure there's nobody still working?' but I went away with that awareness. Maybe it was announced at another shift. I knew the war was over and we continued to do some things, but not for long, and bit by bit there were fewer and fewer there, and I left.

"I was one of those people who wanted to go on making a living welding. I went over to San Francisco and into the various welding shops, and the men looked up from their work. Of course, they were the men who hadn't changed their jobs during the war. They were the ones who stayed at home and were working in the regular commercial shipbuilding, and they gave the same smiling embarrassed look as if they were four years behind when looking up at a woman walking in—how ridiculous that she could do a job welding. I was looked on with a certain smiling indulgence.

"I had that sense for the first time of being a woman again who was being judged for that, not for my work. In the shipyards, there was not any of that. Everybody was respectful of everybody for what they were doing, and that's all there was to it.

"So I went around from place to place looking for a welding job and there was nothing so I went back to being a nursery school teacher for a while. Nursery school, at that time, anyway, was absolutely wonderful, very creative.

"Now I don't even know where my welding equipment is. I would love to have done something."

After her freshman year at Linfield College in a small town outside Portland, Oregon, Rose Coffield Swanson moved back to the city to earn money to pay for the rest of her education. She started working in restaurants, where she had experience, but she saw that the "big money" was beginning to show up in the war industries. The local high school offered a six-week training course to learn the necessary skills for war jobs.

"I didn't have to pay, but they didn't pay me. We had a choice of being a welder or a machinist and several others. To be a welder, you had to pay $40 to get your equipment and I didn't have the $40 so I decided I'd be a machinist. They said you could get your tools slowly, one at a time. I took that course and when I finished it, I went to work in a machine shop. I went to work on my nineteenth birthday.

"It was Iron Fireman in Portland, and it originally made parts for an automatic coal furnace, but during the war it was a job shop for Boeing, Douglas—all the aircraft companies. It also made locks for sea locks, to open and shut for ships, and bomb fuses for bombs, many things.

"I was on a milling machine, basically, and I made a flange that was part of the bomb bay door release for all the Boeing bombers, from the B-17s up through the B-29s, over the two and a half years I was there.

"Now, the men, in order to be a machinist, they had to work on different machines, and in three years' time they'd be a machinist. But the women, they definitely intended to keep us right where they wanted us, and they put us on the same machine. Although I worked a shaper and did a few other jobs, I basically stayed on that milling machine.

"We didn't like it. We had one woman on a lathe that was better than all the men, and they were earning more money, and they really fought about it, that there was a set limit that they never paid women over, I think $1.10, $1.25 an hour.

"I think I started in at around 65 or 70 cents an hour, which was twice what I was getting in the restaurant. I thought I was rich. I worked up to $1.10.

"There was another bit of discrimination that I remember now, and at the time I'm sorry I didn't realize how bad it was. A gentleman that had worked on the lathe disappeared, and somebody said, 'Oh, they found out he was part black and they let him go. The union doesn't allow any blacks in here.' To begin with, I didn't think he looked black, and, second, I didn't know they didn't allow it. I'm sorry to say at the time I didn't realize what a terrible thing it was. I've thought about it a lot since.

"I liked working there. We were in a shop, not out in the shipyards. It was a big building. It was heated and warm and well lighted, and the guys were just real good to me. There I was, a nineteen-year-old girl, and there were only about six women when I came, and they were all women to me, old. Obviously, they weren't old, the early ones were about ten years older than I was. So I got a good welcome and never felt discriminated against in that sense.

"In fact, I apologized to some guy who had to show me the machine and work with me, and he told me quietly that the other guys were more than willing to do it.

"I lived with a girlfriend and her mother, and eventually I married within a year and stayed in Portland. When I got pregnant, probably by the time I was three or four months along, I quit because I couldn't imagine working in that condition. Isn't that a joke? They had a baby shower for me over the lunch hour, and they were almost all men there, and they were just as neat as they could be. They said that was very unusual for the men to come to a woman's shower in those days. That was something. That was a little different. That showed they were concerned about you.

"After the war, I settled down with my family like most of the women did, but I was aware that I could earn money and wanted to. After the kids got a little bigger, I phoned the machinists' union and asked about getting back in and they told me there was, to their knowledge, no woman working in a machine shop in the city of Portland. Very coldly. So I found out right off the bat I wasn't going to get back at that work again."

. . . .

Gladys Poese Ehlmann of St. Charles, Missouri, was shocked by the abruptness of her dismissal from Emerson Electric Company, in St. Louis, where she started working as a punch press operator making parts for bomber gun turrets in 1942. "The war was over on August 14 and we went in on the 15th. They lined us up and had our paychecks ready for us," she said. Immediately, the company began retooling its operation for peacetime activities, and the extra defense workers were not needed.

Ehlmann did not look for another job right away because she expected her husband home soon from overseas. But on discovering that his return would be delayed, she applied for a job as punch press operator with what was then McDonnell Aircraft Corporation.

"I applied for that position since I had experience on it. But they had monstrous presses, and only men were allowed to operate them because there was a lot of heavy lifting and things like that that I was too small to do. I am five feet two. Some of the presses were about two stories high. The ones that I worked on at Emerson, they were about ten to twelve feet high down to about seven foot and 120 tons.

"So I started working in the blueprint department, trimming and folding blueprints anywhere from an 8½ × 11 inch page to, I think they were 36 × 18 feet. We had to fold them all so they would fit in the file cabinet drawer. I stayed there until the first part of 1946, when I got pregnant with my daughter. Before I was called back to work, I got pregnant with my son, so I stayed home with my children until my son was in kindergarten. Then I worked again, starting in 1954.

"When I was working, I got used to being with people and I liked being around people, and the eight years I was home with my children, I developed ulcers. I went back to work and the ulcers went away.

"If my husband hadn't gone into the service, I probably would have just stayed home and been a hausfrau.

"When I started back, I started in the blueprint department, but they had a slow time and I was transferred into record keeping. I liked the records very much. I kept most of the records for the Gemini spacecraft.

"I enjoyed the work. About two weeks after I retired in 1979, my supervisor called me up and asked if I wouldn't come back. I said, no, I'd had enough."

When Marjory Cropley Hollis took a drafting job during the war, she did not expect to fall in love with the work. Her first drafting job was at Alameda Naval Air Station near Oakland, California, where she did mechanical drafting of machine parts. She went back to teaching when she and her husband moved to Sacramento. But he was transferred, and she broke a teaching contract to follow him to San Diego. Not wanting to break another teaching commitment in case they moved again, Hollis applied for a drafting job advertised in the newspaper.

"It was on North Island on a military base. I remember walking into the drafting room with fear and trepidation, wondering what the people would be like and if I could do the job. The first few weeks were so easy. Most of it was copying machine parts that were being slightly altered and then proceeding from there into other kinds of things. Eventually I was creating wiring diagrams for planes that were being turned into hospital airships, flying to look at sites for property acquisition maps, recording the location of military buildings on maps of Army and Navy bases, and thoroughly enjoying it.

"There were usually just men in the drafting department, but the younger men who would have been doing that job were being put in the service, so they started hiring women. I was the first one they hired. The men were very helpful, attentive. There were one or two who I learned not to go into the storage room with; it was too dark and they were too friendly. It happened enough so I was a little annoyed. I also put on some weight because they were forever bringing donuts and some such things—treating me well. I never imagined these attentions would carry over into my own home but they did.

"We lived in a beach cottage and commuted by ferry to North Island. That was fun. The dolphins played around the boat and all. There were no locks on the cottage doors. It was on Mission Bay before the bridge was built. We entertained some, including inviting people over from my job. Once, after Virg had left for the East Coast, men from work came over, climbed in the windows, and made free with the place. They came with bottles of booze and partied; I had to say no, I didn't want any company, I was fine. Just go on home. One of the men crawled in bed with me—that did it. I think this must have happened quite often with young women who were working in men's jobs.

"When the war was over, I thought I would like to stay in drafting, but I knew men would need jobs when they came back, and I knew I would need more training to become an architect. I had a credential in teaching, so the obvious solution was to go back to teaching, which I did enjoy.

"But when Virg was going to Stanford and we needed more funds, we were in Martinez, California, and I worked for a lumber company drawing house plans for people who came in either to build new houses or extend the houses they had. I had a drafting table set up in the dining room and drafted plans there. On two different times, I've redesigned my present house so that it changed considerably, and I always found that enjoyable. I'm still fascinated with new homes and people's plans for changes in their homes."

When he was called overseas, Dorothy "Sunny" Lockard Bristol's husband was worried something might happen to him and suggested that

she acquire a skill. She had completed two years of junior college and had a long-standing interest in art, so she enrolled in a special drafting program for women at Cogswell Polytechnic College, then in San Francisco.

Her first job was at General Engineering and Drydock Company in San Francisco on the swing shift. When her husband joined the Air Force, she moved with him to Connecticut and found a job with Sargent Locks and Hardware as a "tracer" because, as she said, "they did not allow women to do 'real' drafting." Dissatisfied with that job, she went to work as a detail draftsman for Winchester Repeating Arms Company, where she was respected by the older male gun designers. Bristol continued as a drafter after the war, by then living in California.

"Drafting was considered a man's job in no uncertain terms. When there weren't many men available for jobs, they looked toward women with the feeling that, 'Oh my God, we have to have *some*body.' They really didn't hide their feelings very well.

"I saw that in the trade school. They wouldn't come right out and say, 'We're desperate,' and all that, but it was their whole attitude. The male instructors were *flabbergasted* that we did so well in the various courses: drafting, math, piping diagrams, foundry methods, and the like. In fact, we did better work than the few males who were there.

"Some of the worst discrimination I ever ran into was with the oil companies. When I applied for a job, I was told, 'Well, you do beautiful work, but we really prefer a man, and if we can get a man, we'll hire him. Otherwise, we'll give it to you.'

"At that time, because the war was still on, they couldn't get a man so they did hire me. Once I was on the job, they were pretty good. Again, at that particular time, there were older men and they seemed to be more tolerant. I think they may have seen the need to get things done.

"But when the young ones started coming back—I continued working because I was then divorced and had a child to support—

that's when the remarks really began. Like, 'Well, all you women ought to be home cookin' dinner.' Plus, putting up the calendars with the cheesecake. It was the really young men who were the worst.

"The hard part was holding onto our jobs when the men came back. We were all expected to go home. And those of us who were not married, we were expected to marry. In fact, at one point, I was the only woman working in the drafting room at Standard Oil. But then two other women came in. One was married and one was single and the boss decided we weren't making enough money. He tried to get us a raise and he called us in and said, 'I'm awfully sorry, but the three of you really do wonderful work and I'm proud to have you here, but because you're women I just couldn't get a raise for you.' He told us that. 'I did my best,' he said.

"That was the same man who said he'd rather have a man but couldn't find anybody who did the kind of work I did so he hired me. Actually, he was pretty foul mouthed and smoked a nasty cigar, but he appreciated me and he complimented me on my work."

Continuing as a drafter after the war, Louisa Ilges Zeidler of St. Louis, Missouri, had a much different experience. She worked at Bussmann Manufacturing Company until 1951, when she quit to start a family. A year before, she married a man she met at the plant after he came back from the service. "I worked until the furniture was paid for and then I quit," she said.

Zeidler started at the plant as a factory worker ten years earlier, right after graduating from vocational school. Her family had just lost her father and she needed to take any job she could get to help out at home.

"I ended up in a factory doing the things women had been doing all along—assembling small parts for fuse adapters. It was mostly all women. The men were more or less the foremen and the mechanics and things like that. Even now, I think it's still women who do all the little things at Bussmann's except for automation.

"The war came and the men were going into the service. The company had lost their draftsman. My forelady knew of my art background and asked if I'd like to try the drafting job. I took the job and succeeded well.

"I dealt with well-entrenched men who had been foremen in all the departments for years. They seemed to accept me. There were five men foremen and five ladies. The laboratory where I worked had five engineers that I had to work with. No one gave me any trouble, but I don't know what they really thought. I became the whole blueprint department. We revised the system while I was there.

"My only problem was the pay schedule. I was put on an hourly pay arrangement. In the factory, I worked on a piecework basis and did pretty well. The drafting pay was not near the factory pay and I'm sure it was not what the men made before me. So, I told them, either I make what I did on my piecework job or I'll go back to the factory. Eventually, they increased my pay.

"I was the whole drafting department until the war was over, the drafting department, the blueprint department, the whole bit. Then after the war, I worked directly with one engineer and indirectly with two or three others. We all got along fine. I got married in '49 and I think I worked a year or so after I got married.

"I've continued with my artwork through the years. I do china painting, oil painting, and watercolor. During the war, I'd decorate the envelopes of my letters with little figures, thinking not only the people I was writing would enjoy it, but the fellows in the postal office would get a kick out of it. I have a cousin in Oregon and I do it for her too, and she says the mailman waits for the letters, he enjoys them so much."

10

• •

Time to Quit

"**I** couldn't get out of that job fast enough!"

Joyce Taylor Holloway's reaction to leaving her wartime job was more vehement than most but reveals the sentiment of many women holding defense jobs who left them without regret when the final factory whistles blew on August 14, 1945. They regarded those years as an interlude of patriotism, or financial gain, or excitement, or all three.

Hired to replace men who were serving in the armed forces and to supplement the manufacturing industry that grew during the war years, the women's departure was automatic once those needs no longer existed. They would resume their traditional roles of wives, mothers, and homemakers and be happy in that pursuit. This was true for professional women as well as factory workers. They felt privileged to attain stature beyond what women had experienced in the past but considered that work a one-time experience rather than the launching of a lifetime endeavor.

Children left with grandparents or neighbors or placed in various day-care arrangements came home to mothers eager to cook delicious family dinners and stitch up matching bedspreads and curtains.

Women without children or husbands often were eager to have both, and the years after the war saw a flurry of marriages followed by the infamous baby boom. Home became the highest priority for many women, especially with the end of food and gas rationing, and they

reveled in their new peacetime role of creating warm homes and families while putting the grimness of the war behind them.

Haunted by a premonition that her husband would not return from
the war, Joyce Taylor Holloway acted on his suggestion that she leave
private employment as a bookkeeper and take a job with the federal
government. She was hired to work in the optical shop at Mare Island
Naval Shipyard in Vallejo, California, her hometown. She worked
with periscopes, telescopes, binoculars, and range finders. A newly
invented film was applied to the glass, and she remembered that there
"is a certain point at dusk and at dawn where it's very, very difficult,
no matter how good the instrument is, to pierce through that strange
time, that strange light. The new film helped make the vision of the
person using the instrument much clearer."

In April 1945, at the time of the Okinawa invasion, mail from her
husband became scarce. While she did not know about the invasion,
she felt something had happened. She and her mother attended her
brother's graduation at the United States Naval Academy in Annapo-
lis, Maryland, and on their return in May, still found no mail.

A month later, her brother and his wife visited her in Vallejo before
he reported for duty at a shipyard in San Francisco and during that
visit came to see Holloway at the optical shop. Excitedly, she began
introducing him to her co-workers, before he interrupted her, saying,
"Just a minute, just calm down a minute, here. I have something to
tell you." A telegram had arrived at their home that morning stating
that her husband was seriously wounded. The next day, a second
telegram was delivered with the tragic news that he had not survived.

"That was in June, and in July I went back to work as soon as I could.
I worked until the day after they dropped the first atomic bomb, and I
thought, 'Oh, this is all going again, and I don't want to spend the rest

of my life working in pants and wearing a bandanna on my head.' So I began to look around for another bookkeeping job in civilian employment while still at the shipyard. I realized that when the other women left defense work, the competition for employment would become greater.

"Then came the day of surrender, and everybody at the shipyard was just delirious. It was pandemonium in our department. Many in our department were enlisted servicemen, since only they could handle and classify the instruments. We just worked on the glass. When the war ended, they could go back to their lives. It was wild, a lot of fun. Except that I just thought, Oh boy, it's too late.

"Then this one lady who had been so good to me, and I'm sure she just said it unthinkingly, said, 'Well, it's too bad it happened. If the war had just lasted eleven more months, I would have had my home paid for.'

"And that did it. I've never forgotten that statement. I went right downstairs and said, 'The minute that this thing is signed, I'm through.' As I remember, it was around Labor Day that they signed the surrender on the *Missouri*, and that was my last day. I couldn't get out of that job fast enough. Actually, I think 70 percent of the women were delighted to get out of slacks and bandannas."

While she was in college in the Midwest, Eila Ahnger Weisman answered an advertisement for an air traffic controller trainee. Sent to Chicago Midway Center, she was one of the first women air traffic controllers in the country. Keeping the planes apart was stressful.

"The country is divided into regions, or centers they used to call them. The centers control air traffic on the airways between cities. The airways are like highways in the sky. Chicago Midway Center controlled traffic on airways going to Minneapolis, Detroit, St. Louis, and Indianapolis. This is not the same as working in a tower, which controls traffic as it is landing and taking off from the airport.

"The salary was $1,800 a year at that time. After all, that was a lot of money. I went down to the Cincinnati Control Center and got my training and then came up to Chicago and actually taught in a training school here for three months. Once I had a class of twenty-nine girls and one man, and the man's name was Wolf. That item got into someone's column in the newspaper.

"After that, I was at the Chicago Airway Traffic Control Center.

"It was a whole different world, the way I felt about it at the time. I remember this was a government job and there was not supposed to be any discrimination against women. I deserved to be a controller, so I'm going to be a controller. But the atmosphere wasn't conducive to that sort of thinking. But I knew it was a federal agency and that they shouldn't discriminate against me, so I sort of demanded that, although I wasn't terribly assertive. But I must have been assertive enough, because they promoted me.

"We were so accepting of the position of women. I was always very feminist in my attitudes, but I didn't articulate it particularly. I was in the same mold as most women at the time. You want to find a handsome man and marry.

"Actually, as far as men's attitudes toward us go, after the war a number of men came back who were pilots and became trainees, and they seemed even more resentful of us women than the older guys who had been there all the time and hadn't gone away to war. Those older guys were indulgent of the little girls. We were cute little twenty-two- or twenty-three-year-olds, and they found us charming. But the young ones, I think a lot of the veterans coming back—and I don't blame them—here they were with two or three little kids at home struggling to make a living, and here I was with a job as good as theirs or better. They were resentful.

"You had to work around the clock. Eight-hour shifts. Worked seven days in a row, on one shift. Then two days off. Then seven days on, two off, seven on, then four days off.

"It was a very stressful job. I'd come home some nights and think something was wrong with my jaw, because I'd been clenching my teeth for eight hours. When the weather was bad, it was really horrendous. Often the weather was good and you gave clearance, the aircraft could see each other. But during bad weather you had to bring them down the stacks from one thousand to another thousand feet down to where they could be turned over to the tower to land.

"I remember one day a B-24 crashed into a gas tank two miles south of the airport—it was a checkpoint. When they came in they'd say, 'I'm over the two-mile tank' so we'd know exactly where they were. There were various visual checkpoints around the airport. Well, I cleared some other airplane and this B-24 came along and hit the two-mile tank. I thought it was something I had done, but it wasn't.

"We were responsible for the lives on the airplane. If we actually did something really stupid, we could be indicted for manslaughter. So that was always in the back of your mind. You didn't want to hurt anybody anyway. It was very stressful, often. Radar was coming in when I left.

"When I was pregnant—with civil service you get a lot of sick leave and you could accumulate that forever—I think I left after my seventh month so I had two months before and two months after. I remember the senior controller, he was the boss, and he kept calling me out toward the end, saying, 'When are you going to quit? Are you coming back or aren't you?' I kept him guessing as long as I could.

"But I didn't go back. Once you have one of these little creatures—they're so precious. And it wouldn't have been acceptable. It would have been okay at work, but among my friends, it wouldn't have been accepted. They would have criticized me."

Among the thousands of people who left mid-America for defense work on the two coasts were Leila Bacot Dunn and her husband, Dee.

*They closed up their Booneville, Arkansas, farm, packed their neces-
sary belongings, and drove to Stockton, California, for the much-
advertised shipyard employment. Dee was a blacksmith, and Leila
became an electrician. Their son was in Navy training in California,
further incentive for their move.*

"When I first started to work, they had a school, and the first thing the
instructor started us out on was twisting wires. Well, I was raised on a
Texas farm, where my father had taught the girls to do outside work
and the boys to do housework. He told us, you never know when you
might need this. So the instructor came back, and I had my wires just
like he showed me, and he said, 'Well, you sure caught on to that fast.'
I said, 'I've been twisting wires for a lot of years.' Of course, the
copper wires were a lot easier to twist than barbed wire.

"Before I left, I was a full-fledged electrician. I was hooking up
motors, running wires to outlets, a lot of jobs, all inside the ships.

"At the time the war ended, I had been transferred from the shipyard to the Naval Annex since ship construction was down and they
were laying people off. At the Annex, we handled shipments coming
back from war zones, personal stuff, everything. Watches, scissors,
everything piled in boxes. It looked like they'd raked things off the
shelves and shipped it all home. My job was to sort it all out. I worked
there until the boys began to come home and they got men to do the
work. I felt like when the boys were coming home they needed jobs
and it was time for the women to quit. I could get along without a job."

*A desire to serve her country during wartime prompted Elizabeth Har-
bour Oden to quit her schooling at the American Institute of Business
in Des Moines, Iowa, and apply for a job at a nearby munitions plant.*

"That was such a patriotic war and we all wanted to do our part. My job
was to make sure the cartridges were loaded properly in boxes. They

programmed us to say that these were cartridges, not bullets, and you'd be surprised how they handled them. They would just take them from a cart and dump them onto a table that had sideboards on it.

"Then we had little boxes that I think probably held about twenty cartridges. We would take our two hands, scoop up the shells or cartridges, and the ones that were upside down would automatically fall out, and we'd take them and make sure the primer was on top. That's the part that was dangerous.

"Eventually, they moved me over to a machine that cut the box dividers and put the dividers together. Then my job was just to sit there and make sure that that machine didn't jam. And the machine would go fine until I turned to say hi to somebody, and I looked back and it's jammed. That could be so embarrassing because that was all I had to do, just sit and observe the machine.

"The women were from all walks of life, and some were housewives that probably had never worked before. There were all types of women. However, there was not a lot of socialization because we were from such different levels of education and whatever. So I don't recall that I made any real close friendships with anybody that I worked with there.

"People were so patriotic. All through the plant, there would be signs saying 'Loose Lips Sink Ships.' We were always on our guard. We were always told to beware who you talk to, beware who you give information to. The atmosphere for everybody was keep your mouth shut.

"I didn't stay any more than two years. I feel I have an active mind and that became very boring. I was not disappointed to leave the job. I had decided I wanted to go back to school. I found that the money wasn't worth it to me. I would rather have had the education and an office job. I felt I had done my part for defense."

At seventeen, Vi Kirstine Vrooman responded to the call of patriotism with the driving enthusiasm of a Coast Guard officer's daughter. In

1943, she became a riveter at the Boeing Company in Seattle, Washington.

"I wanted to do my bit. My father was across the ocean fighting a whole bunch of strange people, and we were all very patriotic. Very much so. We were all into the war.

"Boeing had a two-week training period in which they made you feel wanted, and instilled patriotism, like, get out there and buy bonds and win the war and build those planes. We were making B-17s. You were really pumped up.

"I'll tell you, at seventeen, I had to be the best-looking riveter in the country. My family was classy so instead of getting the kind of clothes that most people would wear—anything they wanted really—I got what amounted to designer overalls. I used all my money to buy those nifty overalls. I learned to tie head scarves very well.

"The guys were exempt from the service because of defense work and families, and they were courteous and kind and caring about this little kid with this funny little riveting gun. Nobody hit on me. Nobody.

"The biggest thrill—I can't tell you—was when the B-17s rolled off the assembly line. You can't believe the feeling we had. It was incredible. Everyone in the place felt, 'Yeah, we did it. We did it!' Boeing was a nifty company to work for. We were all so proud. We were there for a reason—to win the war—it was what we could do. *We* helped win the war. We felt we were nifty. We *were* nifty.

"All the people from Oklahoma coming west—it really happened. They came. The money was good. I think I was making $98 a week. Probably more than my dad was making. He was in charge of landing craft in the Mediterranean. Our days were full with ten-minute breaks where I learned how to smoke with those women from Oklahoma. And a half hour for lunch.

"After the war, most of the workers went back to Oklahoma. And when the guys came back, the women all went home and did the

dishes. There was no question about that. None of the women said, 'I
don't want to lose this job. I want to stay here and do this. I want to get
this big money.' They didn't. It was like an unwritten law. They just
packed their little tool kits and went back home.

"I didn't have any problems about it at all. It was like you were
holding your job for your husband, maybe he was sick or something.
We were supposed to go home and get married and have babies. I've
talked to some people and find there was some resentment among the
women, but the women I worked with all felt that this is the way it is:
the guys are coming back and the women went back to jobs as little
secretaries and nurses. It was different for me, of course. I was younger than most. And riveting and welding weren't exactly the kind of
jobs that women would stay on in, anyway. Not what women would
ordinarily do."

*Elizabeth Szilagyi Morrison had no thoughts of continuing after the
war when she applied to work at Eastern Aircraft in Linden, Massachusetts, formerly a General Motors automobile factory. The plant
was shut down immediately after the armistice and reopened within a
year to manufacture automobiles.*

"All the women got jobs there, and I got one there. Everybody was
participating in it patriotically. I applied and was hired right away and
I stayed there until the war stopped. My husband was in the service,
and my mother took care of my two daughters.

"I worked as a template maker. You'd make the template and from
the template, they'd make the part from aluminum or steel. The templates were something for the wing. I don't remember exactly. But you
didn't only make one kind. You did a variety of different kinds.

"In a couple of weeks, they showed you how it had to be and how
it had to be precise. They'd bring it to you and bring the paper and all

with the measurements that it had to be, and then you had to go according to that. You had to file it down and then file it on a machine to make sure you got the perfect size and had to figure it out until it came to the sixteenth of an inch. We were working on Wildcat airplanes.

"There were women riveting, too, in the plant, but I didn't want that. The noise and all would drive me crazy, working with a riveting gun.

"It was interesting to meet all the different kinds of people, people usually at home, and teachers and all kinds. Everyone was enthused about working there. Everybody seemed to have that feeling.

"And the saddest but happy day was when we had to leave. We were happy and sad at the same time because I remember when they declared the war over. Oh, my God, everybody just stopped working and just celebrated. But we were sad to leave work, too. The news was announced over the loudspeaker at the plant, and after that, the fore-man came around and said they would stop production on the Wild-cats. Men who had formerly worked for the plant making cars would be reinstated to work on them again. Within a week all production stopped.

"There was no question about whether or not women would be kept on. They wouldn't. But nobody seemed to mind. We went back to our lives."

Velva Butterworth Davis remembers similar abruptness in Kansas City, Missouri, where she worked at a Pratt & Whitney aircraft en-gine plant for about two years, changing shifts every three months and commuting thirty miles each way on two buses and a streetcar.

"I had been working at a shirt factory and quit to go to Pratt & Whit-ney. We were in school for about six months and then I became a gear inspector. We learned all the special tools, micrometer, what a lathe was, and how the metal parts were tested by magna-flux for a minute defect that would not be visible to the naked eye. I could name all the planes that were equipped with Pratt & Whitney engines, but all I can remember now is the 'Black Widow.'

"My job was inspection of the reduction (pinion) gears. It consisted of running the gear roller—a special machine with an indicator that showed how the teeth meshed with the ring gear and how contact would be when they were assembled. We'd have an identifying number etched on every one of those, showing who'd inspected it.

"And when those planes were shot down over there and there was trouble, they'd bring the planes back, part of them. They'd reassemble them and they would be tested in our giant test chamber. When we came to work and heard the roar of the plane that was being tested, we would be very anxious until it was determined whether we were at fault or that it was *not* because of misjudgment or shoddy work. I had brothers in that war whose life might depend on the accuracy of my work, and I was especially dedicated.

"Our days were full when you worked seven days a week, month after month. Hollywood stars would come through and put on shows to get you to buy war bonds to help pay for the war. You helped at the USO and wrote letters and sent packages to the men overseas. It was a time when you were patriotic and everyone wanted to do so much. We donated blood and every once in a while there would be a desperate call for more blood. I gave and wanted to join the 'Gallon Club,' but when I became anemic they wouldn't take any more. I never made it.

"When that last day of work came at the plant, I was happy to quit. It meant the war was over and my brothers could come home. That was the main thing. We went out to my brother's place, out of town, and were there for two days after VJ day.

"The day the war ended, the factory—that was the end. The leadman came out and said the war was over, and we put down our tools and went home and never came back except to pick up our paychecks.

"My husband and I had hoped to go to California, and this was a good time to go. So we sold our duplex, bought a twenty-five-foot trailer and a big 1936 Nash, and came west."

Ann McGhee Wilcox earned considerable recognition for her wartime work painting bombers at Sebring Air Base in Florida. After passing a government test for aptitude with aeronautical and mechanical skills, she and her sister were sent to aeronautical school in Memphis, Tennessee, where they attended class from 5:00 to 7:00 A.M. and then performed hands-on work.

"We started out on the ailerons and elevators, which are the movable parts of the plane. From the metal shop you got this core thing and you built around it with fabric and dope. Dope is the coating that makes the movable parts of the plane very, very strong. It takes layers and layers to build it up. Then you spray paint it and put it on the plane. I got so I didn't work in the shop so much as out on the flight lines spraying bombers with 200-foot hoses and a 10-gallon container of paint, which was very, very heavy.

"I was young and agile so I could do the job nicely, and I didn't have a fear of heights. I could scoot around the top of those bombers like a squirrel. Kind of fun. And the boys would come around and want to talk and I'd say, 'I don't have time to talk. If you want to talk to me, come up and help me work.' If they'd come and work with me, I'd visit along with them. But if they didn't, I'd squirt them with paint and they'd take off.

"The men didn't have any choice but to accept us because we were sent there by the government. They wanted to put me in secretarial positions because I had a little college, and I said, 'No, I trained for this job and I want to do it because it's different.' Plus, it was for the war effort. I could always be a secretary.

"I was painting a plane one day and I had my ladder so I could come down the aileron. I think I was lettering the side with the Army letters. And some smart aleck came along and moved my ladder. So I came down, I was so used to it being right there, I missed it and fell about ten feet to the concrete. I hurt myself pretty bad and recuperated all summer and still could not work, so I went home to Alabama.

"Later I joined my sister and mother-in-law in California and worked at the Oakland Airport processing planes for overseas shipment. We were putting a protective coating on the whole plane so that as the plane goes overseas on the carrier, the saltwater doesn't deteriorate it. After that, I went to Alameda Naval Air Station and worked in the paint and dope shop, and then I had a chance to inspect parachutes for a good long while.

"When the war in Europe was over, I was working at Alameda and we were on our way home. There had been rumblings about things happening that day, the news passed through the shop like wildfire. And when we were actually on our way home, out by the old Montgomery Ward store in Oakland, that's where we were stranded. Nobody moved for two or three hours. Traffic was bad. You could hear every whistle, every bell, everything going.

"And on August 14, my girlfriend and I went to San Francisco to see a stage show and all of a sudden we looked up Market Street and all traffic had stopped. There was a wave of white coming down the street. We suddenly realized it was all sailors. A few soldiers were sprinkled in. I was swept off my feet, carried on shoulders for blocks. They wouldn't let me down. I had to find my girlfriend later. It was exciting, but it was scary. I had worn my sister's hat and lost it.

"I didn't mind leaving the job. I was ready to find my soulmate and settle down and raise a family. I felt, and still do, that the best family life is when mother stays home."

Lillie Cordes Landolt spent the war years making 55,000 bullets a day at an ordnance plant in Des Moines, Iowa. Before the war, she

worked as a telephone operator for four years in Gilmore City, Iowa,
until she got married.

"There were no jobs. We were more or less on relief because that's
about all there was. We moved to Des Moines because WPA [Works
Progress Administration] had a training project down there teaching
people to rivet. They sent my husband down. We had five children,
including a brand-new baby.

"The first weekend he came back to town, he came home and he
said, 'I'm not going back if you don't go back with me.' We were a
very, very close family. I quickly threw things together. I never saw
my house again. I piled all five kids in the car and didn't know where
I was going to go when I got down here, but we found a hole to crawl
into.

"We got out looking right away and found a place that was half a
house. A woman lived in half of it and she rented the other half out,
and we made do. It was furnished.

"He learned the riveting but during that time, an ordnance plant
opened here in Des Moines. Even though we had five small children,
I went to work at the ordnance plant, and I really loved it.

"Making bullets was interesting. I had a huge machine. The ammunition is made in many parts, and the part we worked on was the
bullet, which started out as brass, maybe a half inch across, quite
thick, and not very deep, just kind of a cup. It went through a series of
punches. Probably about six or seven punches pulled it down to about
two and a half inches in length. We made armor-piercing and incendi-
ary bullets.

"My husband's job was right next door, but they had what they
called a fire wing. This was a dangerous place to be, and they put on
the casings, which were the large brass cases that the bullets went
into, and they were filled with powder. He filled them with powder. I
worked on fifty calibers and so did he. Then there was one building of
the factory that made thirty-caliber bullets.

"There were all kinds of people, every kind of person you could think of. Everyone that needed a job was out there. There were an awful lot of young women because so many of the young men had been taken overseas. My husband, with five children, wasn't, and he was in his early thirties, so he wasn't taken. But there weren't an awful lot of men around. I was treated fine by the men who were there, but there was a lot of hanky-panky. The girls needed men and the men needed girls, so they just found them.

"Every seven weeks, we changed shifts. To take care of my family, we found a lady who had been a schoolteacher, in her sixties, and she knew she wasn't competent to take a job in the plant, but she wanted to do her part. She loved children and we had good children and she was happy to come and take care of the children. She actually lived with us. We had an extra room and she lived with us around the clock and raised my family, I might say, for four years.

"When the war was over, I left the ordnance plant and my husband left the ordnance plant. We went on a little vacation. Then he got a good job and I opened a dressmaking shop from my home. I always had time for my kids. I wanted to be home with those kids. They were too precious."

Frances Keller Blanchet went to work at the Kaiser Shipyard in Port-land, Oregon, after her father told her there were a lot of women working in the shipyard and she wasn't doing her patriotic duty. He worked there as an electrician, on leave for the war from the Veterans Hospital. Her mother also worked in the shipyard.

"I had to go downtown to the union office, and the man there said I should be a welder. But I couldn't wear my glasses under the goggles. I became a shipfitter. That's the person who puts the ship together, fits all the little parts. I started down in the shop where they order all the materials for the ships from the outfitting dock. It was a very interesting thing.

"I could read blueprints. The first question they asked was whether I knew how to read a blueprint. My father was the sort of fellow who could never figure anything out so I had helped him. Plus, I'd been sewing all my life. So I could read a blueprint and down there in that little room I ordered all the materials from the outfitting deck. I think they had seventeen ships they were building. Those were the Victory ships.

"I didn't have any training. I didn't need it. They just gave me a blueprint and said, 'Order what we are going to need on this ship.' I got everything ordered up that was going to go on that last Victory ship, that was right at the end of the time they were making Victory ships, then they started building Liberty ships.

"I had two little children and my husband was in the service in the paratroops back East. And I took my children to the day nursery every day. They had a beautiful day nursery and schools for the school-age children. Mine were three and two years old. I had to walk about six blocks to catch the bus, took my kids to the day nursery and let them off right there at the gate, and walked down the hill to the shipyard. On my way home, I'd pick up my children and come home.

"I'd imagine there were half men, half women in the shipyard. There were women crawling all over every piece of steel you saw. They knew what they were doing and they built a lot of ships. They were all ages, like my mother was in her forties. A lot of people came from the South and the Midwest. There were a lot of black people, but I didn't know any.

"I had a drunken foreman who was always trying to get into my little blue britches. I just said, 'No, I've got to be true to my husband.' He just liked to talk that way to all the girls. Actually, everyone treated the other person as an equal. I never heard of any who didn't think the women could do the job. I think women can do just about anything men can do, except maybe heavy lifting.

"Then one day from those loudspeakers up on the high posts came the announcement that the war was over. Everyone threw their hats up in the air and got drunk. That day was the end. They shut down the shipyard. We were glad the war was over and went back home. Working at the shipyard made me think I could do more—gave me a lot of self-confidence. I never wanted to go back to that particular kind of work, though. Nothing colder than cold steel in the wintertime."

As the U.S. involvement in the war increased, Lois LaCroix Barber graduated from Northwestern University in Evanston, Illinois, with a degree in economics and found two interesting jobs in her field.

"It was extraordinary—that brief period. It surprises me still, how I happened to fall into those two jobs. It was an unprecedented time for women to find jobs that were traditionally held by men. We seized the opportunity for a career and made the most of it, knowing that when the war was over the men would forge ahead of us again, particularly in business and finance.

"As an economics major I was thrilled to get a job with an investment counseling firm, although they made it very, very clear to me that I was their last, most desperate choice for doing what turned out to be grubby work, writing information they sent out to the clients.

"They'd always been able to get young men from Harvard and Yale, and I was really a desperate choice. I was properly humbled and grateful, so that made up for my other lacks. The men turned out to be helpful, treated me as a respected colleague. I think a young woman there would be treated much better than an older woman.

"There was a woman, the typical corporate secretary who knows everything and everyone, who was very helpful to me. She and I sat in a large open area, whereas the men all had private offices. It defined our roles. Young men from Yale would have probably sat in that open

space, too, but they could look through the door to the private offices
and know that some day one of them would be theirs.

"The wages, however, were very low and I realized there must be
other opportunities. One came along as assistant to the chief economist of the Office of Price Administration in Hawaii. The wages were
double. I went to Washington to be hired, then I went by train across
the country to San Francisco. You couldn't get any kind of a room
anywhere in San Francisco. I was fortunate to have a very kind cousin
take me in. I was told not to tell them where I was going and when I
was going.

"It was a big convoy. You saw the other ships all around. Absolute
total blackout on the ship. We had to go very slowly because some of
the ships were cargo ships. It seems to me it was two or three weeks
going across.

"My boss was a very bright woman who once taught at Vassar. I
remember one touching comment—maybe a compliment—she once
made to me. 'I keep forgetting you're not a Vassar woman,' she said.

"My special charge was handling price control of restaurants. I got
to know prices and merchants. Prices were rolled back to March 15,
1941. It was a wonderful job. I went to every corner of the islands, all
of them. We met regularly with the businesspeople and discussed new
regulations, kept them informed. They were very responsible.

"I have great respect for the hard work and sincerity of the government people, most of whom had given up high-paying jobs in private industry to work for the government. We regulated prices of
everything from the Japanese woman who sold soup on the curb to the
big famous restaurants and hotels. They were all cooperative. One of
the men I relied on for prices of meat could look at a half-eaten steak
brought to him in a napkin by a customer who questioned the price
and identify what part of the animal it came from and what the restaurant should therefore charge for it.

"I remember a friend who wanted to write a book about those
times. He worked for one of the government offices and his job was to

destroy the confidential trash, but he was keeping material from it for his book!

"When the war was over, I was happy to settle down with home and family. Our friends just after the war all seemed to have three or four kids and were looking for Victorian houses and really getting back to the home. We were all old enough now so we were eager to have our families. I have three, two fifteen months apart and one two years later. It was time."

11

New Directions

People's lives change directions for many reasons: education, marriage, jobs, relocation. A math student takes a course in science and discovers a new passion; a New Yorker marries a Californian, and one of them changes paths; AT&T transfers a Michigan worker to Texas. These are all within established parameters. By contrast, some wartime jobs brought about more dramatic and unexpected changes.

Opportunities opened up for some women during the war that they had never even thought of. They worked in jobs women would never have considered—or been hired for, if they had applied. In some cases, the wartime work gave women skills that they used in related interests after the war, leading these women to new and gratifying paths.

Joyce Duncan Russell put her welding torch to steel and produced sculptures while studying for two art degrees after the war. Doris Casey Berringer's stint as a window trimmer was the start of a lifetime of painting. Helen Filarski Steffes and Dottie Wiltse Collins played baseball for Philip Wrigley, establishing lifelong interests in women's athletics.

These wartime jobs produced lasting career and life-style changes. For many women already headed toward careers or strong volunteer commitments, the war jobs solidified their paths.

Mildred House "Hut" Ferree was called "Little House" because she needed six pillows to fly the Stearman PT-19. "Little House" evolved into her current nickname, "Hut." She obtained her pilot's license and driver's license on the same day, and flying became a major part of her life. Monitoring the progress of the bill to militarize the Women's Airforce Service Pilots (WASP) occupied her energies until its final passage in 1977. It was a thirty-year fight.

"Before Pearl Harbor, I was studying journalism and aeronautic studies. I wanted to be a foreign correspondent—a flying correspondent. At the end of my sophomore year I went to work for North American Aviation, which built the P-51, the B-25, and the AT-6 at the field that is now Los Angeles International.

"As soon as I heard about the WASP I applied. Initially I was too young and then I had to get thirty-five hours. I had soloed on my sixteenth birthday in a Piper Cub. I had my pilot's license before I had my driver's license, because I got my driver's license in the afternoon of the same day.

"Later, I applied for the program and was accepted. I took a month off before reporting and was visiting relatives in Texas when I received a wire at home. My mother called me and said, 'It's signed Arnold and Cochran and says unless you are willing to be militarized, do not report for training.' Well, I wanted to be militarized, and I think they wanted a declaration of intent from each of us. Our militarization bill was pending in Congress.

"I responded by showing up. We paid our own transportation; we had no insurance. I'm totally grateful for the flight time and the aviation education experience that I got in the service.

"We received regular aviation cadet training at Avenger Field—six months. Our instructors were under contract to the Air Force. It was a military thing and we were told we would be militarized. It was years before that would happen. One of those who opposed it was a columnist who said that to put a woman in the cockpit to replace a man and do a man's job was unheard of. At a hearing of our bill, a congressman said that women should do the work for which they are so fit: secretaries, cooks, clerks.

"I was one of the last classes. We called Avenger Field 'Cochran's Convent,' site of rattlesnake roundups today. We loved Sweetwater, Texas, and the specialness of the WASP experience.

"My first instructor was the flight commander for primary and he didn't really want students. He screamed and I couldn't learn from him. Fortunately for me, when a couple of the other gals washed out, I was given to an instructor who was just a doll. They were as different as different can be.

"After graduation I was assigned to Operations at Blackland Army Air Base in Waco, Texas. I mostly test-hopped repaired aircraft.

"I'm the governor of the New England chapter section of 99, which is the International Women Pilots founded back in 1929 by Amelia Earhart and that wonderful woman, Louise Fair. She actually was the founder more than Amelia Earhart, but she suggested that Amelia be the first president because she was more in the public eye.

"I've been secretary of WASP and I'm a member of Experimental and Antique Aircraft, which does the Oshkosh show every year, which is the greatest show of all. I'm also corporator of Women Military Aviators, which includes WASPs, Air Force, Navy, Army Air Force, Marines, Coast Guard.

"When Bruce Arnold (General Hap Arnold's son) read his father's memoirs, he felt WASP was unfinished business. He contacted me to get in touch with Congresswoman Margaret Heckler to get her in the fight to pass the bill to militarize WASP. So I did. I worked with her and got WASP members to contact her. She was co-chair of the women's caucus and sent me transcripts of the hearings. It was the one time when all women in Congress voted together."

*Widowed, with three-month-old twins and a four-year-old, Josephine
Solomon Fundoots needed work. She was grateful to find employment
as a burner for U.S. Steel in Farrell, Pennsylvania, making parts for
ships. She transferred to U.S. Steel after a year at American Can as a
drill press operator because of better pay. The confidence she gained
from her experiences at both places directed her to the job she still
holds today, as well as to others she has had through the years.*

"It was tough. It was hot. But it was fun—it was something different.
You had to wear goggles, long sleeves, gloves, so you wouldn't get
burned from the splatter. I was terrified. Then I got used to the job
and knew what I was doing. I had to be careful to keep the light away
from my face and everybody's face. I can't talk without my hands
waving, and when I talked to anyone with that torch in my hand, oh
boy.

"Men treated us well. I never had any problems. Other women
were nice, too. It seems there was a lot of sympathy because of my
loss and my situation. Our town is not a great big town and it seemed
like everybody knew, here is this woman left with three children.

"I can relate one incident. It was winter and the snow was so deep,
the bus couldn't make the grade going up into Farrell. The driver said
he couldn't go any further, so he turned around and went back. 'I'm
going to walk into work,' I said. I needed the money. Remember, there
was no social security or no widow's pension, all this good, good stuff
that they're getting now. So I said, 'I'm walking in.' A great big 250-
pound black man says, 'I'm walking in, too.' We didn't have the fear
we have today. I had to go in there and make that money. Then a
woman that lived on my street says, 'I'll go in with you.'

"The snow was hitting us clear above our ankles. It was really
bad. This gentleman, and he was a gentleman, walked, and the high
fishing boots he was wearing helped him break a trail, as he put it. We

walked behind him. I walked about two and a half miles early in the
morning, still dark, about 5:00 or 6:00 A.M. just to get there to make
those couple of bucks.

"The job gave me a lot of confidence and led to greater work. I'm
the employment coordinator for the Area Agency on Aging now. I'm
one of their top people. I lead the state in placing older workers in
work. I have no education past high school and have gotten commen-
dations from the governor and from the State of Pennsylvania. I don't
know if the work at the steel mill did this or not, but I sure didn't have
any confidence before.

"My family is very proud of me and when I get my picture taken
with the governor, it just makes them proud. I talk to people over fifty-
five who are down and out, and get them trained, and get them jobs.
This is a wonderful program."

*Artist Joyce Duncan Russell used her Liberty ship welding expertise to
create metal sculpture, ten years and two college degrees later. She
was living in Berkeley, California, during the war.*

"I had three children, and my husband was a graduate student trying
to work on his Ph.D. With prices going up we just couldn't make it on
what we were getting. When an article in the *Berkeley Gazette* asked
for women interested in learning to weld, I jumped at the chance. I
was adept at any kind of hands-on work and learned fast. I think they
only kept me about two days for training.

"As soon as I could strike an arc with their equipment, they sent
me out to the shipyards, where all I did was strike an arc and do what
they called tacking the beams down. I guess they were I-beams, must
have been twelve inches tall and spread out, and that made the
strength of the ship. The shipfitters were laying down lines where the
beams should be, and I followed them around, and when they said

'here,' I made a tack there and tacked it down to the plate they were working on.

"At the beginning, as men came down the line, they'd whistle and make remarks and that kind of routine. Finally we women got tired of that, so one day we took our lunches and we lined up on the edge of the platform and sat there, right down the line, and every time a man came by, we'd whistle and make remarks, and it didn't take them long to get the point.

"I graduated from tacking to doing more advanced work in welding, which was interesting. It was interesting until it started to rain in the winter. I was prone to get pneumonia at the drop of a hat. I talked to the leadman and said, 'This is not good for me.' So he transferred me to the toolroom, where I stayed the rest of the year. Then we were beginning to have trouble finding good babysitters, so my husband quit school and got a job as an electrician out there and I stayed home.

"When the war ended, my husband got a teaching job at Chico State, and I was just so hungry for school that as soon as all three of my kids were in school and I had some free time, I started taking classes at the college. It took me a long time, but I finally got my degree, and then an M.A.—in art.

"One professor had done sculpture and got to talking to me, and then one day I met him up on campus. He said, 'Hey, I just bought a welding outfit. When are you going to come and use it?' He started needling me and finally I did go in and use it.

"It was the most frustrating thing I've ever done in my life. I had worked with materials I could mold—clay, concrete, that kind of thing. Steel does not mold. You have to figure out ahead of time what you're going to do. For the first three months, I think everything I made was pure trash. I threw it out. Finally, one day, one thing that I worked on, he looked at it and said, 'Hey, that's pretty darn good.' I had learned how to do what I had wanted to do. I've sold some of my pieces, I still have some.

"When I moved to San Luis Obispo in 1970, I no longer had a place to work with the equipment. So a friend said, 'Look, come join our stitchery guild,' and I said, 'Stitchery? I wouldn't get caught dead.' But I had never seen any contemporary stitchery, and they were always getting in some expert from someplace for workshops. Once I took one of the workshops, I was hooked. So I went from the hard to the soft.

"Recently I heard about some new materials. I read about a man who went into a shop in New Mexico with some of his big beautiful Indian pots, beautifully decorated. The owner was impressed and said, 'These must be very old.' Then the guy who brought them in picked one up and drop-kicked it across the room. He had used bondo—what they use on cars to fix dents. So I made a group of four, about ten inches high. They look as if they're made out of bronze."

Window trimming at the Palace department store in Spokane, Washington, was the wartime job that inspired a new career for Doris Casey Berringer. Traditionally a man's job, window trimming fell victim to wartime demands: men left for the service or to work in better-paying defense plants. With twenty-seven windows to decorate, the department store executives turned in desperation to women, and Berringer brought her artistic talents to the job.

"That job reinforced the creative energy I'd always felt. It was my launching pad to the satisfying things I'm doing today. This experience with working gave me an urge to keep on working, although having three children ten years apart fouled up my career activity along the way. After the war I ended up in advertising and worked at the Crescent department store, where I had a job that I liked so well. It was at a drawing board, the job of my dreams. Whenever I got my paycheck, I thought I should be paying them.

"All this affected the rest of my life. I joined a women's club, which introduced me to a group of artists. I could talk shop with people with the same feelings and outlooks. Art is a big part of my life. At seventy, I went to the community college to study and found the young people very friendly and good to be with. I paint every day and have all through the years.

"When I got to the Palace, I worked with a woman who had come from Portland. Her husband was stationed in Alaska; mine was in Portland. I was her assistant, doing the cards and artwork and helping her trim the windows. All twenty-seven windows were changed every week. We were too busy, really, to think much about the war. Neither one of us was experienced at this at all, of course, but the store was having trouble finding people to do the windows. At least I had some art training.

"We had to send to the warehouses back East for window trimmings, mannequins, and other equipment. We didn't have any props. We had some arms and legs and could get them together all right, and we hired a little boy after school to run the Skilsaw and make the props.

"It was all pretty much of a mess when we first got there. We got brooms and swept the place out, the place under the roof where they stored things. Heavenly days, it was a firetrap. We cleaned the attic and scrubbed up. For $15 a week. We also ran the elevator and helped out in the gift shop when they needed help, and wrapped packages. One time we had to get hold of a company car and drive out to the woods and get some branches and make blossoms out of crepe paper for a spring display. For the Fourth of July window we used an old radio cabinet as a utility shelf holding magazines with covers featuring American flags that were promoting war bond sales.

"One time after we put one of our windows together, we walked out onto the street to look at it, and my co-worker said, 'I think it stinks.' There was a couple walking by us at that moment, and the man said to the woman, 'I wonder what the heck she thinks she knows about it.'

"I've been fascinated with windows ever since. Nowadays they don't amount to much. They used to be more creative. I was drawing fashion sketches at home at night at the same time I was doing the windows in the daytime.

"In the Depression when you graduated from high school, there was nothing out there. But the war opened up opportunities, and this was certainly one for me. Something else about the war—it was a time when Americans pulled together. Now people seem at odds, looking out for themselves. We seem frayed at the edges."

Helen Filarski Steffes started playing baseball in her home town— Detroit, Michigan—when she was thirteen. In 1943, at the World Softball Championship tournament, one of five scouts sent out by Philip Wrigley approached her to play with the All-American Girls' Professional Baseball League. She went home and told her mother, "Some man asked me to play professional ball in Chicago." Her mother said she'd never heard of any women's baseball league in Chicago or anywhere else and that Helen was not going, because Chicago had "Al Capone and everything else."

"I cried and cried. I was only nineteen and you had to be twenty-one before you could go on your own. So I didn't go. 'When I'm twenty-one I'm leaving and I'm going to play ball,' I said. In 1945, I was twenty-one in May and I left. She was worried about me. I'd never left home. I was never out of Detroit.

"Before that, when I graduated from high school in 1942, the war was on and the boys in our class went right into the service. I graduated on Friday and Monday started in the war plant. I was a riveter at Briggs Aircraft in Detroit, working on B-25s. We were working on wing tips. After a year, they made me into a repairman. They needed more repairmen and I was one of the first women repairmen.

"Anything I do, I watch everybody else around, what they're doing. On the break, I used to go by the repairman and watch what he was doing and help him out a little bit. It was quite different than on the line, and I liked it a lot and I was pretty good.

"Whatever is done wrong on the line is repaired by the repairmen. If they would get a rivet in crooked, or something like that, they don't touch it. It just goes right down the line and when it comes for inspection, it's turned down and given to the repairmen.

"The whole bunch of us who played ball worked there. We were like a bunch of tomboys. In fact, we played for Hudson Motor Company. They were doing war work then, too. We played ball at night. At one point, we were playing on about three teams a day. We started work at 6:00 A.M., got off at 2:30, and at 3:00, the ball diamond was right near the factory, so we had a union game at 3:00. At 6:00, we used to have a Catholic Youth Organization (CYO) game. And then at 8:00, we would go to the park here in Detroit and play recreation ball there. We got home about 11:00.

"We were young and we loved to play ball. We didn't have money. With gas rationing, you couldn't go anywhere and this kept us busy and we loved it outside and we just loved to do it. I guess that's what made us better ballplayers. I was at Briggs until I was twenty-one. I played CYO ball and union ball and then Class A ball for Detroit.

"I reported to Chicago that year and had spring training in Chicago and all these girls, little hick gals that never left town, walked into all these girls sitting in the lobby and they looked you over as you walked by. I remember the day I walked in, I was so embarrassed. Fifteen left Detroit at the same time. We all worked at the factory and they tried to keep us, saying, 'Oh, you have to stay here for the war work.' When I was a rookie, I was picked for Rockford Peaches for 1945, and in 1946 I played at Rockford and played for Bill Allington, one of the best coaches there ever was in that league.

"We didn't have a car, so I had to take two streetcars to play Class A ball. When I'd transfer, I'd be standing there waiting for the other streetcar and everybody just staring at me like it was Halloween or something. You were out there in your uniform, your spikes and your glove in your hand and you were out of place. Women were out of place at a time like that. Nobody told me when I was born that I couldn't do this, so my mother approved of it, which was good. I went to a Catholic school so I suffered a lot because at lunchtime I was out there playing ball with the boys, and afterward, I was sitting in the office getting a lecture on what girls should be doing and not doing.

"Four weeks into my first season, a lot of the girls didn't know how to slide, so Bill was teaching us. I was to cover third and a little Canadian was going to slide. They threw the ball to me and I went to tag her and she didn't know how to slide. She jumped. She jumped and got me right in the leg. It put two big gashes just above the knee. That put me out of commission for a little over a week because they took me to the hospital, had me sewed up. Kids nowadays you take them to the hospital, they get a shot to ease the pain. It took three girls laying over me while they dumped Merthiolate. You're about ready to go crazy. I could feel that needle go in and right through the other side.

"The most outstanding thing in my mind is playing Fort Wayne in the playoffs that year. We won the pennant in August. It was Fort Wayne, Grand Rapids, and Peaches, up and down, half a game apart. Every day it was somebody else's. Everybody was calling the other team at night to find out who was in first place.

"I think it was August 20, we won a doubleheader from Grand Rapids. Fort Wayne had lost a doubleheader. So that put us up there and gave us a good grip on first place. That's how we ended the season, we were in first, and then we played Grand Rapids in the first round of the playoffs. Like the World Series, you had to get three out of five of the first round, so I think we played five games and we took them three out of the five. Then Fort Wayne won their division so it was Fort Wayne and Rockford.

"Anyway, I got knocked out in the last game in Rockford and we were up by two games. We won three and they won one. So we had to go back to Fort Wayne for the next two, or three if we had to. My teeth were knocked out and my mouth was all cut up and I couldn't eat. They put me in the hospital and left town. I was listening to the game on the radio in the hospital. They lost the next one, and the next one. The next morning, there was the director, and he said, 'Get your clothes ready. Bill wants you in Fort Wayne.'

"I couldn't talk. But my mouth was the only thing I was having trouble with. I got up and he drove me to Fort Wayne. I played the game, that night. We won and everybody was celebrating and everything, and the director put me back in the car and took me right back to the hospital. We won the championship that year and that was the greatest time. For a rookie to come in on a team like Rockford and win the pennant and the championship was something.

"Professional ball gave me a lot. You learned how to live on your own, away from home. The people we lived with, the woman did a lot of canning and making jelly and I just wanted to learn everything in life I guess, so I helped her. During the day we would make jelly, go and pick cherries for the jelly. I learned to live with people and make friends. I have the most wonderful friends as a result.

"In 1951, I got married, and from 1951 to 1961, I had six children. I raised them and then in 1967, when my youngest went into kindergarten, I started coaching again. I just finished putting in twenty-five years coaching CYO, softball and basketball. We volunteered at first, for about three years we volunteered, and then they paid us.

"Then I got a job. In 1968, I told my family, 'If you don't start straightening up, I'm going to get a job.' Well, they all laughed at me. I had a job at home taking care of them. This went on, so one day I just went out and got a waitress job. If I was going to wait on people, I was going to get paid for it. Here I was waiting on my family day and night and all I got was a headache. I'm still working. Same place. Twenty-six years now. I enjoy it. I really love people and I have a lot of old friendships."

Rose Ann "Tex" Longnecker Barbarite fully intended to be a math major and ultimately a math teacher. But the wartime need for engineers changed her course. A scholarship to Purdue University in electrical engineering paved the way for a broadcasting career.

"RCA was hiring females. This was in '41, men were in the service, so you got a job. I was not the only female working there. I was called an engineering aide. I didn't get the title of engineer. On a résumé they would call it engineer. But they didn't give me that title, and you didn't question it because it just wasn't done in those days.

"I went right from school to RCA. They were recruiting on campus. I have a picture of me with David Sarnoff. It was a wonderful experience. I've never regretted it.

"I remember putting together what we call a breadboard, putting together a chassis in the shop. Our shop man figured I was female and couldn't do it, and I was trying to tell him, 'No, don't twist it any further, it will break,' and he did it his way and sure enough, he broke it. It was just the things that they thought we couldn't do and you had to go along quietly and do it.

"Because I was the only female in the lab, with forty engineers, it stopped a lot of the bad language. This was in Camden, New Jersey, and later I went to Manhattan when they opened the New York Exhibition Hall. We worked on the first microwave. The first cable came from Princeton. My personal experiences will sound as if I'm complaining. Actually I look back on it and laugh now. I made the cover of a magazine. I was a novelty. It was an electronics magazine, more for laymen than a trade journal. They took my picture for the *Sunday Mirror* in New York, and there was a write-up there, because I was a female working in a man's job.

"I didn't think of the men as being patronizing. I look back on it.

Now we have a lot of different terminology for all the harassment and that sort of stuff. Many of them would come to my assistance. We were taught, for example, to stoop to the floor to pick up a television set or anything heavy. There usually would be one man who would come running over saying, 'Oh, you shouldn't do that.' I'm not sure whether it was because women were in the industry or not, but that was the first I ever heard of industrial engineers. Their job was to find out how much time we were supposed to sit and how much time we were supposed to stand in our jobs. They sent me a questionnaire—I filled it out and thought, 'This is ridiculous.' I spent more time trying to figure out what's the maximum weight I should lift, how much time do I spend walking or what.

"I ran an experimental television station, too, and got my FCC license. That was when we were first on the air. The engineering terminal lab, they called it. They didn't train you on the job except to tell you where the washroom was, and here's the key if you need it. In New York we got to repair things for the recording artists—doing favors for the big shots. Arthur Godfrey was very condescending. I couldn't get over that. He used to be my idol. I worked on wiring in John McCormack's place in New York, the tenor. We were sent out on jobs like that.

"I'm not an activist, I don't belong to any organizations, but I don't like someone looking down on me and saying you're a female and you can't do it. Because I've proven to them that I can.

"After my husband died and my kids were grown, I went with the Peace Corps to Belize, and now I can vaccinate a chicken in Spanish."

The war triggered both geographic and professional changes for Cora "Dolly" Orbison Williamson. After she and her husband worked in the California shipyards during the war, they briefly returned to

Oklahoma to sell their ranch and then moved to Eureka, California,
where they opened a small lumber mill. Having worked at the Kaiser
plant in Richmond, California, she was able to help the Kaiser family
dispose of surplus equipment when she got to Eureka.

"The Kaisers kept in touch with me for quite a while. I declared all
their surplus material while I was in Richmond. They gave me two or
three men to help me.

"When I got to Eureka, I was able to get different things for our
plant and for the city—especially things they needed here to get gas
to our plant. We helped the city get a lot of material. I had the catalog
and they bought some pickup trucks, ladders, pipes, and a lot of
equipment. I was able to get this for the city, things they couldn't have
purchased for a year.

"All of us—my husband, my son, and I—became leadmen at the
shipyard. I was the first woman shipfitter in California, and then the
first leadwoman.

"At first the men in Yard Four were a little hesitant to accept me
in shipfitting because that had always been a man's work. But I'm
strong and I was young, had a lot of endurance, and my husband was
a contractor, so I did know blueprints and I always drew the plans for
our homes. When they learned I could read blueprints, I taught blueprint reading in the yard for about six months, to both men and
women who came into the yard.

"As a shipfitter you have the templates and we laid out all of the
steel and marked it and we had the boys with the cranes, they picked
up the plates and they stored them in the racks. It was all marked and
we built the ATL. They were little ships that carried the guns and
tanks and all. They let down in front. Our last contract was the refrig-
erated cargo carrier. They were slick, neat, pretty little ships, cargo
ships that carried all the frozen foods. I was the foreman, and burners
and welders worked for me. I taught all the men and women how to
do it.

"When we came to Eureka, I worked as an office manager for Sequoia Products Company. My husband went to work for the plywood plant here, helped build it. Louisiana Pacific.

"Then when my husband died, I worked as a real estate salesperson. I helped a real estate broker here, audited their books, and they wanted me to go into the real estate business so I did. That was something different than I'd ever done. I've been a broker for about thirty years. I've done real well in real estate. I've quit beating the bushes and am in investments. I'm eighty-eight years old, still working."

Irene Smith Galley's career sprang from the tragedy of war—of necessity. She took over her husband's insurance business on a temporary basis when he went overseas, and when he did not return, she continued it permanently. Galley and her family were living in Omaha, Nebraska, when the United States entered the war.

"When the company said I could take over his job, when he first left, I said 'Oh, sure,' but I never dreamed it would really happen. I guess the best thing that ever happened—you're forced to do things.

"I was sent to Chicago and was there for two weeks. It got you acquainted. My daughter was about eight years old, and I knew a little bit about insurance, but not much. My husband was trying to tell me about endowments, and twenty-payment life, and things like that. So we talked about it a lot. Once, it was about that time, she said, 'Oh, I hope you don't talk about insurance.' We were going someplace.

"The idea was that I would take his job while he was overseas and give it back when he returned. But he didn't come back, so I continued his job. I continued about a year, maybe fourteen months.

"Other offices had some women, but not very many. I had to learn a territory, the streets. I went out to Bellevue, the edge of Omaha. I don't know how I ever did it. Some of it I enjoyed, some of it I had to force myself to do.

"We'd check into the office every day to deposit the premiums and then go out. I had a lot to learn. I was raised on a farm, one of the oldest. I had a twin brother. I did finish high school and then my family moved to Columbus, Nebraska. So it was a learning thing for me, coming to the city. We moved to Omaha in 1940.

"People then had premiums of like 25 cents a week, 50 cents a week, or a dollar for families. The black people, they were very faithful about saving their money for that, the burial. My husband talked about that. And the black ladies were very kind to me. But one lady thought it was terrible that I was taking a man's job. And one lady, I didn't feel badly about it, but she said that she lost her son. I told her I lost my husband, and she said, 'You can get another husband, but I can't get another son.'

"When the men in the service were coming home, one took my job, and I went to work in the office. The man who took my place had worked for the company before.

"I'm not a pushy salesman, so that all sounded good. Besides I didn't like to leave my daughter, and you had to be out in the evening to make sales and see people, contact families. I did have a lady stay with me for a while. All that was hard on me. I hated to leave her at night. So I went in the office, but I took a pay cut."

Dottie Wiltse Collins and baseball are inextricably linked. She started pitching softball when she was six years old in southern California and continued throughout her school years. She played ball while employed in a defense job with Payne Furnace Company, where she worked in the office during the day and the factory at night. One of her coaches was asked by the Wrigley organization for names of

women who could play for the All-American Girls' Professional Base-
ball League.

"He picked five of us to come back and try out for the league. We
went to Chicago and, in fact, all five of us made it, and in the winter
months I went back to my job in California. We were like a knit family
out there.

"During the war years we also worked at night—Rosie the Riveter. We would go in in the morning and work in the office and then at
five o'clock we'd break and have a bite to eat and then we'd go to the
factory and work in the factory—I don't even remember what I did
now, but I was working some kind of machine—and we'd go over and
stay at a woman's house who sponsored us.

"My first year playing ball was 1944; 1943 was the first year of the
league. We were treated fantastically because of the way Wrigley presented the whole thing. When I was a young kid I was always known
as a tomboy. Always had the jeans on and the baseball cap. And
people did frown on it. I didn't care one way or the other. Mother tried
to put me in dresses. But it didn't work.

"Wrigley wanted ladies who could play baseball. And he really
worked hard at it with the rules and regulations. We were not allowed
to wear slacks or shorts in public, we weren't allowed to drink or
smoke in public, and things like that. He presented it in such a way
that the public accepted it.

"The men baseball players accepted us, too. As a matter of fact,
we outdrew the world champions—the Zollner-Pistons. Their audiences went way down. They're a great bunch of guys and most of them
are still around town. But they recognized the ability we had and were
willing to accept it.

"The people had to get used to it. I said more than once when it
first started and the men came to the game, expecting to do a lot of
laughing, that after they saw our ability, they would change. That did

happen. It turned out to be a family affair and it was Mom and Dad and the kids and Grandma and Grandpa.

"It was the greatest thing that ever happened to me—other than my husband and kids. We were doing what we loved to do.

"The way things have gone in my life, I lay directly to those baseball years. It teaches you a lot, too. You're able to get out in the public, you're able to talk to people. A lot of people are not able to do this because they've never had the experience. But you're thrown among strangers at all times when you're in the sports world and you learn to deal with that.

"I've been very involved with the Association. Filming of the movie [*A League of Their Own*] started this way. One of the girls in Michigan had a little printing shop. She got to thinking about this one day and had ten or fifteen addresses and she remembered the girls and put out a one-page newsletter, and asked for more addresses. Well, it just kept growing and growing.

"We had our first reunion in 1980 in Chicago. The media was all over us. We laughed. We thought it was very funny. And we went on and we kept finding more ballplayers, and then in 1986 I had the reunion here in Fort Wayne, and again, every newspaper in the country was on the phone with us. Again, we're hysterical over this. But we did sit down and said, 'Hey, if they think we're that important, maybe we ought to do something about it.'

"That's when we formed an organization and set goals to establish an archives, which we have done in the Northern Indiana Historical Society. Then we wanted to see what we could do about Cooperstown. We were not looking for induction. We didn't feel we could crack that nut. But we were looking for recognition. We set our goal for 1990 and it happened in 1988.

"We contacted Cooperstown and I got very friendly with Ted Spencer, who is the curator, and he just went to bat for us. He thought we did belong there. It wasn't easy for him. He had a lot of things to overcome. He finally did, and I think what is so great at Cooperstown

· · · · · · · · · · · · · · · · · · · ·

is that all of our names are there. Not just a display. We didn't push. We took it slow. They have a new director coming in—a younger man more broad-minded, Ted feels. They're hoping to enlarge the display.

"Now that all this is happening, what is so rewarding is seeing the women—how do I want to say it—I've been very lucky in my life. My life has been so full, and I've had so much recognition. But there are a lot of the women who haven't been so lucky. They don't have any family left, and they don't have anything. And to see them come out of their shell and be rewarded by this—they're just on cloud nine."

Men dominated the field of medicine at the time of World War II, but as they left for the armed services, unexpected openings became available for women physicians. In San Francisco, Dr. Dorothy Meeker Aggeler discovered that working in an EKG lab at St. Mary's Hospital suited her well.

"There's no question there was more opportunity because it was wartime. There were jobs offered me just because the men were away. Nobody was going to question what you did, and I was pretty good anyhow. I had a job reading electrocardiograms at a couple of hospitals that I probably wouldn't have gotten otherwise. One of them became what I finally did, so that was nice.

"I never really felt discriminated against anywhere. The only real discrimination I had was rather funny. I was fairly high up in my class at Columbia University, so I applied for an internship at Presbyterian Hospital in New York—that seemed a logical thing to do—but I also rather wisely applied to Stanford and the University of California. I had been here and I had friends here. I didn't get the one at Presbyterian. I was called in by the professor of medicine and he said, 'Miss Meeker, I thought I should let you know that we will not be able to consider your application.' I said, 'Oh, why is that?' He fumbled around. Instead of coming right out and saying, 'You're a woman,' he said, 'Well, you know we have had women in the past but we've had some problems with them.' He meant with having babies, and so that was that, and I accepted this.

"Happily, I was accepted at UC, which changed my whole life and of course I'm grateful for it now. But about three years after that I went back with my husband and went to see one of my old professors, and he said, 'I see you've done quite well and maybe you'd like to know what happened to that internship.' 'Well,' I said, 'actually I was grateful I didn't get it.' And he said, 'There were five people on the committee. Four of them voted for you, but the fifth one was the professor of medicine, and he had the final vote and he didn't want to have a woman. The others said, 'Fine, but if you are going to do this, you have to call her in and tell her why.' Otherwise, I would never have known.

"Then this is very funny. We also had a black woman in our class, a perfectly wonderful woman. She was also refused. They told her that the nursing staff wouldn't have her living in their quarters. She didn't know until a couple of years ago when she and I got together that we had both been turned down for the same job.

"When I arrived on the house staff here in California, there was the man who became my husband. I didn't encounter any discrimination except from one other woman who was always trying to get me to do things I didn't want to do. It was a wonderful house staff, and I think I had the best time of my life when I was an intern with them. You hear all these horrible tales about the kind of hours today, but I didn't have this at all. We worked very hard, many nights. That was the most interesting time, to see patients in the middle of the night. Everything seems more stressful now.

"We also did teach the medical students, and that was interesting because they went all around the year and got through in three years because they didn't have summer vacation. That meant the instructors didn't either. It was a very taxing time.

"My maiden name was Meeker, and I got my degree in the name of Meeker, but then I got married a year and a half later, and we had a wonderful professor, Dr. Moffitt, and he used to come around every once in a while and ask to see patients. He came in one day and I gave him a couple of charts to look at, and he came back and said, 'That's an interesting man. Tell me about him.' I said he had liver disease, and he asked what I was doing for him, and there wasn't very much you could do for him, but I said my husband was doing some studies on him, and he said, 'Who's your husband?' I told him 'Paul Aggeler,' and he said, 'Why don't you take his name then?' I eventually did, but not because of Dr. Moffitt. I changed it at a logical time, at the end of the term.

"I think the one thing that has not been resolved is the hierarchy. Women get all kinds of jobs, but they don't get to be professors very often. This has changed some, but it hasn't changed as much as it should.

"I worked full time until my child was born, and then I took some time off, but after that I never worked more than oh, a little more than half time, for the rest of my career. I recommend this highly for married women doctors, or married women who have jobs. I do think it's nice to be available for your kids. My schedule was such that I could call my own shots. It also meant that I could pursue an interest in art. I used to weave. I had an Ahrens loom and wove yardage that was used in skirts, stoles, suits, table mats, place mats—in wool or linen."

12

Counterpoint:
Children and Grandchildren

The impact of the bravery and resourcefulness of the women who worked in various nontraditional jobs during the war did not end with the armistice.

Although some women never spoke about their wartime work to family or friends, others did, often with much pride. While a few children experienced the war firsthand and saw their mothers working, most children and all grandchildren heard about it only through family folklore. These offspring experienced various reactions.

A couple of children who lived through the war were annoyed or embarrassed by their mothers' employment, or were just generally uncomfortable with the wartime conditions. Others viewed it as part of life, much as most children accept what is around them without question.

The children and grandchildren who learned about the wartime jobs of their mothers and grandmothers through family stories heard tales of adventure and courage that often inspired them to similar gutsiness.

Knowing their relatives as they do, however, most said they are not surprised by the stories of their mothers and grandmothers traveling across the country, living in rustic conditions, or working in beastly hot factories—but they *are* impressed.

Gary Bradley was five years old when his mother, Loretha Tabler Bradley, worked on torpedo engines in Washington State.

"I went to day care during the day while she worked. I think I started kindergarten up there, also. Those were pretty miserable times for me. For one thing, Washington is pretty far north. In winter it was dark and the stars were still out when my sister and I walked, about a mile, to school. We lived in temporary housing that was put up during the war to house people working there at different facilities.

"I think there was quite a recruitment program going on for women to do that. Naturally, when I was that young, I didn't think it was anything abnormal. I thought it was the standard way of doing business.

"My father was gone and, as I say, that was kind of a miserable time for me and probably for my sister, too. During those few years in Poulsbo, I suffered a badly sprained arm, was struck by an automobile, and was nursed through scarlet fever by my mother. I missed my father very much.

"I was probably in high school or college when I realized that what my mother did during the war was not exactly the norm. But my mother was young and my classmates thought she was attractive and seemed impressed by what she had done for the war effort. We had our very own 'Rosie the Riveter.' I was always very proud of her. I love her for that.

"I was also impressed that she worked on engines for torpedoes. I just retired from mechanical engineering. In mechanical engineering, at least the areas that I worked in, there is a very strong attitude that women are not mechanical, that women are not cut out for that kind of work. I always tell people that your sex has nothing to do with loosening or tightening a nut or a bolt.

"I've seen women in engineering get pushed aside because of

these attitudes. Even today, probably less, I think you'll find in engineering and in large organizations, anyway, they try to direct the women into doing paperwork and administrative-type jobs.

"My mother continued to work, though not in mechanics, throughout my high school years. Though she probably didn't earn very much, she maintained her independence.

"I've always been very proud of what both my parents did during the war. I married an independent, career woman whose mother also worked most of her life. My wife, with her mother, fled Nazi Germany in 1939. Her mother worked first at housekeeping in this country and then in the business of her second husband until well after my wife had finished college and was into teaching. Both of our two sons are married to career women.

"I think my mother had a very strong influence on my attitudes and philosophies. I still occasionally enjoy thumbing my nose at the 'conventional wisdom.'"

From 1938 to 1942, Dadie Stillwell Potter attended Our Lady of the Lake College in San Antonio, Texas, while her parents, Roy and Hallie Stillwell, were keeping the ranch together, short of their usual cowboys due to the war. Potter returned to her home region after college, teaching school in the nearby town of Marathon. She got married in 1944.

"Not until I was married and had children did I realize she was so special. I went through a divorce and I had four children. Of course she helped me. Everything she has ever done has been for the three of us kids. My two brothers and me. She struggled and worked and slaved to save this ranch and pay the taxes. We're grateful and admire her for that and we still have the ranch. It's all due to her. She's a remarkable woman.

"She comes from a family of pioneers and she has that spirit. She has not had an easy life, but she strives on. She came down here, and the house my father brought her to was one room. They slept in a bedroll. They didn't have electricity until the fifties. That was thirty years after they had been married. In fact, it was after my father got killed in a truck accident that they got electricity here at the ranch.

"She's done, oh, so many things. She's a writer and she was a stringer for newspapers all over Texas. She's written two books and she's writing a sequel to *I'll Gather My Geese*. The name of it is *My Goose Is Cooked*. It'll take up from '48, when my father was killed, to the present. It'll be published soon. She writes everything with a pencil. She has beautiful handwriting. To this day, her handwriting is smooth and pretty. Lots of old people get shaky.

"She's sharp as a tack. Full of wit. Everyone in the state has a lot of respect for Hallie. She's done so much for everybody, for the government. She's gotten one award after the other, and citations, and certificates. That's what prompted me to go ahead and build this museum. We built the building and dedicated it in '91. That was on her ninety-fourth birthday. We just celebrated her ninety-sixth birthday. She's had recognition. I think it's great. We love people. We have a store and a trailer park and we welcome people.

"She's such a wonderful person and loves people and that's rubbed off on me. Everybody says I'm a lot like her. And I get more like her the more I'm around her. Her optimism has made me very optimistic."

For twenty years, Donna Ehlmann Poeling worked for the same aircraft manufacturer in St. Louis, Missouri, where her mother, Gladys Poese Ehlmann, worked for twenty-six years.

"Some of the names she would mention were familiar to me when I started working there. I worked in the engineering side, where she was more into product support and paperwork when she went back after the war.

"I'm not really sure when I became aware that she was working outside the home. I was in school by that time because she waited until my brother was in school to go back to work. I didn't really think too much about it.

"Now, as a working mother, I hear people talking about how terrible it is that women work outside the home. I'm thinking, 'Wait a minute.' Even now I hear people saying, 'Why don't you stay home and take care of the kids?' And I'm thinking, 'Why?' It's not necessary. Particularly when people use it as an excuse for the crime wave or something like that.

"To me, the fact that the mother was working has nothing to do with how the child was brought up. That was a thing that really hit home. I was a product of a working mother. I knew that the fact that a mother worked doesn't necessarily mean that the kids end up in a penal institution. I didn't have any qualms about becoming one myself. Everybody said, 'How can you leave your baby?' I did stay home for the first year. I'm really curious to see what the next generation is going to be like, because there are going to be so many more working mothers."

Karen York was born after the war, one of two children of Rose Cof-field Swanson, who stayed home in Portland, Oregon, until Karen was in kindergarten. Swanson worked as a machinist at Iron Foreman during the war.

"When I was little, we'd look through photo albums and I saw pictures of my mother with her girlfriends who also worked with her. I asked her about it, and she was very proud that she worked on the planes during the war.

"I always felt I wanted to work outside the home. I think that had the greatest impact on me—that my mother was always working outside the home. And I enjoyed it. I think it gave her a lot of confidence and helped her.

"I think for most young women, not all of them saw their mothers in a profession outside the home. So it really made a difference. It continued with my mother. She knew how much fun she had working outside our home that she did that later. I never resented it at all. My mother went to work because she had a lot of energy and liked to keep busy.

"It helped me growing up. When she was working, I cooked the meals. When she got home, I'd have dinner all done. I was eleven years old. It was a great trade-off because I got paid $5 a month. So I could go out and purchase clothes and things that I wanted. It worked out just fine. It teaches children how to do for themselves and learn how to cook. I wasn't afraid to get in the kitchen and start making pies when I was little. It created more confidence.

"During the fifties, people talked about World War II and what happened. Then later, my husband worked for Boeing and they even talked about the planes that she worked on. I remember her telling me she made one of the parts for the doors, the bomb doors that opened up.

"I went to school in Portland, but when I went off to work for the airlines, it made her decide that she could do much better than working in market research because she was doing a lot of clerical things. She looked at what I was making, with just two years of college, and decided to go to work for the City of Portland. She was discriminated against. So she fought her way to get that job. It has had an influence on me. The profession I'm in, I'm a real estate agent, I have to be constantly thinking for myself.

"I may not have gone as far if I had seen a different role model. It definitely had an impact. My daughter sees the same thing. She's eighteen. She's in a program where they step away from high school and start college a year early. She'll still graduate from high school. She's very determined and she has her mind set and I don't try to step in the way."

Jane Arlene Herman was born in 1948 in Arizona to Jennette Hyman Nuttall, who worked as a crane operator during the war. After spending most of her childhood in New England, Herman now lives in San Francisco, working as a medical researcher and political activist. She remembers looking through family photo albums at age three or four and seeing her mother and her mother's friends during the war. Herman believes she would not have lived her life as she has if her mother had not been, in her words, "extraordinary."

"What I learned from my mother, and I think she learned this sitting up on that crane, was that being afraid was not a reason not to do something.

"I do things even when I'm afraid. I got that from her and my father. When I was very young, maybe eight, I remember going to get bread. I was gone for a long time and my mother said, 'Where were you?' I told her it was really crowded and I had to wait for it to clear out so people would see me. She said, 'Next time you raise your hand and say you're next. They'll see your hand. You raise it.' The next time I was at the bakery, I raised my hand. She gave me tools.

"It was always pretty clear to me what my mother did during the war. When I was four or five years old, I didn't exactly understand what her job was or how she got there, but I knew that she did do that and that it was important. I think it encouraged her in a way she hadn't been encouraged before. Traveling across the country with her sister and her friends, that was not something women were commonly doing.

"I don't think I've ever seen her fail at anything. She's very smart, so she won't do things that are absurd for her to be doing, but when she does do something, she decides she is going to finish whatever it is. And if something had to be done, she wouldn't say, 'Oh, I'll wait until my husband comes home and he'll take care of it.' She would take care of it.

"I had wanted her to be like other mummies, but at the same time, she was much more fun, yet I resented that, too. My mother was the star, and I didn't want her to be the star. I just wanted her to be quiet. But it was also fun. My girlfriends would come over and be dancing and my mother was a wonderful dancer and still is. So she would teach us how to do the jitterbug. She would dance with me and dance with my friends. It would be really fun and we would be laughing, but on the other hand, I didn't want my mother to have the attention. I wanted the attention. I felt like we were in competition.

"This was very difficult for a teenager or young woman trying to find my way in the world to feel like I could never get beyond my mother. At some point, I realized that the competition probably didn't exist. The last sixteen years, I've really been able to pay attention to my mother and treasure her more."

Elmer Becky and his two brothers were overseas during World War II when their mother, Matilda Hoffman Becky Havers, was asked to become a machinist at the New York Shipyard. Elmer was in Italy flying combat as an Air Force photoreconnaissance pilot.

"The first I heard of it was when she wrote me, as she usually did, and told me she was now working in the shipyard. She was the first woman hired by them at the south yard. It didn't surprise me a bit. If they had said my mom had enlisted and was in combat someplace, it would not have surprised me.

"My mom has always been a tomboy. She was one of the first women to drive cars and fly an airplane, had her own airplane. She gave up flying at age seventy-nine and stopped riding her Honda at eighty because it was too heavy for her to lift if it fell over. She still in her mind is that way but she's ninety years old. She still lives alone, has her own house. I called her about a month ago and she sounded out of breath. I asked her—she has a portable phone—'Mom, where are you?' She was up in the attic fixing a broken pipe.

"She told me stories about how the men resented her being there at first. But when she showed them she was capable of doing things, setting up her own work without having a supervisor check it, the next thing my mom wrote was that they had asked her, 'Is there anyone else like you at home?' She recruited her younger sister and the two of them rode a motorcycle to work every day.

"The humorous part about it was my mom said she was making more money at the shipyard than my dad was as a foreman at General Electric.

"I have often expressed to my mom and to everybody else I know that I had a wonderful childhood and a great trainer. Just tremendous. Mom was fantastic.

"I remember her doing a valve job on a 1933 Plymouth and her three boys 'helping' and I was the oldest at thirteen. She never was afraid of anyone. She took us to see every event that ever happened. When the Hindenburg burned, we went to see it. If a whale washed up on the shore, we were taken down to see it. All the way to see the Dionne quintuplets when they were born deep into Canada.

"When she got sick one time and was in bed for a long time, I'd go home from school and see Mom in bed and she'd tell me how to make dinner for Dad, what to let Harry do.

"Mom always managed to go to church. We were all christened

and confirmed Lutherans. I packed a New Testament bible with me
all through the war."

*Barbara Barbash Kendall has found great inspiration in the life of
her grandmother, Bella Neumann Zilberman. Her feelings about the
wartime experiences of her mother, Cecile Zilberman Barbash—who
worked for the government during the war because of her recent
divorce—are more mixed. That was a difficult time for Kendall.*

"I was very upset that she had to go to work because none of my
friends' mothers worked. I was furious because she wasn't in fashion.
I really didn't know what she was doing. I had no idea. It embarrassed
me. I didn't want to tell people she worked for the government. Any
effect my mother had on me was only negative.

"My grandmother was the one that was a little crazy. She was the
first suffragette. She marched for Margaret Sanger. She did all these
wonderful things.

"I think I learned from both of them that you could get out there
and do something. My grandmother lost all her money in the Depression. From the furnishings in her home, she opened an antique shop
in San Francisco and ran it for twenty years. She was creative. She
was an entrepreneur. She never made any money. I guess I identify
with her more than my mother. She had a lot of emotional problems.
She had the intellect.

"She was involved with Benjamin Bufano at a peace foundation.
She was a hippie before her time. All these great things. She was a
friend of Isadora Duncan in the twenties. She was a frustrated actress.

"My mother was divorced at the same time she took this job. It was
a terrible time for me because I had already mentally enrolled myself
at The Hamlin School, a private girls' school. My stepfather said,
'You're not going to have the standard of living that you're used to.

Everything's going to change.' So I was angry. Just because they were getting a divorce, why did it have to have such an impact on my life?

"So, far from looking at my mother and thinking, This is great, it was, Why? She was very proud of what she did. I just couldn't understand it. I always looked at civil service as just the lowest."

Janice Callahan Waggoner grew up in Arkansas hearing stories about her parents' jobs in California during the war. Her mother, Dee Davenport Callahan, worked in a sugar refinery in Crockett.

"I always grew up not thinking of myself as having to have a traditionally female job or be traditionally female. Many of her sisters did the same sort of thing. She went out there with three of her sisters who also worked in California. They moved out there just to earn money basically. It was the old joke story, the Arkies moving to California to get jobs during the dismal times.

"I'm not sure if they worked at the same plant or not. I heard all of these stories about what they did and how they lived and where they worked. It was never traditionally female. I think it affected me in that way. I've never held a traditionally female job. After graduate school, I went to work for the telephone company. They asked me would I be willing to work in the plant department, which at the time was traditionally male. I was in management so I didn't actually climb telephone poles, but that was who I supervised.

"Now I'm an insurance agent. Even though there are now lots of women insurance agents, it traditionally was not a female job.

"My mother was always an income producer in our family. If she didn't work, I don't remember. I had a babysitter and I can remember going to a day-care center. Just exactly the same kinds of things I did with my son when he was little. To me, that was just what everybody did.

"My best friend, her mom and dad owned a grocery store when I was little. I guess among my four best friends, I had one whose mother was widowed and she worked. I had another whose mother was a nurse. I had another two who had stay-at-home mothers. I didn't feel real odd.

"I thought it was really adventurous for my mother to go across the country. I was born and raised in the same state and even though California was easily accessible to me, to think of my mother so many years earlier just getting on a train and going out there and starting a new life—it was adventurous.

"The first time I ever went out there was when I was about twelve. We went out there on a vacation, and I think it was really more like a pilgrimage for my parents. We went to San Francisco. We went to that plant and we took a tour and my mother showed me where she worked and what machine she operated. To me, I thought we were going on a vacation but to them, I think it was something different.

"I still have little souvenirs from that sugar plant. We rode a train to get there, which was really interesting because that's how they used to get back and forth during the war. They drove out there initially. That was probably the last three to five years that you could actually easily ride a train. We rode it up to Kansas City and then got a train to San Francisco. It would have been a lot easier and better to fly, but they didn't want to do that. They wanted to ride the train and they wanted me to ride the train."

The youngest of three boys growing up on a farm in Texas, Bo Blanton heard tales about the wartime adventures of his mother, Lucille Genz Blanton Teeters, who worked as a riveter in an airplane factory. During his childhood years, he saw a strong mother firsthand.

"She told me so many stories, about chewing tobacco and getting in trouble with her supervisors. They weren't allowed to chew tobacco, and she'd get a wad in her mouth and the supervisor would come by, and if they caught you, you'd get fired, so she'd swallow it. Then she'd get sick. I thought it was real interesting that she was tough enough to do that kind of work.

"She talked about her and her girlfriends driving back from New York, where they went to see Dad off. He was a Seabee. She was driving back and someone tried to get in the car and get them with a butcher knife. All kinds of stories.

"We had a farm and we raised cows and she'd go over, even when we were doing cows, she'd hold the cow down while Dad cut—a tough, tough lady. I've even seen her on a tractor. When we were kids, we took hoes over there and hoed for cotton. We did all kinds of things in Texas.

"Before I went to school, she got her nurse's license. She was a nurse.

"All three of us kids, she lost one son last year, but all three of us grew up to be real honest. That's just the way our parents were. They were tough. We didn't steal or take. Everything was yes ma'am or no ma'am. We're affected by the way we were raised. The other day I picked up a wallet and returned it. I wouldn't think of keeping it. They raised us tough. If you wanted a car, you had to earn it.

"I just think she grew up in an age where they were tough old birds. I don't think the old girls today could do as much physically. She came out of a family of thirteen. They had to work the farm or they didn't have anything to eat.

"I think these days we don't have any choice except to have women work, to make house payments and so on. People scream about kids turning out so bad because the women are working, but what else can you do? We have bills to pay."

During the war, both of Jo Droullard Krueger's parents worked at Todd Shipyard in Seattle, Washington. Her father was deferred from

the armed forces for health reasons and her mother, Mary Todd
Droullard, worked as a coppersmith on the British minesweepers and
then as a welder.

"I was born in 1940. We were going to what would now be called day
care, but I think it was a government-run nursery school. I remember
the naptimes and being fed cod liver oil and running in the bathroom
and spitting it out in the toilet.

"I think my mother worked from the time I remember. It was not a
real positive thing for me. From a positive standpoint, it probably
increased our income.

"She never really talked about the shipyard that much. I was very
young. I wasn't really aware of where she was working. I don't think I
was aware that she had done it until I was a teenager and noticed she
had all these scars on her chest. She said it was from welding.

"I recall her talking about there being some flirting—she mentioned that a little bit. She's very beautiful. Very curvaceous. Just very
beautiful and I'm sure she attracted a lot of eyes, and in those days,
I'm sure much more sexual harassment went on than now. It would be
unusual to see someone who's five foot two and petite with long, dark
hair doing a job like that. She kind of looked like Gene Tierney. You'd
think of someone more sturdy working there.

"I think that's what started her on her working life because she
worked from then on. I suppose my model as a woman was to work. I
didn't work at all until my children were up and growing."

Ballplaying was soundly but not forcefully passed on from former
Rockford Peaches third basewoman Helen Filarski Steffes to her
daughter, Diane Steffes Grabowski, who in turn is actively involved in
her children's athletic activities.

"She talked a lot about it. She never elaborated on it. She said that she played, and we believed it. I think she was a pioneer in her day because that was unheard of. I think very highly of her and I have a lot of respect for her.

"She never pushed any of us to get involved in sports. If we wanted to play, we asked her, she never asked us. Although she did become involved with it, just as I do now with my kids, and my kids are ten and seven.

"I am a working mother and I am also actively involved with my children playing sports. My girl plays baseball. My boy plays soccer. It can be done and I'll do it until I'm eighty if I can.

"She coached basketball and baseball in my grade school. Therefore, I got involved. But I never got involved in basketball because I wasn't good enough and I had asthma. Baseball, I always made the team.

"I was a tomboy. They'd kid me. To this day, my husband makes jokes that I still don't know how to bake. I can throw a ball, but I don't know how to sew. But Mom did that. She didn't spend time teaching me that. I can cook up a storm and I consider myself to be a good mother, and I thought she was a wonderful mother and still do.

"I stay active, and what will keep her young longer than anybody is the fact that she stays active with younger people.

"She told us some stuff about playing professional ball, but my mouth hung in 1989 when I heard they were going to get recognized at Cooperstown. I said, 'Oh, come on, it wasn't that big was it, Mom?' Then I started asking questions. 'You played for who, you got paid how much, what did you wear?' And then you really started listening because it wasn't just your mother. You know how kids know more than their mothers do.

"I believed her and then she met with other people. They were having interviews and reunions with the old-timers. It was all so cool, but then I never got to see her play. It was all hearsay. But anything your mom tells you is all hearsay when you're a kid.

"I don't know anybody who doesn't have the utmost respect for her, whether it is friends of mine, or an umpire that's umpiring the game. I've heard people talking about her behind her back, for instance, after games or something. The umpire just shakes his head and says, 'Boy, that old lady knows what she's talking about.' She's the only one out there who's gray but she's the smartest one on the ball diamond."

Even though Ernest Stark's grandmother, Stella Vanderlinden Alway, moved to California from Kansas when he was young, he heard stories about her work as a machinist during the war.

"My folks were separated when I was about seven. I was raised by my dad. Stella is my mother's mother. But my dad had a very high opinion of her. He talked to me about her ambition, her drive, the fact that she would stand up and take a job right alongside a man. She would work with the best of them.

"She left and went out to California when I was quite young. I was aware as a child growing up that she worked with aircraft, building aircraft, repairing aircraft. I grew up with the idea of her out there on the Coast working in what was traditionally a man's field, able to stand up and slap around with all of them.

"When I thought about my grandmother, it wasn't the traditional, stereotypical sort of woman. It was the gal who rolled up her sleeves and threw rivets into an airplane, jacked up metal parts, and things like that.

"She may have been the liberated woman before the liberated woman was in fashion. She left my granddad, he was quite a bit older than she, but she just literally pulled herself up out of the poverty that was in southeast Kansas. She decided she was going to take hold of life and shape it and get more out of it than she had been getting. The impression of the family is, this is a gal that is going to meet the world on her terms, not necessarily on the world's terms.

"She would keep in touch, would send Christmas presents, write letters. When I got older we even became closer, as I got older and raised my family. She started coming back and visiting more frequently.

"Probably she served as an example to my daughters. I'm an old football coach and I raised two daughters. There's quite a folklore among my daughters about their great-grandmother. My daughters have felt that this is somebody who has sort of paved the way for them. Both of them are independent, have careers.

"I think the stories they heard about their great-grandma Stella sort of convinced them that they could be assertive, they could be independent, they could go out and meet the world on their terms, too. She's held with a great deal of respect among my two daughters as a woman who could go out and make things happen in a man's world."

LouAnn Fornataro calls her grandmother, Josephine Solomon Fundoots, "one of the original liberated ladies." Fundoots worked as a burner for U.S. Steel during the war, while supporting three daughters, the oldest of whom is Fornataro's mother.

"My mother's family is women oriented and we seem to like it that way. The matriarch was 'Sitto,' my great-grandmother, Rose, who lived with my grandmother for as long as I can remember. She was a woman who still chased my brothers around when she was in her eighties. A divorced woman with little education, she and my grandmother had some arrangement whereby they could cohabitate in relative peace.

"The story has come to me that when my mother was three, and her twin sisters were born, my grandfather divorced my grandmother on the grounds that she could not give him sons. That was about 1941. So, here was a woman left with a mother and three babies to support at the start of World War II.

"When we're sitting around Grandma's table, talking about nothing, she sometimes drags down her suitcase of pictures. While everyone else searches for early shots of themselves, I look for pictures of Grandma. They are pictures of a woman who always looks like she's going to her executive office—hair done, makeup perfect, seams straight, blouse starched, spike heels, but she's got an infant in each arm and a toddler on her hem. This is a woman who works in a factory making war machines.

"Grandma and I don't talk much about that time in her life. It seems she'd rather not get into it. I can see why. It goes against her basic nature to always be, and look like, a lady. What I see in my grandmother is a person who holds her head high and does what she knows needs to be done, despite her preferences and ideals.

"Of all the things my grandmother has given to me, this is what I find most important—the conviction that I must do what I must do. Through all my life, and especially in my career, I have been able to hold to that. I can only aspire to hold my head as high as my grandmother has been able to do through all her adversity."

As a small child, Edwina Holbrook Leach remembers her mother and father talking about the time they were in California during the war. Her mother, Nova Lee McGhee Holbrook, worked as a welder in the Kaiser Shipyard in Richmond.

"It's just something I grew up knowing. It was just part of my childhood, like being a Methodist. My mother was always a little different. She rode with my father on the motorcycle. Other mothers didn't do this, but she did. She played basketball when I was a young girl, and she was in her thirties and forties. Even today, in her early seventies, my mother still goes dancing and is very agile for her age.

"As a young girl, I was always proud to show pictures of my mom to my friends and tell them that she was a 'Rosie the Riveter.' However, most of them didn't have the foggiest idea what I was talking about. My parents were older than most of their parents because they were married over ten years before I was born. I guess here in rural Arkansas there was very little knowledge that women were working in men's jobs building ships during the war.

"I just always grew up knowing Mom was a real tomboy. She wasn't afraid of anything. She wasn't a sit-in-the-home, bake-cookies type of mother. She was just the type, if she wanted to do something, she just would go do it. She would rather get on top of the house to help my father repair the roof than stay in the kitchen cooking lunch.

"When the war was over and my father came back home, my mother continued to work until just shortly after I was born. She didn't return to work until I was three, and that job began as a temporary assignment and led to a permanent job as a secretary for a medical clinic. She kept working even after my brother was born when I was seven. My father died when I was eleven and about three and a half months later, my four-year-old brother died, leaving my mother and me alone.

"I grew up knowing that my mother had always worked, so I never thought much about the type of work she did during the war. However, looking back, I believe that growing up and hearing that my mother was one of the first women in our country to work in a 'man's' job in the shipyards was my first introduction to an awareness of the inequality of women in the workplace.

"I once held a job as a secretary for a heavy-construction company that was owned by a Native American and his business was classified as a Disadvantaged Business Entity. I was shocked at his prejudice, and the prejudice of other men in his field, toward DBEs that were owned and operated by women.

"And I recently attended a pastor's licensing school, and in a class of twenty-five, we had two women and three black men. The instructors told us that the black men would meet racial prejudice and discrimination in their future, but that their problems would be small compared to the problems the women would face.

"I realize that many people have religious reasons for not believing in women ministers, but most who are asked about their reasons cannot give a biblically based reason. I'm a very feminine-type woman and have no desire to hold a job that has been traditionally thought of as a man's, but I get angry knowing that many women are physically capable of doing anything a man can, yet still they are discriminated against in the workplace."

The People We Interviewed
. . . .

Dr. Dorothy Meeker Aggeler is in a play-reading group and is on the selection committee for the artwork exhibited in the lobby of her Oakland, California, retirement complex. Her part-time medical career allowed time for her weaving, and one of her wall hangings won a prize at a Women Artists' exhibit. (Chapter Eleven)

Marge Young Altschuler went into the restaurant business with her husband in California. Today she lives in Placerville, California, and thinks of ways to bring smiles to the faces of her friends and neighbors. (Chapter Six)

Stella Vanderlinden Alway is supervisor of the Citrus Heights Cancer Station, where items are made for cancer patients. She has traveled worldwide and likes to remember the romantic South Pacific and its tradewinds. She bowls, goes dancing, and has two children and a grandson. She lives in Fair Oaks, California. (Chapter Five)

Liz Arnold learned how to drive so she could sell advertising for the *San Francisco News*, has been in advertising for several years, appears in local little theater productions, and lives in Portland, Oregon. She has two daughters. (Chapter Six)

Rose Ann "Tex" Longnecker Barbarite is still amused by National Broadcasting Company's letter (1951) saying, "We are seriously considering the employing of women as military replacements." She volunteers at the National Institutes of Health for experimental medicine studies and also volunteers as a teacher in a middle school near her Columbia, Maryland home, readying students for ham radio licenses. (Chapter Eleven)

Cecile Zilberman Barbash of Novato, California, retired in 1965, became active in political campaigns, and has devoted her time to geriatric studies and activities. Barbash was appointed a delegate to the White House Conference on Aging in 1981. She also was appointed to the state aging commission, volunteered at the San Francisco office on aging, and served on an advisory council for the aging in Marin County, California. (Chapter Nine)

Lois LaCroix Barber is busy on local committees, is active with Meals on Wheels, and takes special pleasure in working with her husband's aunt, who is involved with United Nations projects, particularly the Commission on the Status of Women. Barber lives in Greenwich, Connecticut. (Chapter Ten)

Jane-Ellen Washburn Bartholomew, as a member of the Hanford (California) Show-Offs, will be happy to show off the town's architectural treasures, among them the Carnegie Library and the handsome courthouse. That is, when she's not busy with the King County Historical Society, or the new art gallery, or the King County Republican Women, or the Heritage League, or the American Cancer Society. (Chapter Four)

Gertrude Clark Beavers bracketed her teaching during the war with five years of teaching before and twenty-three years after. In retirement she enjoys life, appreciates her exceptional family, and does some traveling. She lives in Edgar, Nebraska, and has eight grandchildren and ten great-grandchildren. (Chapter Eight)

Elmer Becky of Sacramento, California, graduated from Drexel University and earned a master's at the University of Southern California. He worked as an engineer for the State of California for thirty-three and a half years and has served in the military for twenty-two years, with the rank of lieutenant colonel. He has six electric trains on 200 feet of track, enjoys working with wood, and has remodeled his home. He has a daughter, three sons, and six grandchildren. (Chapter Twelve)

Mildred Admire Bedell worked in California for several years after the war, at one time as deputy auditor for Contra Costa County, where she got used to writing checks for millions of dollars. She and her husband returned to Missouri because her husband was homesick for their native state. She became a social worker. Their four sons live in California. (Chapter One)

Margaret Fraser Beezley lives in Bellevue, Washington and just retired from twenty-two years of managing her daughter's household, which included a horse, two dogs, two cats, and two grandchildren. Before that, she braved storms and tornadoes in Parson, Kansas, hating every minute but staying because of her husband's job. (Chapter Two)

Inka Sanna Benton lives in Greenbrae, California. Since the end of the war, she has worked as an architect, exhibited her studio photographs, produced slide shows on environmental issues, traveled extensively, and discovered another view of women when she was an urban planner with the Peace Corps in Iran. (Chapter Five)

Geraldine Amidon Berkey, from Painesville, Ohio, now lives in Fresno, California, where she taught elementary school for twenty-three years. In her retirement she writes about children's needs, and her book,

Easy to Read, is a popular text on the subject. Her worldwide traveling began when she won a prize: a trip to Aruba and Curaçao. She has
two daughters. (Chapter One)

Doris Casey Berringer greets each day with another painting. She meets
with others who enjoy art and has gotten college credit in fine art. She
lives in Spokane, Washington, and has three children. (Chapter
Eleven)

Margaret Wolfe Berry had the unique experience of working on the
refurbishing of the B-29 and B-17—the planes she worked on fifty
years ago. The museum volunteer project is part of a fifty-year celebration of the two planes. One B-29 came to the museum in bits and
pieces and presented a riveting challenge. Berry lives in Seattle,
Washington. (Chapter Two)

Frances Keller Blanchet lives in Portland, Oregon, and worked as a
bookkeeper for Terminix International for seventeen and a half years.
She advanced through the offices of the American Legion Auxiliary
and served as president. Her son lives near her, and she has a dog
and two cats. (Chapter Ten)

Bo Blanton is the youngest of three sons born to Lucille Genz Blanton
Teeters. He runs a floral business and enjoys his hobby of raising
Bouviers des Flandres. His mother came from a family of thirteen and
his father was one of twelve, so when the Blanton family gathers every
year just outside Austin, Texas, it is quite a crowd. (Chapter Twelve)

Gary Bradley, an engineer retired from Lawrence Livermore Laboratory,
spends time compiling his family's genealogy and finds there is not
enough time to do all he would like. He has two sons and lives in
Livermore, California. (Chapter Twelve)

Loretha Tabler Bradley loves to do research. She has been working on her family genealogy and helping her son collect information on her husband's family. Her son and daughter have six children between them, and Bradley has four great-grandchildren. She lives in Walnut Creek, California. (Chapter Six)

Dorothy "Sunny" Lockard Bristol spends three days a week at the National Women's History Project ("and it's never enough") as archivist, handling topic files, photo files, and the individual files of more than 1,000 important women. The project is open to researchers. Bristol lives in Santa Rosa, California. (Chapter Nine)

Fern Stephens Brooks was a chemist for ten years, was employed in a film library, and then worked in a laboratory analyzing developing solutions. She does needlework, volunteers with the American Red Cross, has a son and daughter, and lives in Front Royal, Virginia. (Chapter Six)

Lyllus Runyan Butler, in Altoona, Iowa, was asked by her grandson to record the wartime experiences of Grandma the Machinist, for the class at school. She loves people and works with her daughter at flea markets. She has six great-grandchildren. (Chapter One)

Dee Davenport Callahan returned to Arkansas after her California experience and lives in North Little Rock. Twenty years after the war, she and her family visited the sugar refinery where she had worked, and she was delighted to see some of the same faces and to be treated to a gracious welcome and a tour of the plant. She has been a bookkeeper for Central Flying Service, then was self-employed, then employed by Holiday Inn. She has a son and a daughter. (Chapter One)

Alison Ely Campbell raised a family for twenty years and then completed a secondary teaching credential and later a master's. She has had various professions, including graphic arts and teaching. Campbell presently develops training courses for the telecommunications industry. She lives in Los Altos, California. (Chapter Five)

Naomi Turnbough Campbell of St. James, Missouri, stayed with the railroad for a few years after the war, did some office work, and conducted television monitoring for broadcast advertising. She enjoys oil painting and has three trunks of her homemade quilts. Campbell has three daughters and two grandchildren. (Chapter Four)

Joan Ascher Cardon brought her skills as a psychiatric nurse to a job with the Peace Corps in Washington, D.C., where she evaluated volunteers' applications for mental stability, among other traits. She volunteers on library committees and for the Volunteer Bureau and is a director of the Mental Health Association. She and her husband share a love of long-distance sailing, having crossed the Atlantic and sailed both the Mediterranean and Caribbean seas. Cardon lives in Wheaton, Maryland. (Chapter Seven)

Harriet Pinchbeck Carpenter has enjoyed singing throughout her life. A contralto, she has been a church soloist and a member of community choruses. She worked for the Connecticut State Employment Service and is a past governor of the Northeast Soroptomists International. She holds two sociology degrees: a B.A. from Syracuse University and an M.A. from Columbia. Carpenter lives in Pinedale, California. (Chapter Seven)

Frances Park Claypool of Visalia, California, put her wartime electrician's training to good use at home by fixing a derelict $5 washing machine, which she sold later for $130. She volunteered her accountant's talents at the local senior center, figuring income tax for center participants. Claypool loved her camping trips in her motor home. She died in 1993. (Chapter Four)

Patricia Herbert Cody and her husband established Cody's Books in Berkeley in 1956, and her book, *The Life and Times of Cody's Books*, was published in 1992. Before that, she got an M.A. in economics at Columbia University and worked for the *Economist* magazine in London, while her husband got his Ph.D. at the University of London. She lives in Berkeley, California. (Chapter Five)

Marna Angell Cohen and her family left Eastern winters for better weather, settling in Mill Valley, California. She has been a social worker at the University of California Medical Center for twenty-five years. (Chapter Nine)

Dottie Wiltse Collins worked for General Electric when she and her husband needed furniture for the new house, then for an organization called Baseball Bluebook. She keeps busy with the All-American Girls Professional Baseball League, plays golf, and lives in Fort Wayne, Indiana. (Chapter Eleven)

Dorothy Martschinsky Comstock has five children, lives in Versailles, Missouri, and has worked on assembly lines off and on throughout her life—helping manufacture everything from airplanes to lawnmower bags. (Chapter Seven)

Gloria Zamko Conklin has had a career as a commercial artist; her assignments have included fashion illustration. She has lived in the New York area as well as throughout the United States. For the past twenty years, she has been a painter; she now has a studio in Williamsburg, Virginia, where she lives. (Chapter Three)

Gretchen de Boer Courtleigh worked in retail for fifteen years after the war and then became the first woman manager and vice president of a Beverly Hills bank. She was also the first woman president of the Beverly Hills Bankers Association. In her retirement, she travels, reads, and walks for exercise. She has a son and lives in Los Angeles. (Chapter Four)

Lillian Brooks Crawford lives in Florissant, Missouri. She has worked since she was nine years old; before her post office job, she worked at the American Can Company, where they made oatmeal cartons out of cardboard rather than tin to save metal for defense needs. She was also manager of a school cafeteria for twenty-eight years. She has a son and daughter. (Chapter Four)

Opal Braniff Daniels raised her family after the war in the San Francisco Bay Area and worked for Sprouse Reitz and Montgomery Ward. Seven years ago, Daniels moved to Angels Camp, California, to care for her great-grandchildren while her granddaughter teaches school. (Chapter Two)

Sally Boyce Davis worked as a dental assistant and later in the accounting department of an electronics company. These days, she does traditional rug hooking as well as some quilting and sings with the Sweet Adelines, a barbershop chorus. Davis lives in Capitola, California. (Chapter Five)

Velva Butterworth Davis got a job with the Department of Motor Vehicles when she and her husband arrived in California after the war, and she worked there for twenty-two and a half years. In her retirement, she has enjoyed traveling and observing the state's flowers, birds, and other wildlife. She especially appreciates gardening at her Sacramento, California home, growing trees from saplings and even some trees from cuttings. (Chapter Ten)

Goldie Shamchoian Deckwa enjoys the quiet air and the spring lupine on her two and a half acres in Sanger, California. She has worked in the assessor's office and the traffic court and lives with a dog and several Manx cats. (Chapter Six)

Virginia Tredinnick Denmark found that her expertise in weather observation was a useful resource when working with her youth camp in past years, leading courses in nature study. She lives in Springfield, Missouri. (Chapter Two)

Eva Schifferle Diamond is a part-time art teacher, volunteer, and mother of six children. She lives in San Anselmo, California. (Chapter Five)

Helen Kooima Dowling was born in Sioux Falls, South Dakota, has raised a son and two daughters, and has worked in the Washington State Department of Health and Social Services. When her granddaughters interviewed her on a school assignment, she was happy to give her firsthand reports of working conditions during World War II and general experiences during the war. (Chapter One)

Mary Todd Droullard stood on the decks of the ships she was building during World War II and dreamed that one day she would sail on a ship. During her retirement, she has been on more than fifteen cruises, making that dream come true. She has a daughter and three grandsons living in Seattle, near her Issaquah, Washington, home. (Chapter Three)

Faiga Fram Duncan began working at sixteen, telephoning for classified advertisements. She continued working to support her studies at the University of California at Los Angeles and at Berkeley and was a social worker at San Francisco General Hospital. She also lectured on health subjects in Sydney, Australia, now does research for health organizations, and recently pretended to be a polar bear, posing for an artist illustrating children's books who needed a model for action poses. Duncan lives in Oakland, California. (Chapter Three)

Leila Bacot Dunn lived in Texas for several years, caring for her parents, and returned to Sacramento, California, seven years ago to be near her son, now retired. She enjoys handwork: crocheting, knitting, embroidery. (Chapter Ten)

Gladys Poese Ehlmann worked at McDonnell Douglas Corporation in St. Louis, Missouri, for twenty-six years, where, among other things, she kept records for the Gemini spacecraft. She lives in St. Charles, Missouri, and has a son and a daughter. (Chapter Nine)

Julie Raymond Elliott was a hairdresser for several years after the war. She loved ballroom dancing. A volunteer homemaker and health aide for seniors, she became an ombudsperson for elderly people, working with the State of Massachusetts. She had a son and three grandchildren. Elliott died in 1993. (Chapter Five)

Mildred House "Hut" Ferree went back to work when her third child was in school, first for Wellesley College, then Radcliffe. She was Legislative Chair and Education Chair of the Hartford Junior League and is an expert on the WASP and the accompanying militarization legislation. Ferree lives in Manchester Center, Vermont. (Chapter Eleven)

Jennie Fain Folan moved to the Yakima Valley in Washington after the war, where she worked in a hospital and her children worked for fruit growers. Their combined efforts "kept them off welfare." She worked for thirty-eight years straight, including serving as activity director of the Seattle retirement home where she now lives. (Chapter One)

LouAnn Fornataro, a registered architect, has founded her own firm, which holds the distinction of being the first woman-owned architectural firm to consult to the State of New Hampshire. Her other clients include churches, manufacturers, health care providers, homeowners, restaurateurs, developers, and contractors. A graduate of Penn State

University, Fornataro was born in Pennsylvania and now lives in Mont Vernon, New Hampshire. (Chapter Twelve)

Vera-Mae Widmer Fredrickson, an anthropologist living in Berkeley, California, installed an exhibit of Indian culture at Shelter Cove for the Kings Range Conservation area. She has three daughters and knows her granddaughters won't be brought up "feminine." (Chapter Nine)

Ruth Vogler Fritz grew up in Middle River, Maryland. After the war, she and her family moved to her husband's home state, Massachusetts. She raised two children and worked in a shoelace factory, then in a kindergarten, later as a baker, then as a school cafeteria cook. She lives in New Hampshire and keeps active with volunteer work. (Chapter One)

Josephine Solomon Fundoots worked at voter registration and as a civilian secretary in the armed forces after the war. She is proud of her current job, where she finds work for people over fifty-five as part of a senior program. She lives in Newcastle, Pennsylvania, and has three children. (Chapter Eleven)

Irene Smith Galley belongs to a Christian Women's club, enjoys golf and bridge, and keeps up her yard and house, where she has lived for fifty years. She has a daughter and lives in Omaha, Nebraska. (Chapter Eleven)

Betty Kirstine Gannon lives in Aloha, Oregon, raised a family, enjoys gardening, and especially looks forward to occasional reunions with her two sisters, who also worked in defense jobs during the war. (Chapter One)

Maggie Gee reports that an important part of her life is her position on the executive committee of the California Democratic Party. A physicist at Lawrence Livermore Laboratory, she lives in Berkeley, California. (Chapter Eight)

Margaret Schroeder Gibson took a leave of absence from teaching elementary school to teach Morse code to men in the service, and when the war was over returned to teaching children. She has a daughter and lives in Berger, Missouri. (Chapter Six)

Althea Bates Gladish lives in Randolph, Massachusetts. She spent many years after the war caring for ailing parents, sisters, and a husband. Working at the Boston Gear Works inspired her to write a poem, one line of which is, "And the portercable arbor will avenge good old Pearl Harbor." (Chapter Three)

Diane Steffes Grabowski and her family live in Lenox, Michigan, in a log home on ten acres of land. She has been a bookkeeper for an iron works firm in Detroit for eighteen years, plays baseball, bowls, and is busy with Cub Scouts and family activities. She has a son and daughter. (Chapter Twelve)

Florence Barker Hackel lives in Emeryville, California, swims, and is a museum junkie. Beginning with a fourth-grade scholarship to the Chicago Art Institute, she has always been fascinated by art. She recently sold a photograph in a fundraising event, paints in water colors, maybe "sliding back into oils and acrylic." She has had one foot in anthropology and one in home economics and is taking a class on how to become an entrepreneur. She has eight children and nine grandchildren. (Chapter Three)

Joy Hampton works ten hours a week at the Oklahoma Geological Survey—"my convenience, my time, it's my work." She trained all the men in the mud business for ten years, figuring they were more or less resigned to a woman doing this. Mud folk furnish chemicals and "stuff" to keep the material liquid enough to travel through a mile or so of pipe. She lives in Norman, Oklahoma. (Chapter Three)

Matilda Hoffman Becky Havers bought a Piper Cub J-4 after World War II, and flying became a large part of her life. Her plane is now in a museum. She swims, works in ceramics, does her own gardening and housework, and recently celebrated her ninetieth birthday. A resident of Philadelphia, she has three sons and twelve grandchildren. (Chapter Two)

Betty Stuart Hennessey grew up on a wheat ranch in Washington's Big Bend area, near Ritzville. Making fun of the strong winds in that region, she reports that at the time of the war, they "blew off the ranch and came to Spokane," where she remained. She has raised three girls and a boy and has returned to teaching as a substitute. (Chapter Three)

Jane Arlene Herman is a political activist and medical researcher on issues of environmental health and multiple chemical and toxic sensitivities. "It was like I was being groomed to be a feminist," she said about her upbringing. Retired on disability, she lives in San Francisco. (Chapter Twelve)

Nova Lee McGhee Holbrook worked in a café for a while after the war, then as a receptionist and bookkeeper in a rural health care clinic for twenty-six years. Her arthritis does not keep her from going dancing. She lives in Perry, Arkansas. (Chapter Eight)

Marjory Cropley Hollis has taught in school districts of all sizes, ranging from major metropolitan areas to small mountain towns where a colleague hung boys from hooks by their suspenders when they misbehaved. She enjoys reading, traveling, gardening. Hollis lives in Tiburon, California, and has one daughter. (Chapter Nine)

....

Joyce Taylor Holloway and her husband sold their real estate business after thirty-three years in the same location in Sacramento, California. They are active in Masonic and Eastern Star work and love their summer place on the Russian River. They have a son, daughter, and one grandson. (Chapter Ten)

Marjorie Cordell Hoskins does not like sitting around doing nothing, so she has filled a cedar chest with her homemade quilts. Many are being enjoyed by her six grandchildren and two great-grandchildren. She also does piece quilting decorated with embroidery. She has a son and daughter and lives in Nebraska City, Nebraska. (Chapter Three)

Dena Brugioni Johnson stayed on at Ford Motor Company after the war in spite of pressure to make her quit. Union support of women helped her keep her job, which she had for thirty years. She lives in Des Moines, Iowa. (Chapter Four)

Winifred Shaw Johnson was an elementary school music teacher and supervisor and currently works as a substitute teacher. Johnson is president of the local Delta Kappa Gamma chapter and belongs to the American Association of University Women, Daughters of the American Revolution, and the Veterans of Foreign Wars auxiliary. She plays bridge, sings in the church choir, rings the bellchoir, and is a church organist. A resident of Broken Bow, Nebraska, Johnson has a son, two grandchildren, and one great-grandchild. (Chapter Seven)

Barbara Barbash Kendall taught elementary school for twenty-seven years near her San Rafael, California, home. On a summer vacation in England one year, she tasted a raspberry vinegar she liked and decided she could make a better one. She now heads a company that is producing the vinegar along with a variety of salad dressings. She's been doing that for thirteen years. (Chapter Twelve)

Frances McCormick King was advertising manager for Whitney Blake, worked as an editor for *Encyclopaedia Britannica*, greeted newcomers as a Welcome Wagon representative, and has a real estate license. She has four children and lives in Guilford, Connecticut. (Chapter Eight)

Katie Lee Clark Knight left El Paso, Texas, with her husband when he traveled in the construction business. They discovered that Sacramento, California, pleased them most, so they settled there, where she worked for the Bureau of Reclamation. She paints in oil and acrylic, and their home looks like a gallery. She has one son and two grandchildren. (Chapter One)

Jo Droullard Krueger of Seattle, Washington, is an interior designer and has a furniture store featuring the Kreiss collection. She is listed in the *Who's Who of Interior Design*. Krueger has three sons. (Chapter Twelve)

Elanore Bair Kurtz worked seasonally after World War II, drying fruit in Fresno, California. When her two sons were grown, she worked as admitting manager in a hospital; she currently is a temporary employee of the City of Fresno, working as anything from administrative clerk to accounting technician. (Chapter Four)

Cecilia Null Kutna worked as a nurse for the elderly, helping them with shopping, other errands, and medication. She is now a pet sitter and is also available for bird rescue after oil spills. She lives in Gulfport, Florida. (Chapter Eight)

Lillie Cordes Landolt worked in the engineering department at City Hall, as a draftsperson. In the 1960s, she gathered a group of co-workers together and took a trip to Mexico. When they came back, they asked, "Where next year?" Now—forty-two trips later—she talks of many enjoyable travels in Europe. She lives in Des Moines, Iowa, and has five children, twenty-two grandchildren, and twelve great-grandchildren. (Chapter Ten)

Patricia Teeling Lapp, a writer, was assistant director of student publications for the University of California at Berkeley and editor of a magazine for *Encyclopaedia Britannica*. She lives in San Mateo, California. (Chapter Six)

Edwina Holbrook Leach works part time as a secretary and is active in her church, her community, and the local Democratic committee. She serves on the board of a center for mentally disabled adults and volunteers with the fire department auxiliary. A resident of Perry, Arkansas, Leach has two children and four grandchildren. (Chapter Twelve)

Sylvia Rebarber Leff anticipated the future with a television show in the late 1940s in San Francisco called *Frankly Feminine*. She featured interesting women guests and talked about the status of women. She was the first woman dean (1972) at City College in San Francisco. She lives in Walnut Creek, California. (Chapter Two)

Caryl "Jeri" Johnson McIntire returned to the Roy Rogers Rodeo after the war, riding, singing, playing western music, and doing public relations for the group. She left the rodeo to get married and worked on her local newspaper. She hikes with the Appalachian Mountain Club, enjoys oil painting and gardening, and volunteers with the Humane Society to find adoptive homes for rabbits. McIntire has a daughter and lives in Milton, New Hampshire. (Chapter Seven)

Margaret Christensen MacLaury has two sons and two daughters. She lives in Woodacre, California, and loves listening to music, playing the piano, and spending time in her sunny country kitchen. (Chapter Two)

Mildred Daniels Maguire raised seven children, has nineteen grand-children and great-grandchildren, operated a resort at one time, and worked for a seed company. She likes to crochet and produces a ready supply of caps and afghans. She lives in Angels Camp, California. (Chapter Two)

Jane Ward Mayta is a native of California whose family arrived in cov-ered wagons in the early 1800s. She worked with her husband in their general contracting business after the war, doing office work and driv-ing everything from a sports car to a one-and-a-half-ton truck. She has two children and lives in San Mateo, California. (Chapter One)

Eleanor Boysen Morgan is a Peace Corps volunteer in Jamaica. Inspired by one of her two sons to join the Peace Corps, she is on her second tour of duty. Morgan most recently lived in New York City. (Chapter Nine)

Elizabeth Szilagyi Morrison loves to cook, reads constantly, and has knit a wardrobe for her new great-grandson. Her favorite travel destina-tion is Puerto Rico, where she walks on the beach and plays in the casinos at night. She has two daughters, three grandchildren, and one great-grandchild. She lives in Ashburnham, Massachusetts. (Chapter Ten)

Lorraine Gaylord Moscow has decided not to run again for mayor of her village, a post she has held for eighteen years. A recent hip operation may delay her return to jogging. She taught math for twenty-two years, including a class for adults called "Math Without Pain." Moscow has four children, fourteen grandchildren, and five great-grandchildren and lives in Grand View–on–Hudson, New York. (Chapter Seven)

Audrey Ward Norman volunteers these days, providing services for which she used to get paid. She helps seniors and disadvantaged people with their income tax, having previously been a tax consultant. She lives in Troy, Missouri. (Chapter Eight)

Jennette Hyman Nuttall has two daughters and a son, lives in Las Vegas, Nevada, and managed her father's bakery for a period after the war. She also was manager of hardware and automotive supplies for National Hard Goods in Massachusetts and traveled throughout the United States purchasing goods for 200 concessions supplied by National. She loves to dance and travel and thinks standing on a glacier in Alaska is one of her more exciting travel experiences. (Chapter Eight)

Elizabeth Harbour Oden studied at business school after the war. She has worked in accounting and medical transcribing at the University of California at Davis Hospital in Sacramento, California, advancing to the rank of supervisor in the accounting department. She has an adopted son and lives in Sacramento. (Chapter Ten)

Madeline Bartlow Ontis returned to Mare Island Naval Shipyard during the Korean War and had the same boss in the ordnance department that she worked with during World War II. She was a psychiatric technician at Napa State Hospital, has three children, and is writing a family history. Ontis lives in Napa, California. (Chapter Four)

Mary Jo Davis Owens worked for a grocery chain in St. Louis, Missouri, for thirty-three years, staying on during three ownership changes. She was head checker and bookkeeper. The athletic events of her eight grandchildren keep her busy. (Chapter Six)

Gwen Porter Palmer taught school after her daughter was born, but when her son came along she stayed home with her kids. When her children became teenagers, she started tutoring and substituting, eventually going back to teaching full time. She lives in Pleasant Hill, California. (Chapter Six)

Alice Dickie Perry was a nursery school teacher and has been in theater for most of her life. She is learning to relax, finds pleasure in being with people, and is keeping physically alive and mentally alert. She lives in Sausalito, California, and has a son and daughter. (Chapter Nine)

ElvaRene Daughhetee Plimpton is one of eight siblings, all of whom were teachers. She lives in Salt Lake City, Utah, where she and her husband volunteer for environmental projects. (Chapter Four)

Donna Ehlmann Poeling is a technical writer in the field of commercial refrigeration. Prior to this, she was an engineering administrator at McDonnell Douglas, the same company where her mother worked for twenty-six years. Her "fun thing" is to come home and play with her computer. Poeling has a seventeen-year-old son and lives in St. Charles, Missouri. (Chapter Twelve)

Mary Entwistle Poole taught school before and after her wartime job at a California shipyard, a career that included teaching in a rural high school and a one-room school. Poole enjoys gardening and camping. She has a son and two daughters and loves having her three grandchildren live just up the road from her in Tiburon, California. (Chapter Seven)

Dadie Stillwell Potter taught school prior to her marriage and has worked with the family business ever since, in Alpine, Texas. She manages the Stillwell store and RV park and was instrumental in establishing Hallie's Hall of Fame, the museum honoring her mother, Hallie Stillwell. (Chapter Twelve)

Florence Stoll Protte watches for bargains at yard sales, likes to do a little gambling on the riverboats, does crafts for her granddaughter's school, and maintains friendships with people she worked with during the war. She became a nurse after the war, working at it for fifteen years. She lives in St. Louis, Missouri. (Chapter Five)

Rita Stangle Reker lives in Fresno, California, has three daughters and a son, and was one of the first women to work for the McDonald's hamburger chain. She has viewed in person all U.S. presidents since Franklin Delano Roosevelt, except Richard Nixon. (Chapter Four)

Geraldine Collogan Richey was recently elected mayor of her town— Carbon, Iowa—and volunteers at a nursing home. She enjoys square dancing and country line dancing, is involved with genealogy, is treasurer of her church, and works in the county recorder's office when they need her. (Chapter Six)

June Fine Roberts went to Texas after the war to visit her grandmother for a couple of months and stayed two years. She was a radio commentator and wrote ads for the radio station. After moving to California, she did social work in San Jose and Sacramento, was a secondary school teacher and an adult education administrator, and is now a farmer in Reedley, raising plums. She has a son and daughter. (Chapter Eight)

Lucille Gray Rogers retired in 1979 from a bookkeeper's job and in her retirement has traveled on bus tours throughout the United States. Branson, Missouri, and the Southwest have been favorites. She likes to read and is busy with church work. She has two sons and three granddaughters. (Chapter Six)

Phyllis Jack Rohrer of Tacoma, Washington, has worked off and on at department stores and variety stores. She has three sons. The oldest two, while growing up, proudly told their friends in school that their mother was a riveter. (Chapter Three)

Jackie Moxley Romaine of Swansea, Illinois, was the first female silk screen operator at Emerson Electric Company, a job she held after the war. She works two days a week at a printing firm established in 1844 in Belleville, Illinois. She has two sons. (Chapter Three)

Joyce Duncan Russell lives in Paradise, California, and has three children. Her artist's spirit rejoices at the discovery of new materials, the latest of which is bondo. (Chapter Eleven)

Mary Smith Ryder became so adept at installing radio equipment in fighter planes that when the Korean War came along, the airplane manufacturers took her back. She worked during the Korean War, stayed out to raise three girls, then returned to work during the Vietnam War. She retired in 1986 and lives in North Highland, California. (Chapter Two)

Phyllis Kenney Skinner and a group of similarly energetic senior citizens constructed the New Harmony Senior Citizen building completely on donated funds, grant money, and energy. Skinner volunteered secretarial help and, when needed, shoveled sand and gravel to make cement. (Chapter Five)

Peg McNamara Slaymaker has been an active volunteer and was involved in her children's activities during their growing years. She especially enjoyed being on the board of the Garden Club of America when living in New York. She now lives in Santa Rosa, California. (Chapter Two)

Annie Green Small went from her native Shreveport, Louisiana, to the Marinship yard in California and lives today in Marin City, her first California home. She worked at the Vogue Cleaners and has had several other jobs. She loves children and has four of her own, fourteen foster children, eighteen grandchildren, and fourteen great-grandchildren. (Chapter One)

Bill Smith is an electrician with California Steel Industries and lives in Oak Hills, California. (Chapter Seven)

Dorothy Henderson Smith raised a family for twenty-five years and went back to work for twenty years as a geologist. She is still active, having recently completed a study of a field to determine whether it contained a reservoir of oil. She recalls that when other girls were spending money on clothes, she spent it on flying and got her pilot's license. Smith lives in Norman, Oklahoma. (Chapter Five)

Dolores Kelsey Sorci, at the end of the war, "pickled" the planes, stored the trainers in hangars, and took a brief job in Salt Lake City's ZCMI department store. The next years were with American Telephone and Telegraph, which transferred her to Burlingame, California, where she still lives. She volunteers at the Peninsula Hospital, does quilting, and makes doll clothes. (Chapter Four)

Ernest Stark is a professor of human resource management at Bellevue College in Bellevue, Nebraska, and president of a consulting firm, Industrial Relations Affiliates. He lives in Fort Calhoun, Nebraska. (Chapter Twelve)

Helen Filarski Steffes delights her audiences when she gives presentations about women's baseball—"they never heard of it!" She's worked as a waitress in a restaurant for twenty-six years, where she is considered a celebrity because of the movie *A League of Their Own*, about the women's baseball league. She has six children, lives in Harper Woods, Michigan, and has coached women's baseball for twenty-five years. (Chapter Eleven)

Hallie Crawford Stillwell is on hand to greet visitors to a West Texas museum established in her name honoring her impact on the area surrounding the ranch that she has worked since 1907. Stillwell was the justice of the peace for Brewster County for fifteen years near her Alpine, Texas, ranch. She is a journalist and author and has two sons and a daughter. (Chapter Seven)

Rose Coffield Swanson knew from working at men's jobs during the war that she could handle what Portland, Oregon, was offering, but she had to convince city officials first. As the first woman field representative in any bureau in the city, her job was to explain and enforce city regulations. She also has done public opinion polling and market research interviewing. Swanson lives in Portland. (Chapter Nine)

Winifred E. Tanges was a closet Trekkie for years until she discovered how useful the Star Trek episodes were in teaching science fiction to her junior high and high school English classes. She was secretary to the school board for nine and a half years and taught high school English for twenty-five years. She lives in Virginia Beach, Virginia. (Chapter Eight)

Lucille Genz Blanton Teeters lives in Bangs, Texas. When her husband came home from World War II with severe diabetes, she felt she would be raising her three sons alone and took a course in licensed vocational nursing, then became director of nursing at a nursing home. (Chapter Three)

Edith Wolfe Tepper joined the WAVES, and after the war, accompanied her husband on his business trips. After his death, she worked with her brother in his wholesale business. She writes poetry for the newsletter of her Houston, Texas, retirement center. (Chapter Two)

Wilhelmina "Mina" Eckey Terry volunteers at her local library, taping bar codes to the books for inclusion in the computer program. She has been a teacher, belongs to a literature study group, and enjoys gardening. She has a son and daughter and lives in Waterville, Maine. (Chapter Nine)

Rose Judge Toomey volunteers as an usher at a local theater, has driven for Meals on Wheels, and has been a counselor for seniors. With nine grandchildren, there is no lack of opportunity for babysitting. She has four children and lives in Beverly, Massachusetts. (Chapter Six)

Vi Kirstine Vrooman is especially proud to be a volunteer at Davies Hospital in San Francisco, where she lives. She works two days a week in the personnel department. She reads and travels often to visit her daughters. (Chapter Ten)

Janice Callahan Waggoner worked for Southwestern Bell before her marriage. Her husband's work took them to Belgium for several years. She now has her own insurance agency and likes to travel. Waggoner has one son and lives in San Francisco. (Chapter Twelve)

Margaret Furey Walsh is the second vice president in the American Legion Auxiliary and is the Chapeau in the 8/40, a sister organization. They raise funds and contribute time to children with asthma, tuberculosis, cystic fibrosis, and other lung disorders. Walsh lives in Jamaica Plains, Massachusetts, and has two sons. (Chapter Six)

Eila Ahnger Weisman of Evanston, Illinois, reports with some pride that she passed the CPA exam the first time she took it and worked in the field for twenty years. After completing a course in real estate in 1986, she has embarked on another career, but she admits she's pursuing it casually, just making sure she's not sitting around doing nothing. (Chapter Ten)

Marie Templeton Westcott resumed a teaching career after the war, and during the past few years has been documenting her life experiences and the communities where she has lived on tape. Westcott was ninety-three years old when she shared her recollections. She lives in Schenectedy, New York. (Chapter Seven)

Doris Whitney is an expert in pre-Columbian studies and recently served as a docent for the Teotihuacan pre-Columbian exhibit at the M. H. DeYoung Museum in San Francisco. Whitney gives lectures and slide shows on various South American cultures and is available as a tour guide for friends and colleagues on trips to South America. She lives in San Francisco. (Chapter Three)

Kay Kane Whitney and her husband maintain twenty-two acres and a big house adjoining a national wilderness area in North Bend, Washington. They occasionally see bears, cougars, and coyotes. Whitney worked part time as a medical secretary and later as a teacher. She has five children and twelve grandchildren. (Chapter Five)

Ann McGhee Wilcox enjoys traveling in the United States and fondly remembers a trip to the Sawtooth Mountains in Idaho, where they caught fish every day. She sews, gardens, and paints. She lives in Woodland, California. (Chapter Ten)

Cora "Dolly" Orbison Williamson was chosen to cut the opening-day ribbon at the dedication of the Marine Museum in Eureka, California. After World War II, she was office manager of the Sequoia Products Company, and she has been in real estate for thirty years. She has three grandchildren, and at ninety, has gone into investments, "still working." (Chapter Eleven)

Elizabeth Harrell Winter has been a teacher, librarian, and choir director. She plays bridge and enjoys life. She has traveled all over the world and loves coming home to the mountains and foothills of her town: Alpine, Texas. (Chapter Two)

Nancy Baker Wise taught English at the junior high level and creative writing to community college students. She worked in public relations and has been an environmental activist. Wise is the author of *Marin's Natural Assets: An Historic Look at Marin County* and numerous magazine and newspaper articles. She lives in Novato, California, and has a daughter, a son, and four grandchildren. (Chapter Eight)

Polly Ann Stinnett Workman was on the Democratic Central Committee in Las Vegas, Nevada, moved to Canada where she managed a hotel, and returned to California in 1969. Currently a resident of Fresno, she enjoys being a foster grandparent, which involves craftsmaking and sewing for disadvantaged adolescents. (Chapter Seven)

Karen York worked for four years as a flight attendant with United Air Lines, then graduated from the University of Washington, and now is a real estate associate broker. She and her husband enjoy their weekend and summer residence near Mt. Rainier. Residents of Bellevue, Washington, they have a son and daughter. (Chapter Twelve)

Louisa Ilges Zeidler has won trophies for her painted ceramics as well as her oils and watercolors, most of which feature birds and flowers. Her envelope cartoon figures entertain friends who receive her letters. She belongs to an art group and likes working in her garden outside her St. Louis, Missouri, home. (Chapter Nine)

Bibliography

Baber, L. "Liberty Ship Capital of the World." *Daily Shipping News*, June 1991 (supplement).

Bailey, R. H. *The Home Front: U.S.A.* Alexandria, Va.: Time-Life Books, 1977.

Barrett, J. *Since You Went Away: World War II Letters from American Women on the Home Front.* New York: Oxford University Press, 1991.

Casdorph, P. *Let the Good Times Roll: Life at Home in America During WW II.* New York: Paragon House, 1989.

Chin, S. A. "WWII Gave Her Dreams a Chance to Soar." *San Francisco Examiner*, Sept. 19, 1993, p. D-6.

Douglas, D. *United States Women in Aviation 1940–1985.* Washington, D.C.: Smithsonian Institution Press, 1991.

Gluck, S. *Rosie the Riveter Revisited: Women, the War, and Social Change.* Boston: Twayne, 1987.

Hartmann, S. *The Home Front and Beyond: American Women in the 1940s.* Boston: Twayne, 1982.

Hoffman, M. (ed.) *World Almanac and Book of Facts, 1993.* New York: Pharos Books, 1992.

Jones, J. *World War II.* New York: Grosset & Dunlap, 1975.

Keegan, J. *The Second World War*. New York: Viking Penguin, 1989.

LeBaron, G. "Women's History: It's Whatever the 'Market' Demands." *Santa Rosa Press Democrat*, Mar. 29, 1992, p. A2.

Leth, B. "Mary Poole Recalls Heyday of Sausalito's Shipbuilding." *Tiburon Ark*, May 1, 1991, p. 6.

Macy, S. *A Whole New Ball Game*. New York: Holt, 1993.

Mulvey, D. *We Pulled Together and Won!* Greendale, Wis.: Reiman, 1993.

Northwestern Alumni Association. *Northwestern University Remembrances: The War Years and NU's Response*. Vol. 2: World War II Commemoration. Evanston, Ill.: Northwestern Alumni Association, 1993.

O'Brien, K., and Grice, G. (eds.). *Women in the Weather Bureau During World War II*. Salt Lake City, Utah: National Weather Service, 1991.

Potter, J. (ed.). "What Did You Do in the War?" *Nebraska History* (Nebraska State Historical Society), winter 1991 (entire issue).

Pratt & Whitney. *The Pratt & Whitney Aircraft Story*. In-house company publication. East Hartford, Conn.: Pratt & Whitney, 1950.

Raffensperger, G. "Remember the WACs." *Des Moines Register*, Aug. 29, 1992, p. T-1.

Ross, N. L. "When the World Was at War." *Washington Post*, Dec. 5, 1991, Home sec., p. 16.

Snyder, L. *The War: A Concise History*. New York: Messner, 1960.

Sulzberger, C. L., and others. *The American Heritage Picture History of World War II*. American Heritage, 1966.

Weatherford, D. *American Women and World War II*. New York: Facts on File, 1990.

Williams, R. "Zest of the West." *Texas Highways*, Oct. 1991, pp. 14–20.

Wollenberg, C. *Marinship at War: Shipbuilding and Social Change in Wartime Sausalito*. Berkeley, Calif.: Western Heritage Press, 1990.

Index